Seven Stars

TEXAS A&M UNIVERSITY MILITARY HISTORY SERIES

93

Joseph G. Dawson III, General Editor

Seven Stars

The Okinawa Battle Diaries of *Simon Bolivar Buckner, Jr., and Joseph Stilwell*

EDITED BY *Nicholas Evan Sarantakes*

Texas A&M University Press
College Station

First edition

The paper used in this book meets the minimum requirements
of the American National Standard for Permanence
of Paper for Printed Library Materials, Z39.48–1984.
Binding materials have been chosen for durability.
♾

Library of Congress Cataloging-in-Publication Data

Buckner, Simon Bolivar, 1886–1945.
Seven stars : the Okinawa battle diaries of Simon Bolivar Buckner, Jr., and Joseph Stilwell / edited by Nicholas Evan Sarantakes.
p. cm. — (Texas A&M military history series ; no. 93)
Includes bibliographical references.
ISBN 1-58544-294-1 (alk. paper)
1. Buckner, Simon Bolivar, 1886–1945—Diaries. 2. Stilwell, Joseph Warren, 1883–1946—Diaries. 3. World War, 1939–1945—Campaigns—Japan—Okinawa Island—Personal narratives. 4. World War, 1939–1945—Personal narratives, American. 5. Generals—United States—Diaries. I. Stilwell, Joseph Warren, 1883–1946. II. Sarantakes, Nicholas Evan, 1966– . III. Title. IV. Series: Texas A & M University military history series ; 93.
D767.99.O45 B83 2004
940.54′252294′0922—dc22

2003015128

In Memory of
Ross Stillwell
(1967–2001)

Philmont Ranger, 1986–1987

Contents

Illustrations

Preface

The diaries of these two generals are quite different from one another. Buckner wrote his account in a prepared logbook that had the dates printed at the top of each page. Stilwell, on the other hand, wrote his journal in a small, spiral flip-top notebook. As the editor, I faced a number of difficult decisions in attempting to create standardization for the reader without altering the unique flavor of either record. First, I deleted some material, mainly personal in nature, from the text. Historians and the public have no legitimate reason to intrude into the privacy of either general or his family. As a result, I removed passages that mention such things as personal health, family legal matters, dreams, and romantic feelings. I also excluded trivial issues of little importance. Anything reasonably affecting command decisions remains. All places where material has been deleted are marked with three asterisks.

Two entirely different, very busy men serving in stressful situations wrote these diaries. Needless to say, given the circumstances, there were a number of flaws in their composition. Indecipherable or grammatically confusing material was removed and marked with an ellipse. I silently corrected all misspellings in the text, particularly the names of individuals. In a few cases, where Buckner or Stilwell clearly made such errors purposefully, or where they are so grossly off the mark as to leave doubt what word is intended, the incorrect spellings remain. I also silently corrected a number of punctuation errors when the intended meaning was obvious. Corrections having the potential to change the text's meaning appear in brackets.

The differences in the two generals' writing styles serve as a second reason for my making many of the corrections silently. Buckner's writing is more formal, with complete sentences and definable paragraphs appearing on every page. Marking the changes made to his journal was a realistic proposition. Stilwell's record is quite different. He rarely wrote in complete sentences and he often underlined words without necessarily intending to give them more emphasis. He also relied heavily on the dash, sometimes as a substitute for either a period or a paragraph break, and at other times as simply a dash. He also used map symbols and numbers for military units, and even wrote a few words in kanji characters. His entries are peppered with rial without even trying. In the middle of the week I went to Gilroy, California, to have dinner with my cousin, Margaret Hays, and her husband, Jim, in their new home. (The drive there was an adventure in itself. Kate and Chuck loaned me a car and, for the first time in ten years, I was required to cope with a standard transmission. I wound up stalling the car a lot.) That afternoon, while looking at items about Stilwell's death, I noticed that his deputy commander in the Sixth Army was a general named Hays. I knew that Jim's grandfather had been a general, so I asked the obvious question when I finally arrived at their house in the sputtering car. It turned out that Jim's grandfather had indeed been Stilwell's deputy. Jim had a number of historical items about his grandfather and showed them to me that evening, including a typed manuscript of an unpublished memoir. Jim's grandfather, Lt. Gen. George P. Hays, had an interesting and full military career in which he was awarded the Medal of Honor, commanded the 10th Mountain Division during the World War II Italian campaign, and met the likes of Theodore Roosevelt and Richard Nixon. His association with Stilwell was brief, but it confirmed what I had suspected: The Sixth Army's main mission in the immediate postwar period was overseeing the downsizing of the U.S. Army in the western United States.

I am fortunate that I come from a military family. The diaries of these two generals are loaded with military terms. Stilwell even used map symbols as a form of shorthand. I literally had inhouse experts to call on to explain most of this jargon, namely: my father, Lt. Col. Nick Sarantakes, and my brother, Capt. Andrew Sarantakes. Andy also designed the charts used in this book. A friend and former roommate, Brett Huffman, answered my questions on naval matters. Major Tom Schonberger, a friend of mine from my days at the Philmont Scout Ranch helped with air force terminology. I also imposed on the research and teaching of my colleagues in the history department at Texas A&M University–Commerce. Peter Messer, Ricky Dobbs, and Isaac Land took time away from their own labors to proofread various sections of the manuscript. Toward the end of my work on this project, Randy Papadopoulos, a friend of mine from the 1999 West Point Summer Seminar in Military History, helped me track down information and identify individuals that I discovered I had overlooked. Sal Mercogliano, another friend from that West Point experience, shared ideas about the importance of logistics. His comments had an enormous impact, helping me see the context in which Buckner had to operate. Siva Vaidhyanathan, an old friend from our undergraduate days at the University of Texas, gave me generous assistance on questions concerning copyright law. M. Taylor Fravel, a colleague from the 2000 Summer Workshop on the Analysis of Military Operations and Strategy sponsored by the Institute of War and Peace Studies at Columbia University, is fluent in Chinese. He checked my kanji translations—these characters are used in both Japanese and Chinese—and saved me from making a huge mistake. A friend from my graduate school days at the University of Southern California, Regina Lark, got me a copy of an article from the *Ryudai Review of EuroAmerican Studies* in which an early version of Buckner's letters appeared. This title is exceptionally obscure: only three institutions in North America subscribe to the journal, and one of them is the library at the University of California, Los Angeles. Regina works at UCLA's Center for the Study of Women and was able to get a copy for me when my efforts through interlibrary loan failed.

For the most part, I had no need of financial assistance for this project. Most of my research work was done on trips taken for other reasons. As a result, this was a cost effective undertaking. In 1997, however, when I had to return to the San Francisco Bay area to work exclusively on the diaries, the office of the vice president of graduate studies at Texas A&M–Commerce provided a small grant that made this trip possible. The office also provided another grant to pay for the photos appearing in this book.

I am in the debt to all the people and institutions mentioned above. I have often seen other writers, while continuing to accept all responsibility for any remaining shortcomings, claim that their books would never have turned out as well had it not been for the assistance of their friends and colleagues. Having now worked on two booklength projects, I truly understand and share such sentiment.

Finally, this book is dedicated to the memory of another friend of mine from Philmont, Ross Stillwell. Ross was a distant relative of Joseph W. Stilwell, despite the different spellings of their names, and shared many traits with his kinsman. Both had real intellectual talent, were good about following a regular physical fitness regimen, and were exceptional leaders. The major difference was in temperament. While General Stilwell had the well-deserved nickname "Vinegar Joe," Ross was one of the most positive and inspirational people I have known. His death, which came just as I completed work on this manuscript, was a loss that was widely and deeply felt.

Okinawa Campaign Chronology

Date	*Event*
September 4, 1944	Lt. Gen. Simon Bolivar Buckner, Jr., assumes command of Tenth Army
September 26	Buckner informs Adm. Chester W. Nimitz, commander in chief, Pacific Ocean Areas, that distance and logistics make an invasion of Formosa unfeasible.
September 29–October 1	Nimitz meets with Adm. Ernest J. King, chief of naval operations, and informs King that his command should seize Okinawa rather than Formosa.
October 3	The U.S. Joint Chiefs of Staff order Admiral Nimitz to seize Okinawa.
October 5	Nimitz informs his command that Okinawa is now their objective.
October 9	Nimitz assigns Tenth Army the task of seizing Okinawa.
March 21, 1945	Western Island Attack Group carrying the 77th Division sorties from Leyte Gulf.
March 24	Southern Tractor Flotilla carrying XXIV Corps sorties from Leyte Gulf. Planes and ships of Task Force 58 begin the bombardment of Okinawa.

March 25	Northern Tractor Flotilla carrying III Amphibious Corps sorties from Ulithi.
March 27	Transport and covering forces of the Joint Expeditionary Force sortie from Leyte Gulf and Ulithi.
April 1	Okinawa campaign begins. Tenth Army lands on Higashi Beach unopposed.
April 2	Forward elements of the 7th Division reach the east coast, severing the island in two.
April 4	XXIV Corps units make first contact with Japanese defensive fortifications in southern Okinawa.
April 6–7	Japanese begin Operation Ten-Go, the coordinated use of kamikaze suicide pilots against U.S. ships operating in the waters off Okinawa. Each attack wave is codenamed *kikusui*. The first *kikusui* assault launched employs 355 planes.
April 12–13	Kikusui 2 strikes with 185 planes.
April 15–16	Kikusui 3 assaults with 165 planes.
April 16	6th Marine Division begins battle for control of Mount Yae Take and the Motobu Peninsula in northern Okinawa. 77th Division invades Ie Shima, an island off the coast of Motobu.
April 18	Pulitzer Prize–winning newspaper columnist Ernie Pyle killed on Ie Shima. Buckner moves Tenth Army command post ashore.
April 19	XXIV Corps launches assault on Japanese positions. Japanese Thirty-second Army holds, turning back the Americans.

April 20	III Marine Amphibious Corps finishes taking northern Okinawa.
April 21	Ie Shima declared secure.
April 23	Japanese increase artillery fires on night of April 23–24 to mask the withdrawal of troops from the first Shuri line.
April 24	Tenth Army seizes first Japanese line.
April 27	Buckner assigns 1st Marine Division to XXIV Corps.
April 27–28	Japanese launch Kikusui 4 with 115 planes.
May 1	1st Marine Division relieves 27th Division on the front line in southern Okinawa.
May 3–4	Japanese launch 125 planes in Kikusui 5 operation.
May 4	Japanese Thirty-second Army launches counterattack against Tenth Army.
May 5	Japanese counterattack halted.
May 7	III Amphibious Corps takes over western sector of front lines in southern Okinawa and regains control of 1st Marine Division.
May 10–11	150 Japanese planes take part in Kikusui 6.
May 11	Tenth Army launches assault on second Shuri line.
May 12	6th Marine Division elements assault Sugar Loaf Hill. Joined by Half Moon and Horseshoe Hills, 230-foot Sugar Loaf Hill dominates the open country leading to Shuri Ridge and the second Japanese defensive line.

May 17	Change in command structure makes Buckner directly subordinate to Adm. Raymond A. Spruance, commander of the Central Pacific Task Forces, also known as the Fifth Fleet.
May 21	Marines take Sugar Loaf Hill, which guards the entrance to Shuri and the Japanese Thirty-second Army's headquarters. Japanese begin withdrawing from the Shuri line, which takes until May 29.
May 23–25	Kikusui 7 initiated with 165 planes.
May 24	Marines enter Naha, capital of Okinawa. It is the largest city ever captured by the Marine Corps up to that point in time.
May 27	Fleet Adm. William F. "Bull" Halsey replaces Spruance as commander of the Central Pacific Task Forces. Fifth Fleet designation changes to Third Fleet. Buckner now reports directly to Nimitz.
May 27–29	Japanese launch Kikusui 8 with 110 planes.
May 29 (in United States)	*New York Herald Tribune* publishes an article in which correspondent Homer Bigart criticizes Buckner's "ultra-conservative" tactical leadership.
May 29	1st Marine Division takes Shuri Castle, centerpiece of the second Japanese defensive line and former Thirty-second Army headquarters.
May 30 (in United States)	Syndicated columnist David Lawrence uses Bigart article as the basis for a column blaming heavy battle losses on Buckner.
June 3	Gen. Joseph W. Stilwell arrives on Okinawa on an inspection tour.

June 4 (in United States)	Lawrence writes another column demanding an investigation into Buckner's handling of the campaign.
June 5	Tenth Army reaches third and final Japanese defensive line.
June 3–7	Ninth *kikusui* attacked launched with fifty planes.
June 7	Stilwell and his party depart Okinawa.
June 10	Buckner offers surrender terms to Lt. Gen. Ushijima Mitsuru, Thirty-second Army commander, but receives no response.
June 15	Coordinated Japanese resistance ends; Thirty-second Army ceases to exist as an effective fighting force. Buckner holds press conference in which he defends his conduct of the campaign.
June 17	Nimitz releases press statement defending Buckner: "During the operation each service took loses and each service inflicted great damage to the enemy. Comparisons between services are out of place and ill-advised."
June 18	Japanese artillery barrage kills Buckner. Maj. Gen. Roy Geiger, commanding general of the III Amphibious Corps, assumes command of Tenth Army; becomes first marine officer to command a field army in combat. Stilwell meets with Gen. of the Army Douglas MacArthur, commander in chief, U.S. Army Forces, Pacific, and turns down offer to serve as his chief of staff.
June 19	MacArthur and Gen. of the Army George C. Marshall, U.S. Army chief of staff, begin correspondence regarding naming of Buckner's

	successor. Marshall instructs MacArthur to choose between Stilwell; Lt. Gen. Alexander "Sandy" Patch, commanding general, Seventh Army; Lt. Gen. Lucian K. Truscott, Jr., commanding general, Fifth Army; Gen. George S. Patton, Jr., commanding general, Third Army; Lt. Gen. William Simpson, commanding general, Ninth Army; or Gen. Jacob Devers, commanding general, Sixth Army Group. MacArthur states that he would prefer Lt. Gen. Oscar W. Griswold, commanding general, XIV Corps, but that he will accept Stilwell if his choice is limited to the list Marshall provided.
June 20	Marshall informs MacArthur that Stilwell will be Tenth Army's new commander. Stilwell advised of the transfer upon his arrival in Hawaii.
June 21	Geiger announces island secured.
June 21–22	Japanese muster forty-five planes for Kikusui 10, the last major kamikaze attack in the Ryukyus.
June 22	Flag-raising ceremony at Tenth Army headquarters marks the capture of Okinawa.
June 23	Ushijima and Lt. Gen. Cho Isamu, Thirty-second Army chief of staff, commit suicide. Stilwell assumes command of Tenth Army. Mop-up campaign begins to eliminate last vestiges of Japanese resistance.
June 30	Mop-up operations end.
July 2	Stilwell announces end of Okinawa campaign.
August 6	Atomic bomb dropped on Hiroshima.
August 9	Atomic bomb dropped on Nagasaki.

August 15	Japan announces acceptance of surrender terms.
September 2	Surrender ceremony held on USS *Missouri* in Tokyo Bay. Stilwell present to witness the event.
September 7	Japanese forces in the Ryukyus surrender at Kadena Air Base (location later renamed Stilwell Park).

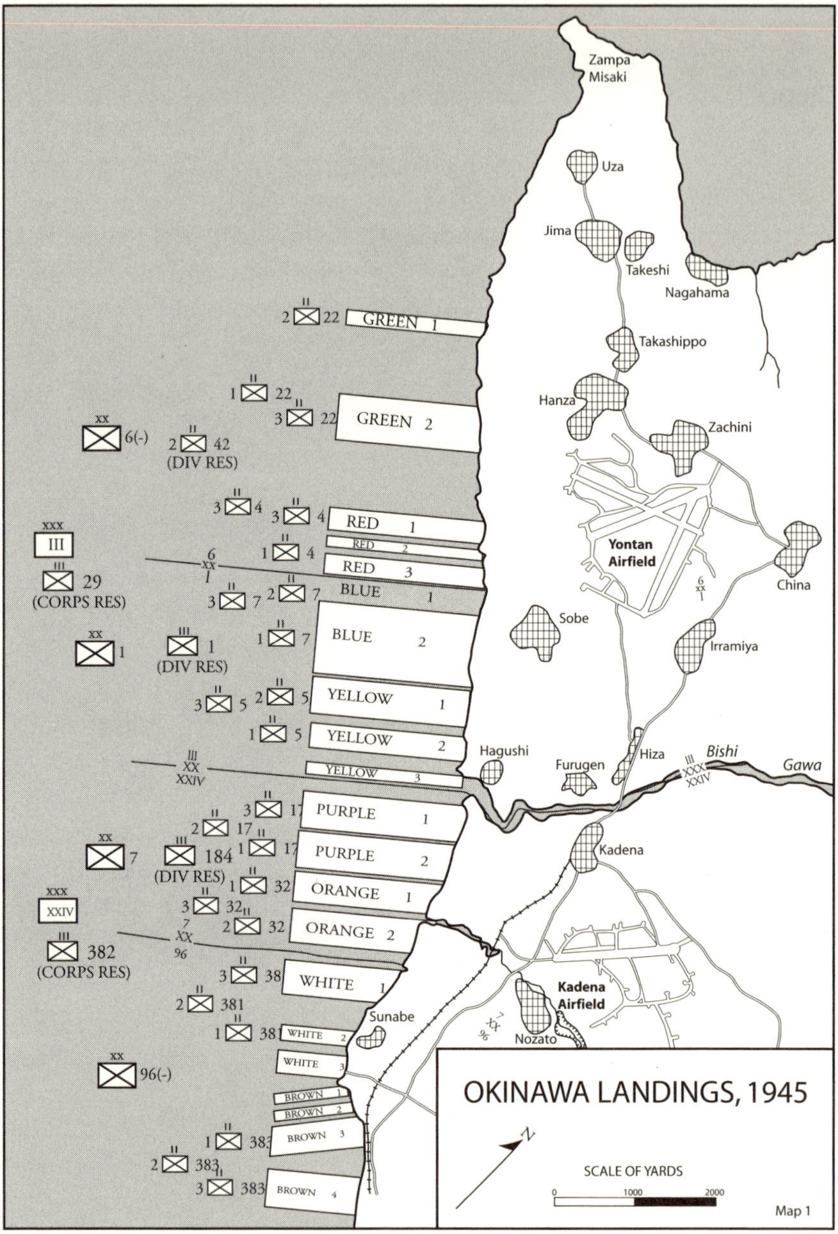

Map 1. Okinawa Landings, 1945. Map by Frank J. Martini, Cartographer–Media Developer, United States Military Academy.

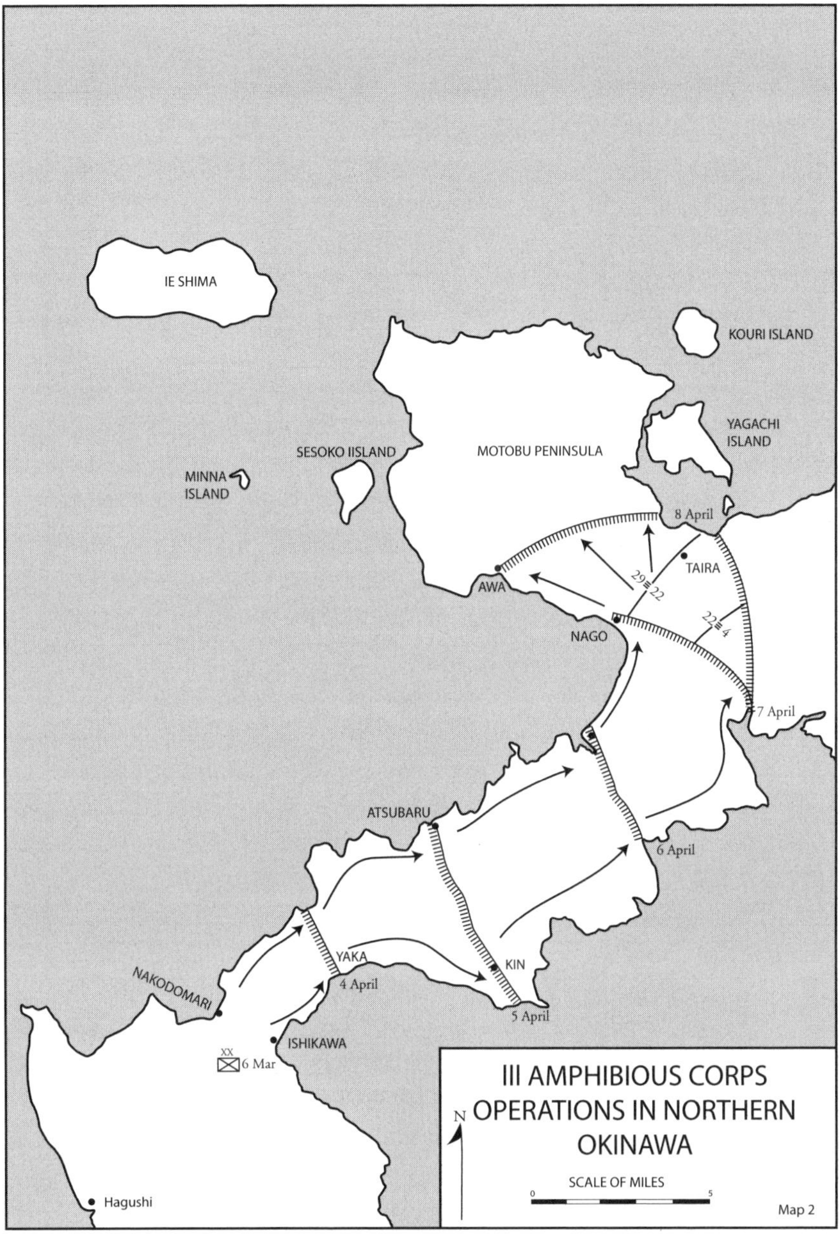

Map 2. III Amphibious Corps Operations in Northern Okinawa. Map by Frank J. Martini, Cartographer–Media Developer, United States Military Academy.

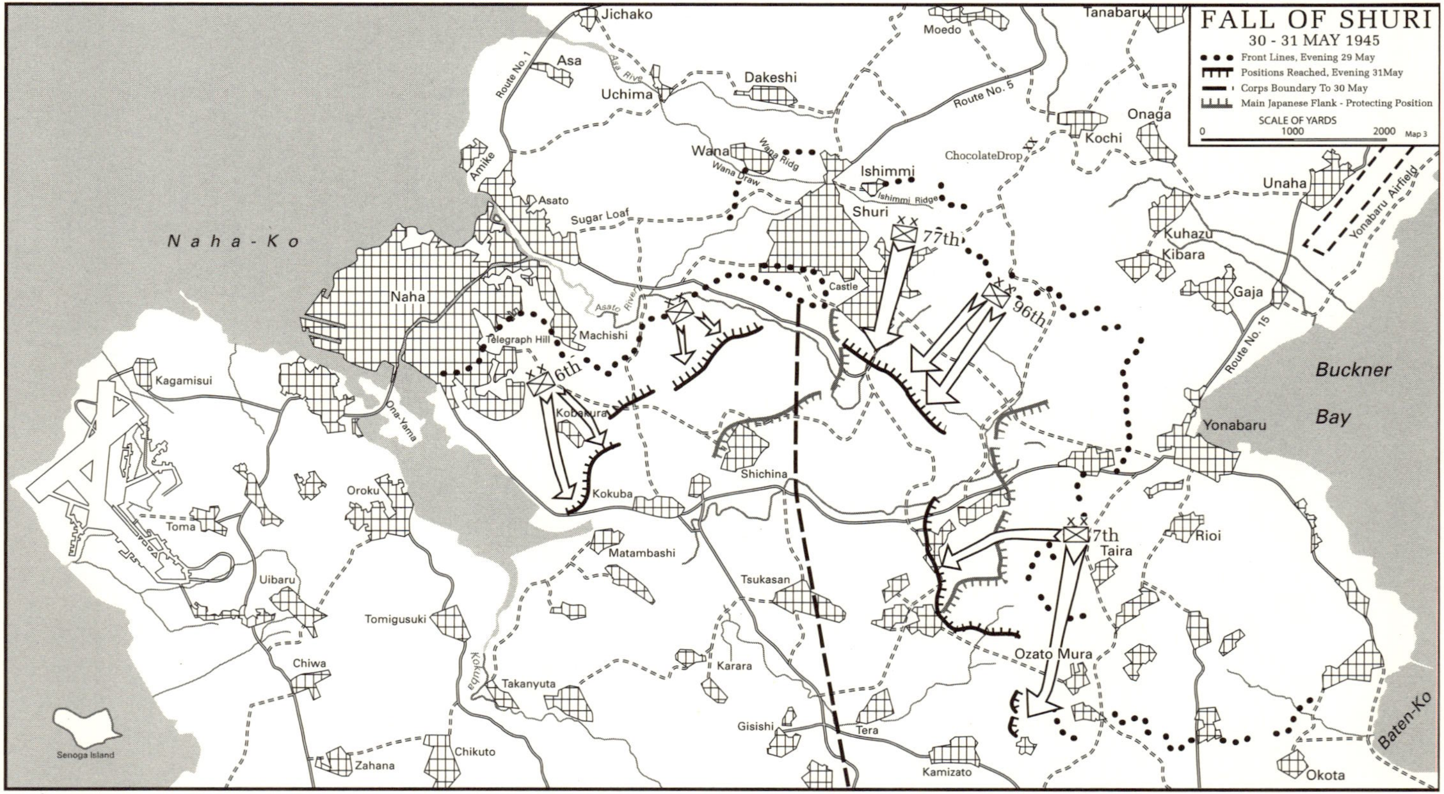

Map 3. Fall of Shuri, May 30–31, 1945. Map by Frank J. Martini, Cartographer–Media Developer, United States Military Academy.

Seven Stars

Introduction

On April 1, 1945, the U.S. Tenth Army, commanded by Lt. Gen. Simon Bolivar Buckner, Jr., invaded Okinawa. For the next three months, this unit, a combination of marine and army formations, fought the Japanese Thirty-second Army for control of the island. The battle for Okinawa was one of the most costly American campaigns in World War II, and has the distinction of being the single bloodiest conflict in the history of the U.S. Navy. As the clash neared an end, Buckner died in an enemy artillery barrage. General Joseph W. Stilwell replaced him as the Tenth Army commander and oversaw the mop-up stage of the campaign. During the course of the next six weeks, Stilwell prepared his command to take part in the expected invasion of Japan. When that ancient empire suddenly capitulated and formally surrendered on the deck of the battleship *Missouri,* Stilwell was there to witness the ceremony. He returned to Okinawa afterward and helped supervise the demobilization of U.S. forces stationed on the island.

The diaries of these two generals with their seven stars are important for three reasons. First, as history, these journals offer a new window into the last days of World War II. Since the shooting stopped, far too much scholarship has focused on the role of the atomic bombs in bringing the hostilities to an end. Okinawa was the last land campaign of the war and preparations were under way to carry the fight to Japan itself. These operations were important elements in the shaping events of that summer. Much to the dismay of historians, military regulations of the day prohibited the keeping of diaries for understandable security reasons. Those of us who work for the muse Clio are fortunate that Buckner and Stilwell chose to ignore the regulations and kept personal journals. Although there have been many studies of the Okinawa campaign, none of their authors examined the conflict from the commanding general's perspective.[1] A. P. Jenkins, however, published portions of Buckner's diary and letters in two lesser-known historical journals, but those publications had an exceptionally limited audience.[2]

A second reason these diaries are important is that they are a record of high-level leadership in combat. The ultimate mission of any general in the combat arms branches and many of those in combat support branches is to lead soldiers in times of war. Most military officers who aspire to high command spend the majority of their careers in peacetime service, training for that eventuality. Short of any actual previous combat experience, simulations and exercises are the only ways to prepare for the next war. Mentor-protégé relationships between senior and junior officers often facilitate this process. One of the best ways to learn how to be a high-level military leader is to serve as a general's aide. From these positions, junior officers get to watch and observe the art of leadership firsthand. There are relatively few such jobs, however, and those who serve in them normally do so in peacetime. The opportunity to watch a general command during a period of hostilities is quite rare, which makes these diaries all the more unique because they offer an original, firsthand account of high-level combat leadership.

Finally, these journals offer a unique opportunity to witness the conduct of joint operations. The term *joint operation* refers to a military action in which two or more services work together to achieve an objective. The different services join together to maximize their firepower in order to accomplish that which air, land, or sea power is unable to achieve on its own. Armies, navies, and air forces—particularly when they serve different nations—have their own distinct ways of training, organizing, and employing their men and equipment. Even similar services defending the same nation—the U.S. Navy and Coast Guard, for example—have distinct institutional cultures stemming from their different histories, missions, and purposes. The Tenth Army, composed as it was of a marine amphibious corps and an army corps, by its very nature conducted joint operations. As Adm. Alan G. Kirk, commander of the Western Naval Task Force at the invasion of Normandy, made clear in his D-Day after-action report, success turned on some fragile elements: "A firm tradition of mutual trust and confidence now exists, but this record could easily be marred in special instances by the personal incompatibility of two commanders of different services. There is no effective guarantee of success—it takes one to command and two to cooperate; and the existence at a remotely high level of a supreme commander cannot ensure cooperation against the will of subordinates." An appreciation for the differences in the traditions and views of the various units scheduled to work together was a fundamental element in the success of a joint operation. "Only by working, training, and fighting together could the military and naval cultures and the emerging air force culture be merged into a successful joint command," historian Adrian R. Lewis observes.[3] The Tenth Army never had the opportunity to develop an institutional culture of its own, making Buckner's work all the more difficult.

As army commanders, Buckner and Stilwell had two different missions. The priority of those two tasks changed with the passage of time, and their diaries reflect the shifting importance of each mission. The first objective was to take and secure the island. The second was to prepare Okinawa to serve as a base for future operations against the Japanese home islands. In the course of trying to fulfill these two missions, Buckner and Stilwell devoted much of their attention to six areas of concern.

Perhaps the biggest concern that each man had was logistics. By early 1945, the United States was experiencing supply shortages in the Pacific theater. The shortcoming lay not in production or the availability of merchant shipping, but in port capacity. The major West Coast port cities—San Francisco, Los Angeles, Seattle, and Portland—lacked sufficient storage facilities, staging areas, labor, and railroad networks to handle the increased demand for supplies as the war effort moved farther and farther away. In the words of the official army historians studying this issue, merchant shipping had become "the most critical of Allied resources." In addition, the German Ardennes counteroffensive caused the U.S. Army to send all available infantry units to Europe, depleting America's strategic reserves. As a result, the Tenth Army barely had enough men and supplies to attack Okinawa, and then only after changing loading doctrine. Operation Iceberg absorbed almost all of the assault lift in the Pacific, with much of the shipping sailing from Saipan, the Philippines, and the West Coast of the United States. Supply problems could easily develop if port capacity and development on Okinawa did not go according to schedule. As a result, Buckner had to worry about issues such as opening up new beaches, the quality of the road network, the speed of the advance on the ground, kamikaze attacks, and weather conditions—all of which affected a supply effort with little margin for error. Supply problems thus affected decisions made about operations on the island. For example, Tenth Army's marine units began running short of food. On June 4, the 96th Infantry Division shared its rations with the 3rd Battalion, 1st Marines, which allowed the sea soldiers to eat that day.[4] Despite the transition to a one-front war, most of these problems remained when Stilwell took command. In the United States, logistical shortfalls required that shipping began leaving for the Pacific not only from West Coast ports, but also from those on the Atlantic and Gulf of Mexico. The kamikazes were gone by the time Stilwell took over, but he still had to worry about stragglers, which were a constant threat to the security of the supply dumps the army was building up in preparation for the invasion of Japan. The Army Air Forces also wanted to use Okinawa as its main base against Japan, increasing the demand on the island's fragile supply system and adding to the problems with which Stilwell had to contend.[5]

A second theme that is developed in the pages of each diary is the importance of strategic and political issues. Buckner made his feelings about domestic affairs clear. Even though his father was a newspaper editor for a time after the Civil War, he saw the press as a nuisance and made no effort to cultivate reporters. This attitude contributed, in part, to controversy about his decision not to launch a second landing on Okinawa's southern tip. His conservative views on social issues, specifically race, are consistent with those of a southerner at the time. He also wanted the United States to retain control over Okinawa in the postwar period. The island's strategic location would allow the United States to project its influence into the western Pacific and contain the advances of a variety of foreign powers.

Stilwell's attitudes toward many civilian matters and institutions were quite different from Buckner's. Known publicly as "Vinegar Joe" for his sharp, blunt comments and views, Stilwell pulled no punches in writing his private record. Although no longer associated with the war effort on the Asian mainland, he still recorded his views about the situation in China and information that he received from visitors.

Unlike Buckner, Stilwell was adept at handling the journalists who visited the island. His direct, uninhibited remarks endeared him to reporters. The suggestion that he confided in only a few correspondents needs reconsideration.[6] Reporters were an important source for information about events in China, and Stilwell's conversations with the many publishers visiting the island gave him an opportunity to influence public opinion about important postwar issues. Journalists were also important to him because they kept the public informed. Stilwell believed that the strength of the U.S. war effort was its citizen soldiers. Although he made several derogatory remarks about racial groups, he had an encompassing view of America that was inclusive of different ethnic groups.

Tactics is another subject both men addressed in their journals. Buckner displays a single-minded devotion to army doctrine and his mission to take the island. He planned to use the weight of his heavy artillery to destroy the Japanese. He told reporters that although progress was gradual it was certain: "Constricted terrain and powerful natural defenses make this a slow proposition but a sure one. A careful study of the terrain shows avenues of infiltration against which the Japs can bring least resistance. Thus strong positions are gradually pinched out and then the process started all over again. This way we are saving men. Our men are too valuable to be sacrificed because of impatience."[7] To this end, Tenth Army began using what Buckner graphically described as "blowtorch and corkscrew" tactics. Pioneered by the marines before being developed further by the army, this tank-infantry approach was an example of the two services learning from one another. Cannon-equipped tanks and flamethrower tanks delivered suppressing fire and moved forward with infantry teams. The latter often suffered light casualties while delivering supporting fire that prevented the Japanese from targeting the tanks or sending out soldiers with satchel charges whose job was to dive under the tanks as suicide bombers. The infantry would then use explosives to seal off the caves in which the enemy sought shelter.[8]

Tactical doctrine was not dogma, however, and Stilwell was critical of Buckner for sticking to frontal assaults and his heavy emphasis on artillery. His background as the unorthodox chief of tactics at the Infantry School at Fort Benning, Georgia, twenty years before is evident in these pages. When he first arrived on Okinawa, Stilwell held no command assignment, was free from the press of responsibility, and had the freedom to look at events with a fresh perspective. As a result, the entries in his journal were often longer and more informative than Buckner's.

Another theme that comes through Buckner's journal is the importance of good interservice relations, which one way or another was going to be a critical element in the outcome of this joint operation. Buckner worked hard to get along well with the marines under his command. He even designated his senior marine subordinate, Maj. Gen. Roy S. Geiger, the III Amphibious Corps commander, to be his successor in case he became a casualty. The two generals got along well with one another. "There was never any friction," a marine staff officer observed of Buckner's visits to III Amphibious Corps. "He and General Geiger got along very well."[9] Indeed, the two had been friends ever since they attended the U.S. Army Command and General Staff School together as majors during the interwar period.[10] The two generals' long association was an important element in the operation of the Tenth Army. Factors such as the personal relationship between commanding generals can often be a critical element in the success of a joint operation.[11] Oliver P. Smith, who gained fame as a Marine Corps commander in World War II and Korea, offered a slightly more complex description of army-marine relations. Smith, who served as Tenth Army's marine deputy chief of staff, wrote shortly after the war: "Relations were very cordial and the Army staff had no particular cause to criticize what the Marines were doing." The relief of Ralph Smith, an army general, by Holland Smith, his Marine Corps superior, during the Saipan campaign was still a sore subject for many and the Tenth Army staff, embroiled in yet another joint operation, knew better than to revisit the issue. "In their relations with the XXIV Corps the Army staff could be absolutely frank," Oliver Smith observed. "I did note, however, that the Army staff members were very careful in my presence, not to criticize an Army unit or to make invidious comparisons. I, of course, was on my good behavior and scrupulously avoided making any invidious comparisons. All this may seem strained, but if you are going to conduct joint operations successfully you have to tread softly."[12]

The two services learned much from one another during the course of the battle. The most important example was the development of blowtorch-and-corkscrew tactics. There were other instances: marine artillery copied innovations army units had developed to hit well-protected enemy positions, and the army's infantry was more than willing to call in marine fighter-bombers to hit the fortified positions they faced.[13] These exchanges and good personal relations, while important, hardly resolved major differences between the two services—a reflection of their different institutional cultures and honest differences of opinion on how best to approach tactical problems. The Marine Corps believed much more in maneuver than was called for in army doctrine. The Marine Corps in 1944 assigned three Browning automatic rifles to each infantry squad, allowing the squad to divide into three fire teams, each supported by an automatic weapon, and thus approach objectives with more firepower and mobility. The marines also used tactical airpower to a far greater degree than the army. Forward air controllers—aviators serving in an infantry capacity—requested and directed air strikes by communicating directly with the pilots. The result was that marines were able to get ordnance dropped on targets within just a few hundred yards of friendly positions. Army Air Forces pilots, on the other hand, were reluctant to perform tactical missions and normally needed a larger safety margin than the marines.[14] Another example of the differences between the two services was the logistical infrastructure of a combat division. Despite a number of revisions to tables of organization and equipment, marine divisions were short of vehicles—both tracked and wheeled—used to deliver needed supplies. Army units helped supply the leathernecks, but this problem became worse as the marines moved farther and farther from the beachhead.[15] As a result, marine divisions moved slower than their army counterparts. However, since both were using the blowtorch-and-corkscrew method against Japanese fortifications, Buckner tended to treat them the same.

Buckner's failure to appreciate the differences between the units under his command might never have come to much had it not been for the Navy Department's manipulative efforts to control news coverage in the Pacific. Each factor in its own right was the cause for some resentment and limited grumbling, but like two inert chemicals, they became explosive when combined. Marine Corps advocates claim a second landing in southern Okinawa—a purely marine operation—would have brought the campaign to a quicker end. This contention is, of course, a counterfactual argument that no historian can, or should, try to answer. It is interesting to note that similar questions were raised in Hearst Corporation newspapers about the human cost of taking Iwo Jima. An enraged group of marines charged into the offices of the *San Francisco Examiner* demanding an apology for the insult to the good name of the Corps.[16] Since then, publicists have turned the battle of Iwo Jima into one of the finest moments in Marine Corps history. Such a transformation in public attitudes toward Okinawa has never taken place. More importantly, this contention ignores certain historical facts. The issue had no partisan dimension when it was originally debated. An army general made the original proposal, and marine commanders on Okinawa were divided about its merit.

Staff work is another subject to which Buckner and Stilwell devoted much time and energy. Tenth Army was an organization with little cohesion. Its major subordinate units came from different services and had never served or even trained together prior to the attack on Okinawa. Buckner and his staff officers had to wield this diverse group of soldiers and marines into a well-tuned organization. Although all of Tenth Army's corps were veteran units, most of the army staff officers had little or no combat experience or troop duty. Buckner selected many individuals from the ranks of those who had served with him before. This lack of experience especially concerned the XXIV Corps's division commanders. Oliver Smith made a similar observation. Something of an outsider as a marine, he held his Tenth Army colleagues in high regard. "Basically all of the staff were well grounded professionally, and, considering their initial lack of cohesion and their lack of combat experience, they did a very creditable job."[17] Buckner also insisted that the staff undergo a strong physical conditioning program. "He wanted his staff to be tough and would accept no excuses," Smith wrote after the war. "I believed and still believe that he was on the wrong track. The program General Buckner de[vis]ed was suitable for battalion commanders but not for staff officers, many of whom had passed their fiftieth birthday. Any army staff officer is subjected to considerable mental strain but he can do with a reasonable amount, only of physical conditioning. For the older officers the program resulted in broken collar bones, broken arms, sprained ankles, and charley horses."[18] Stilwell devoted considerable energy to remaking the Tenth Army staff after he took command. Like Buckner, he wanted a staff that he knew. During the summer of 1945 there was a massive personnel turnover in the Tenth Army headquarters.

A final theme in each diary is the writer's concern about the pending invasion of Japan. This concern was closely tied to the press controversy. General of the Army Douglas MacArthur had reservations about Buckner. MacArthur thought Buckner had sold out army interests to the navy. He recognized, however, that Japanese resistance was the main reason for the long, bloody campaign. Nevertheless, he talked with Stilwell about assuming command of the Tenth Army when the Joint Chiefs first transferred the unit to his theater command. For his part, Buckner thought MacArthur needlessly complicated interservice relations in an effort to enhance his own prestige. Although he realized his relationship with MacArthur was poor and made efforts to improve it, he expected to retain command of his army and fight in Japan.

When Stilwell took command of Tenth Army the battle for control of Okinawa was basically over, but he still had to oversee the mop-up operation. Far more important, though, was his leadership of the effort to establish Okinawa as a base for future operations against Japan. The Americans made use of the island in two ways. First, Okinawa quickly became a forward air base for bombing missions over Japan. General of the Army Henry H. "Hap" Arnold, commanding general of the Army Air Forces, told a meeting of the American, British, and Soviet chiefs of staff that he expected to station anywhere between two thousand and thirty-five hundred planes on the island. Moreover, the B-24 and B-29 bombers stationed in the Ryukyus would have a longer range and heavier payload capacity than those stationed elsewhere.[19] The United States would also use Okinawa as a forward staging area for the coming invasion of Japan. Preparing his army for this operation was Stilwell's main concern. He focused on little else during the month of July. Planning and training absorbed much of his time as he worked in an atmosphere of urgency and concern. Tenth Army had learned how to wage cave warfare and the procurement of the proper equipment for this type of combat was a top priority. He also began bringing in staff officers with whom he had previously worked, thus making Tenth Army his own. His papers are full of letters from officers wanting an assignment for what most thought would be the war's last major campaign.

Stilwell was bitterly disappointed when the conflict suddenly ended in August. All he had ever wanted was to lead troops in combat. It seemed to him that he had wasted his career. China did not count; it had been a futile effort. His days were soon filled with tedium. Letters from home, sunbathing, and good food were as important to him in breaking up the boredom as they were to the soldiers under his command.

These journals naturally reflect the different career paths Buckner and Stilwell followed. Buckner was in his late fifties when he assumed command of the newly formed Tenth Army in 1944. Other than the graying of his thick hair, his features showed little sign of age. His solid physique reflected the amazingly good athletic condition in which he kept himself. A naturalist, and a party goer of the first rank, Buckner's hawklike nose was the only feature that took away from his jutting jaw and dark, blazing eyes, which make it easy to understand his success as a womanizer.[20]

Buckner's early career was average at best. He spent it living in his father's shadow. Simon Bolivar Buckner, Sr., was a West Point graduate who earned the three stars of a lieutenant general during the Civil War. However, having acquired his rank in the Confederate army, his military career ended with the war. The elder Buckner entered politics after the war and became the governor of Kentucky and later the vice-presidential nominee of the "Gold Democrats" in 1896.

Simon, Jr., graduated from West Point in 1908 after his father secured an appointment for him from none other than the president of the United

States, Theodore Roosevelt. He saw no combat in World War I, and spent most of the interwar period as either a student or instructor in U.S. Army training programs and schools. Although he became an aviator during the Great War and was deeply interested in tanks, he remained an infantryman. While serving in these training and educational posts, Buckner absorbed and then disseminated U.S. Army doctrine that emphasized the decisive role of artillery in combat. According to this approach, the best way to destroy the enemy was through the use of overwhelming firepower in a head-on confrontation. The infantry's mission was to find and hold the enemy. The artillery would then destroy the opposing force. These tactics required matériel superiority for success, thus the need for a long logistical tail. During the battle on Okinawa, he explained his approach for winning to a group of reporters: "We're relying on our tremendous fire power and trying to crush them by weight of weapons."[21]

Buckner returned to West Point several times as an instructor during the interwar period. In the early 1930s he was the commandant of cadets—a position roughly equivalent to being the dean of students at a civilian university. During this time he developed a reputation as a stern disciplinarian. He allowed his cadets few luxuries. Buckner confiscated their cologne and after shave and screamed at his charges whenever they blundered. In one episode, he observed Cadet Maxwell Taylor walking around the grounds of the school arm in arm with a young lady. Taylor had two days until graduation and was intentionally flaunting the regulation prohibiting public signs of affection. Buckner knew the cadet's status, called Taylor into his office, and yelled at him, threatening to block his commissioning. The cadet spent the next forty-eight hours extremely uncertain about his future. Taylor survived Buckner's wrath, graduated, married the lady in question, and went on to become a four-star general and chairman of the Joint Chiefs of Staff.[22]

When war came a second time, Buckner spent most of it in Alaska, an area of only secondary importance. He had numerous clashes with the naval commander for the northern Pacific, which almost ended his career. In 1944, however, he received a third star and command of the new Tenth Army, even though its objective and mission were still uncertain.[23]

Although there were some occasional similarities, Stilwell's life and career were quite different from Buckner's. He grew up in Yonkers, New York, attended West Point, and played football at a time when the Military Academy was one of the dominant powers in college football. Like Buckner, he was a lifelong physical fitness fanatic.[24]

His early career went as well as could be expected in the small U.S. Army of the day. As a cadet he showed proficiency in several different languages, and the army sent him to China to learn Mandarin early in his career. He served as a liaison officer with the French army during World War I and saw combat while on detached duty. After the war, Col. George C. Marshall and China became large influences on his career. As the assistant commandant of the Infantry School at Fort Benning, Marshall instituted a small revolution in training. Stilwell was an unorthodox chief of tactics who emphasized creative problem-solving skills rather than a mandated solution to a specific problem. This style of training had a huge impact on the army, since many of the instructors and students going through the school eventually went on to hold important commands in World War II. Stilwell returned to China as the military attaché and his Chinese language ability greatly improved.[25]

When war broke out, Marshall, who became army chief of staff in 1939, considered Stilwell to be the best general in the service. He planned to make him the overall U.S. commander when American troops went to North Africa and then Europe. Then China intervened. Generalissimo Chiang Kai-shek, the president of the Republic of China, asked Pres. Franklin D. Roosevelt to send a general to China to serve as his chief of staff. Marshall reluctantly gave Stilwell the assignment because of his language ability. As a result, the command of U.S. troops in North Africa and then Europe that would have been Stilwell's went instead to Dwight D. Eisenhower, then a brigadier general and head of the War Plans Division.[26]

China was an exasperating theater of peripheral importance. The United States and its Allies had fundamentally different interests and strategies in the region. Roosevelt wanted China to contain the bulk of the Japanese army on the Asian continent while the army and navy approached Japan through the small island chains of the western Pacific. Chiang, on the other hand, wanted to use the Americans to destroy his Japanese enemies while he prepared for the coming showdown with the Chinese Communists. Chiang was more than willing to accept American lend-lease aid, and came to expect it as his due. He never came to understand that the Americans expected a return on their investment, however, and so was unwilling to use the new matériel or send his best units into combat. Corruption was also a major problem. Local commanders were often more interested in increasing their personal wealth than in fighting the Japanese. Major General Claire Chennault, the Fourteenth Air Force commander, worsened Stilwell's relations with Chiang by claiming that airpower alone could defeat the Japanese. The British complicated matters even further. Their goals were to preserve and retake their colonial empire and then defeat the Japanese. The Chinese Communists were the only group with aims close to those of the United States, but a number of political issues limited their cooperation.[27]

The differences between the Allies came to a head in 1944 when a Japanese offensive threatened to overtake the Fourteenth Air Force's airfields. Roosevelt issued an ultimatum demanding that Chiang give Stilwell command of the entire Chinese army. Chiang agreed at first, then retreated slowly, asking that the United States send a mediator to resolve the differences between himself and Stilwell. Finally, he said he would agree to American terms if Stilwell were replaced. From a distance the request seemed reasonable, so Roosevelt recalled his general, claiming that personality differences between Stilwell and Chiang rather than policy differences between the United States and China, were at fault. Stilwell returned home and, under orders from Marshall, made no public comments about his recall. He became the commander of the Army Ground Forces, a position in which he was responsible for the training of all ground combat troops in the United States. In May, 1945, with the war in Europe finally over, he went to the Pacific on an inspection trip—hoping all the while that MacArthur would give him a troop command.[28]

Part I

Buckner

1944

September 2

Had conference with Adm. Nimitz, Vice Adm. Spruance, Vice Adm. Turner and others Re: my coming project.[1] Spruance expressed doubt as to advisability of project and suggested a smaller island. Adm. Nimitz said that unless our project went through we would be tied to a southern project that would make the war last another year.[2]

September 4

★ ★ ★

Richardson's order assigning me officially to Army published today (at last).[3]

September 7

Sherman got back from Washington with no assurances of an early decision regarding my project.[4] Target date now set at 2 weeks later than first planned.

★ ★ ★

September 13

After morning naval conference Adm. Nimitz spoke to me about the Ralph Smith incident and my board report, regretting that Richardson had sent a copy to Washington to Gen. Marshall.[5] He wanted it all cleared up here. I agreed with him and called his attention to personalities involved and assured him that inter service feeling existed in my army. I also mentioned later the impropriety of my writing a personal letter to Gen. Marshall, thus short-circuiting Richardson. Adm. Nimitz agreed but hoped that Gen. Marshall would make it appropriate by bringing up the subject himself.[6]

★ ★ ★

October 3

Adm. Nimitz got back after his S.F. conference with Adm. King.[7] Looks like our present plan will be changed or deferred for lack of available service troops.[8]

★ ★ ★

October 7

Adm. Nimitz after sounding out my attitude on the Smith vs. Smith controversy and finding that I deplored the whole matter and harbored no inter-service ill feelings, announced that I would command the new joint project.

★ ★ ★

October 11

Got authority from Adm. Nimitz to organize separate island commander and staff.

* * *

October 27

2:00 P.M.: With Cowart went through obstacle course in 49 minutes.[9] Post informs me that many staff members are unable to get more than half through the course—poor condition.[10]

* * *

November 1

* * *

10:30 A.M.: Presented my combat plans to Adm. Turner and Adm. Spruance.

November 6

Fred Wallace arrived as my island commander.[11] His oldest son has just been killed in France, so I am letting him go home to see his family for two weeks. Meanwhile getting him oriented here and in touch with Colladay who has had similar experience.[12]

December 23

Gen. Trunesdell, Commandant at C&GS school spent morning discussing my organization and staff methods.[13] Says MacArthur wants all land troops in Pacific under one man (obviously himself).[14]

* * *

1945

January 6

* * *

Approved tentative orders for my operation. Annexes later.

January 8

2 P.M.: Presented alternate plan to Adm. Turner who accepted it.

* * *

January 9

Inspected AAA units. Lunch with Brig. Gen. Handwerk.[15] Most units looked well. Group HQ need more training as soldiers.

Brig. Gen. Garvin, Chief of Staff of XXIV Corps and several staff members arrived from Leyte to discuss plans.[16] Sent message asking Hodge to join them.[17] I shall postpone my planned trip of January 15 to see him but go a few days later to inspect my Divs. Looks as though our troops loaned to Gen. MacArthur for the Leyte campaign would be difficult to get back. I cautioned Adm. Nimitz of this when the XXIV Corps was sent there.[18]

January 17

Took Hodge to see Adm. Nimitz and had conference there regarding service units and rehabilitation of XXIV Corps. Adm. Nimitz decided to send a message to Gen. MacArthur insisting that latter live up to his agreement regarding the release of the Corps. Also decided to send Gen. Feldman to Leyte as his representative and Gen. Englehart as Gen. Richardson's.[19]

Got letter from Richardson intimating that he did not have full confidence in Wallace as my island commander, the he had not been the former's choice and asking that I state in writing whether or not I felt satisfied with him. (Evidently an attempt to shift the blame to me if he did not do well). I replied by stating that my only dissatisfaction with his work was the result of Richardson's being slow in furnishing him with an adequate and competent staff—thus dropping it squarely back into his lap. I also asked for Richardson's suggestions in the event that Wallace should not prove satisfactory just to see if he had a candidate.

February 7

⋆ ⋆ ⋆

Sent letter through Richardson to Adm. Nimitz asking that Gen. Geiger take over the Tenth Army should I become a casualty.[20] His reaction will be entertaining since he mortally fears and distrusts the Marines.

March 1

At the conference this morning were Pat Hurly (Ambassador to China), Gen. Wedemeyer, Adm. Cooke (Chief of Staff to Adm. King) and "Wild Bill" Donovan.[21] The first three were on their way back from the Roosevelt-Stalin-Churchill conference in Crimea.[22]

Had lunch with Richardson who had all the visiting firemen there. Afterwards had conference with Gen. Donovan in Fielder's office.[23] He wants to send representatives with the Tenth Army. I questioned him on what services they could render but was non-committal and told him that it was a matter of policy that Adm. Nimitz would have to decide.

★ ★ ★

March 3

Told Adm. Towers that I might use some of Bill Donovan's agent as secret service *after Phase I.*[24] Willing to take one man and try him out. Could take him on March 15. . . . Experienced no great enthusiasm but willing to try him.

★ ★ ★

March 4

★ ★ ★

Called on Richardson who said he was still awaiting word from War Department regarding command succession in case I became a casualty (pocket veto).

★ ★ ★

March 7

★ ★ ★

After supper there [at Adm. Charles H. McMorris's house on Guam] Adm. Spruance, Adms. Davis and McMorris had a conflict with us on air command relationships which was entirely satisfactory and flexible enough for all purposes.[25]

★ ★ ★

March 8

★ ★ ★

The Navy lives well ashore. They make themselves far more comfortable than the Army. Their houses are better, they are well furnished, including rugs, curtains, double and single beds, wicker and overstuffed furniture, mess china, mess boys and every comfort. At Adm. Nimitz mess now presided over by Adm. McMorris, the officers assembled at 6:30 for cocktails and have a very gay party before 7:00 P.M. (1900) dinner.[26]

★ ★ ★

March 9

From Leyte comes word that SWPAC has declined again to live up to agreements. This time concerning replacements for the XXIV Corps.

March 11

★ ★ ★

Had 11:00 A.M. press conference. Long emphasis on equal publicity for all services and the desirability of reaching down as far as possible to lower units and NCOs. Also including staff officers who are usually overlooked.

★ ★ ★

March 12

★ ★ ★

After lunch we went out with Adm. Turner in his barge and boarded our command ship the *Eldorado*. . . . We sailed shortly before six, a long looked-forward to occasion.

After sailing, Turner took me aside and dwelt on the difficulties and uncertainties of our mission which he characterized as a "son of a bitch" and asked what I thought about it. I expressed confidence and started to argue him out of his misgivings. I found then that he wasn't worried at all, but was trying to find out if I was.

After supper, Turner talked to Post and myself about the shore party set-up of the Marines whom he has less confidence in along these lines than he has in Army units. He said that the Marine shore party work at Iwo Jima was poor, particularly that of the V Corps and the 4th Div.

★ ★ ★

March 13

All day the *Eldorado* zigzagged westward escorted by the destroyer *Putnam*. Some of the gun crews drilled with dummy shells on a dummy gun, the idea being to acquire speed in loading. The skies are clear, the trade wind is with us and a moderate swell gives a little life to the ship. The destroyer stays a mile ahead of us.

★ ★ ★

There is very little life in the sea—no birds and only an occasional lonely flying fish.

After supper, Adm. Turner repeated his conversation of last night almost verbatim. He is still leery of shore parties and thinks the Marines know little about moving their supplies off the beaches and won't take experienced advice.

He doesn't consider Generals Geiger nor Schmidt very intelligent.[27] He regards Erskine as the best Div Commander in the V Phibcorps and doesn't admire the other two.[28]

Buckner to Adele Buckner, March 13

I am beginning this letter now and including news that can not be released at present.[29] This permits me to write things down as they happened and to mail the letter when the news can be appropriately divulged.

Yesterday I left Guam with about a dozen key members of my staff on board the joint command ship from which I will eventually disembark when my army goes ashore to fight. With me is ~~the~~ [strikethrough in original] Vice Admiral who will command the amphibious expedition, put us ashore, give us supporting gunfire and support us with escorts carrier planes until we can take enough air fields to stand on our own feet and fly in our own planes ~~in~~ [strikethrough in original] and support ourselves. The command ship and the admiral are just back from Iwo Jima were they performed a similar service for the V Marine Corps.

Major elements of my command will be a marine corps of three divisions and some more army divisions in reserve to be landed when and where the situation demands. In addition, there will be numerous corps, army and service troops to support the combat elements air units to join when we capture or build the necessary fields. My divisions are composed seasoned and experienced troops. In fact, I seem to be the only raw recruit in the crowd when battle experience is considered. However, the others should raise the average.

We are headed for the Philippines where I will watch some amphibious rehearsals of our landing operations and pick up the army corps in time to start for the objective. The marine corps embarks elsewhere and joins us. I have already visited both corps.

Escorted by a destroyer, our ship has been plowing westward all day through a moderate swell, constantly zig-zagging to worry any Jap submarine that try to torpedo us. I have seen only three flying fish since leaving Guam and no birds of any kind. I finished up a book called *Japan and the Japanese* and got a good start on *The Pacific World*.[30] When I finish writing this, I shall look over plans for what I shall have to do if I accomplish my present mission. [Buckner wrote this letter over a period of several days, dating each new portion of it. The sections are included after each day's diary entry.]

★ ★ ★

March 14

A couple of small balloons were released before lunch and shot at by the anti-aircraft guns aboard. The shooting was rotten.

★ ★ ★

March 15

★ ★ ★

Smoothed out the trigger pull on my pistol.

After supper I read and also got about caught up on my letter writing, if such a thing is possible.

March 16

About 9:30 A.M. we came into Leyte Gulf and went to a berth opposite Adm. Kinkaid's Headquarters of the Seventh Fleet. Harbor full of ships of all kinds.[31]

★ ★ ★

We . . . drove out to XXIV Corps HQ. The Corps and most of the staff were on amphibious rehearsals but we saw Gen. Garvin, Chief of Staff, and Talley and some of our staff.[32]

At 6:00 we went to Kinkaid's for dinner. Adm. Kaufman,[33] Commanding the Naval District was there. There was much speculation as to the future command set up in the Pacific and whether MacArthur would take over for the eventual attack on Japan. Kinkaid thinks he is very sound strategically but overlooks important operational details.

March 17

During the morning, we went over to where the XXIV Corps was having a landing rehearsal with the 7th and 96th Divs. A hard rain came up and make it impossible to carry out air support missions.

★ ★ ★

Buckner to Adele Buckner, March 17

> We got into Leyte yesterday and I saw Adm. Kinkaid of the Seventh Fleet; Eichelburger, commanding the Eighth Army, and his chief of staff Clovis Byers. The last two sent you their very best. Today I watched amphibious rehearsals for my landing and Gen. Hodge, commanding my XXIV Corps.

March 19

During the morning our staff manned battle positions and we observed another amphibious landing by the XXIV Corps. They were 15 minutes late crossing the line of departure and Adm. Turner said he was going to relieve the LST Div commander responsible for the delay.

Gen. Mulcahy (USMC) commanding my land based aircraft arrived from Honolulu and joined us aboard.[34]

I told Dumas that he might go to Manila to see his sister-in-law who had been a captive in Jap hands since the outbreak of the war, provided he could fly up tomorrow and return next day.[35] He wants to supply her with funds. She is still at Santo Tomas, where she was confined.

March 20

Dumas couldn't get plane transportation to Manila, after all.

The morning was uneventful, except for a visit from Gen. Bruce (77th Div) and Rear Adm. Kiland who is taking him to his objective.[36] Bruce, as usual, is rarin' to go and is looking well ahead for action. I much prefer a bird dog that you have to whistle in to one that you have to urge out. He is of the former variety.

★ ★ ★

I gave Hodge a quart of scotch and a pistol slide with a stainless steel front sight. He let me have the second volume of *Lee's Lieutenants* by Freeman to read.[37] I started it when I was last with him in January.

March 21

Today the 77th Div (Bruce) started for the target. At last our advance guard is headed for the enemy with no intermediate stops. Bruce is rarin' to go.

From 2 to 5 P.M. we went to the *Teton,* Adm. Hall's flagship and listened to a critique of the amphibious rehearsals.[38] There was a general feeling of confidence and assurance at the meeting. I saw Arnold (7th Div) and Jim Bradley (96th Div) at the meeting.[39] After the first hour, the benefit arrived from critiques progressed in accordance with the law of diminishing returns.

Don Prior of the combined American radio networks wants me to go on the air with him and Adm. Turner when we are on the target, just as he did with the latter, Holland Smith and Schmidt at Iwo Jima.[40] I would much prefer to keep quiet but saw no way out of it since Turner accepted.

Buckner to Adele Buckner, March 21

For several days I have been watching practice landing exercise on the beaches here, attending critiques and getting impatient to move on. Last night, I had dinner ashore with Gen. Hodge, commanding the XXIV Corps. Archie Arnold, Jim Bradley and Bruce are the division commanders in the corps. Tomorrow night, Adm. Turner, Eddie Post and I dine with Eichelberger. He is off today watching a landing to mop Japs on another island. The Japs fortify the old Spanish towns and we have to destroy them to get at the Japs. I am afraid that Manila, Zambonaga, Cebu, Iloilo and Ilo will all be gone before the Japs are destroyed. Large parts of these towns have already been burned by the Japs.

Today was a great day. I was the convoy with my leading division move out on its non-stop trip to strike the enemy. Those of us who are to follow for the main landing got a great thrill out of it. Mulcahy, a big red-faced Irish Maj. Gen. of Marines who commands my land-based air force was standing near me when the convoy slowly steamed by with its escort of destroyers darting about on the watch for submarines. He looked up with a broad smile and said "Here goes the kick-off for the big game."

March 22

Had a rough, rainy trip to and from Eichelberger's dinner.[41] He had just returned from his Iloilo expedition. The Japs left the city and took to the hills. About 2/3 of the city and all of the water front has been burned. Eichelberger drove into Iloilo in a jeep. Maj. Gen. Irwin and an Australian brigadier were also at the party.[42] Byers was away.[43] On the way back the cockswain of the Admiral's barge got lost in the rain and Adm. Turner took over and got us back.

March 23

We stormed over toward the Samar coast this morning and took on fuel from an oiler.

Further details came regarding Adm. Mitschner's strike in the Japanese Inland Sea.[44] The fact that he could cripple warships there is a real landmark in the war. It means that the Japs now have no safe anchorage anywhere in which they can restore or hide their fleet. Their intelligent men can't help realizing this.[45]

Buckner to Adele Buckner, March 23

Six of us had a most enjoyable dinner with Eichelberger last night. He had just flown back from the capture of Iloilo. The Japs took to the hills leaving entire water front and two-thirds of the city destroyed.

March 24

Today was spent having a command post exercise using the actual messages that were sent during the first Iwo Jima assault day. It was an excellent way to shake down the staff and teach them what to expect.

Messages were picked up to the effect that the Japs had located some battleships near Okinawa and that they had made at least one air attack on our mine sweepers. Nothing came directly from our forces, although the sweeping and bombardment were to have begun today.

March 25

Our LSTs and tractor outfits moved out this morning. Being slower than the transports, they need a head start. They will meet us on the objective.

Buckner to Adele Buckner, March 25

> Yesterday my staff manned all their positions on the command ship and had a command post exercise using the actual messages sent and received during the first days attack and I have seen attack and landing on Iwo Jima. It gave them all a good idea of what kinds of messages and events are likely to come up on the day of our main landing.
>
> Our carrier forces and battleships have struck our objective and our mine sweeping was due to begin today. Tomorrow, my leading division lands to secure the Kerma Retto, a group of small islands just southwest of Okinawa. We will forfeit strategic surprise by this but it is necessary for the fleet and will strengthen the main attack and landing.
>
> We are now having an air alert in San Pedro Bay—possibly a Jap snooper trying to check the movements of our big fleet here at dusk. This is our third since we have been here.

March 26

Early morning messages indicate that the bombardment, minesweeping and air attacks came off as scheduled. UDTs report only 1 moored and 6 floating mines and beach conditions in the Kerama Retto about as expected. Only rifle fire at UDTs and only 1 casualty.

10:00 A.M.: We had a demonstration of the use of 5 lb. TNT charges against Jap underwater swimmers. We dropped one in 60 feet of water and killed a good many small fish.

Intercepted local message indicate that the 77th has a good foothold in the Kerama Retto but nothing direct from him.

A message from Adm. Mitschner says that Okinawa is honey-combed with caves, tunnels and emplacements and predicts a very tough job for us. Tomorrow we start on a great adventure.

Buckner to Adele Buckner, March 26

* * *

> I have seen a good deal recently of Eichelberger who commands the Eighth Army here. He is busy mopping up the southern islands. Clovis Byers is his chief of staff. Eichelberger looks well but is irritated over having to do the cleanup job after Kruger has had the interesting part of the campaign. I hope to have better luck with the Tenth. There is plenty of fresh ground to be broken and some of it is none too soft. The fighting will be more and more interesting as we press forward into the Mikado's domains. Iwo Jima is an example of how heavily a small island can be fortified. The marines had a tough time there because every inch of the island was defended by solid rock and concrete emplacements. The Marines did a good job in taking it and its capture compensates for the heavy losses. In actual numbers the marine casualties equal those of Lee at Gettysburg. This will give you some idea of how heavy the fighting was.[46]

* * *

Buckner to Adele Buckner, March 26

> Fragmentary messages tell of a foothold on the Kerama Retto by our leading divisions. Adm. Mitchner also says that the recent air reconnaissance shows Okinawa to be honeycombed with fortifications. He predicts a tough job for us. [Buckner wrote two letters to his wife on this date.]

March 27

At 10:45 A.M. our convoy weighed anchor and moved with an air of dignified confidence on its non-stop trip to close with the enemy. When we were well started a message came to the effect that a sailor in the *Eldorado*'s crew had just been designated to attend an officer's training school. We signaled to a PT boat which came alongside. The sailor slid down a ladder which we lowered, someone threw his bags into the PT boat after him and the little craft took him smiling toward shore.

In the afternoon we briefed all the war correspondents aboard and had some anti-aircraft practice at sleeves by planes from our escort carriers.

Just before supper, word came from Bruce that the landing of the 77th

Div in the Kerama Retto was progressing well and that he had captured 38 suicide boats hidden in caves.

March 28

Finished reading the third volume of Freeman's *Lee's Lieutenants: Gettysburg to Appomattox*.[47] A tragic epitaph to a nobly defended cause.

Buckner to Adele Buckner, March 28

> Word came that the Kerama Retto had been occupied according to plane with very few casualties. Two hundred fifty 1-man "suicide" attack boats were captured in caves along the shores. Twelve strangled native women were found in one cave.

March 29

The gun crews of the ships in the convoy practiced following planes from the carriers that stimulated strafing attacks. Our ship also launched its paravanes to see if they were in order and that the crew knew how to use them.

Adm. Turner now spends all his time and takes his meals on the flag bridge. His staff said that he had never messed with the troop commander's staff until the two weeks that he was with us from Guam until the convoy left Leyte.

March 30

Number of suicide boats captured in Kerama Retto now reported as over 300.

Had abandon ship drill in PM.

Had a submarine contact and passed one or more floating mines. During the afternoon a destroyer came alongside and delivered mail via breeches buoy.

Buckner to Adele Buckner, March 30

> A submarine contact and a couple of floating mines were reported by our escort vessels.

March 31

Ely came aboard from a destroyer in a breeches buoy.[48] Had just left Adm. Blandy task force with the 77th Div and had the latest pictures and UDT reports.[49]

Tomorrow is Easter Sunday, my father's birthday and the day of my first battle. I hope that I shall be able to look back upon it with the same degree of enthusiasm with which I anticipate it.

Attended Easter services at 8:15 P.M. and turned in early so as to be fresh for tomorrow's events.

BUCKNER TO ADELE BUCKNER, MARCH 31

> Colonel Ely, my G-2 and son of Gen. Hanson Ely, came back from the Kerama Retto on a destroyer and boarded us with a breeches buoy. He had the latest pictures and reports of the landing beaches. These, he reported, had been distributed to every battalion that is to land tomorrow. With members of my staff, I am attending Easter services this evening. Tomorrow is our big day—incidentally my father's birthday.

April 1

Rose at 4:30 and had hot cakes for breakfast by way of getting fortified for a day of fighting. The weather was good and the golden sunrise was not for Japan. Shortly before six some Jap planes attacked. Seven were shot down. Apparently we shot down an eighth that was ours.

The crescendo of the bombardment, culminating in the rocket discharge was a magnificent spectacle. From start to finish the landing was a superb piece of teamwork, which we could watch from the 50-yard line in the command room on the flag deck. We landed practically without opposition and gained more ground than we expected to for three days, including the Yomitan and Kadena airfields. Arnold's 7th Div made the furthest gains and got half way across the island. The weather continues [to be] good and we have nearly 10,000 troops ashore with negligible casualties.

At about dusk several suicide planes came in. The *West Virginia* and one other ship were hit. We set up a smoke screen around our ship. Tonight the sky is constantly lighted by star shells.

The Japs have missed their best opportunity on the ground and in the air. When their counter-attack comes we will be holding strong ground.

After a careful analysis of Okinawa's geography, Col. Yahara Hiromichi, senior officer in charge of operations of the Japanese Thirty-second Army on the island, accurately predicted the location and size of the American invasion force. In a memo to his commander, Lt. Gen. Ushijima Mitsuru and the chief of staff, Lt. Gen. Cho Isamu, he argued that the Thirty-second Army lacked the strength to defend the beaches. Since the northern half of the island was mountainous, making it impossible to build military bases or airfields there, he recommended that the army concede it to the Americans and defend only the southern portion of the island. He suggested they allow the Americans to land on the beaches

unopposed and take the island's north end. Ushijima and Cho agreed with Yahara's assessment and adopted his proposed strategy.[50]

Buckner to Adele Buckner, April 1

> From the opening bombardment and air attack to the landing of the last tank and gun our assault against Okinawa today was as beautiful a piece of teamwork as I have ever seen. Opposition was light, the Japs evidently having expected us to land elsewhere on the island. We gained more ground today than we had hoped to get within three days. This included two air fields Some of our ships were hit by planes but none sunk. The enemy has launched no counter attack so far, but we have gained ground that will give us strong positions. We should be able to hold and later expand. I consider the day highly successful. We have nearly 60,000 troops ashore and will land more tomorrow.

April 2

A Jap plane was shot down at dawn by AAA.

The 7th Div got entirely across the island today. Being well ahead of the 1st Mardiv on its left, it could not turn south abreast of the 96th Div which was attacking in that direction against gradually stiffening resistance. Some opposition was met by the left of the III Phibcorps. Weather excellent.

I have decided to order up the 27th Div from Ulithi to land on the east shore about April 10. Hodge came aboard during the afternoon.

Adm. Spruance is trying to hurry us in the capture of Ie [Sh]ima. This would gain no time in completing the field and would use up the army reserves before the main fight starts.

In a letter to an old friend, Spruance commented: "I doubt if the Army slow, methodical method of fighting really saves any lives in the long run. It merely spreads the casualties over a longer period. The longer period greatly increases the naval casualties when Jap air attacks on ships is a continuing factor. However, I do not think the Army is at all allergic to losses of naval ships and personnel. There are times when I get impatient for some of Holland Smith's drive, but there is nothing we can do about it." Spruance's biographer, however, disagreed with the admiral's assessment, arguing that Okinawa was better suited for army units.[51]

Main Jap forces are apparently in the south and heavy fighting should start within two days.

At dusk 12 suicide planes attacked Kerama shipping. The struck and damaged 4 transports. Ships in our vicinity put up a smoke screen.

A slightly injured Jap plane landed today by mistake on a field that we had captured. He was shot when he started to run and the plane was captured.

Buckner to Adele Buckner, April 2

> We got across to the east coast of the island today, cutting it in two. Resistance is stiffening somewhat on both flanks but the Jap commander failed to counter attack this morning. A slightly damaged Jap plane landed today on a field that the pilot did not know we had captured. He was "very sorry please." So far, the Jap's apparent misconception of our plan, his failure to oppose our landing have made things easy for us, but very hard fighting against a strong system of concrete and underground defenses is still ahead of us. However, we are here to stay.

Buckner soon realized what Ushijima planned to do with his army. In an April 24 conversation with Post and Col. John Stevens, an army historian assigned to Tenth Army, Buckner said he suspected that the Japanese conceded the landing for one of two reasons: seizure of the small islands off the coast of Okinawa convinced Ushijima that the Americans would land in the south, or he realized his best chance of defeating the invaders was to engage them in the heavily fortified zones, avoiding the danger of being out maneuvered in the open areas behind the beaches.[52]

April 3

Yesterday 11 women armed and in Jap uniforms along with some soldiers tried to attack 96th Div FA positions and were killed.

Disapproved Hodge's request to have 77th Div land and cover his rear. (He probably wants to assure himself that it will remain in his corps).

All units progressed satisfactorily. The 7th Div got turned south and the 1st Mardiv reached the east coast. Resistance still light.

The 27th Div was sent for to land on the east coast about April 10. It is at Ulithi.

The 2nd Mardiv ordered to land April 5 on beaches north of those now used by III Phibcorps. Geiger came aboard after lunch in fine spirits.

At sundown our fighters reported that 25 Jap planes started toward our ships but after 13 had been shot down, the rest left.

Buckner to Adele Buckner, April 3

> Good progress continues against light resistance. Main defenses appear to be in the south and heavy fighting will probably begin tomorrow

or next day. About 13 planes were shot down while attacking our ships today at sunset and others driven off. No ship was hit.

★ ★ ★

Everything is now going well and so far my opposing general has not displayed any noticeable degree of military brilliance. At least, he has not yet done [any] of the things that I hoped he would not think of. I hope he keeps this up.

Thoughts of my responsibility for so many lives are always sobering, but the fine fighting qualities of my men fill me with enthusiasm in my present task.

April 4

Air raids reported so far have come at dawn or dusk, many suicide planes. Numbers as follows:

April 1	15 attacked	11 shot down
April 2	30 attacked	12 shot down
April 3	71 attacked	26 shot down

Wind today shifting to north and slightly slowing up unloadings. Work progressing on air fields.

Hodge, Geiger and Adm. Reifsnider came aboard.[53]

I was unable to go ashore as I had planned due to two conferences on future operations.

Troops are beginning to [encounter] enemy positions to the south. Bradley well ahead of Arnold. The latter in very rough ground. The Marines cleaned up everything to the north and started up the isthmus practically unopposed. Some evidence of looting and vandalism. I issued further instructions to stop this.

Handelman of the International News Service wants a statement from me to issue on V-E Day.[54] I told him I knew nothing of V-E Day and wouldn't tell anybody if I did. Too many people have already talked too much on that subject.

April 5

Cold north wind, rain and some swells. Very little unloading as the result. No planes attacked this group.

Had conference with Geiger and Adm. Reifsnider regarding Phase 2. Also conferred with my own staff regarding Phase 3 and what is to follow.[55]

Sherrod, who was in Alaska as a correspondent came to see me.[56] He is on his way to N.Y.

The 3rd Mardiv continued to advance northward against negligible resistance. A few Okinawans had been given guns. They don't know either how to fight or how to surrender. They shoot a few rounds and go into caves but won't come out and have to be killed. The 7th and 96th Divs moved slowly against increasing resistance.

The civil population remains docile. Two men who killed their wives because the Japs told them they would be raped to death became very hostile to the Japs when they surrendered themselves and found this not to be true. One attacked a Jap prisoner.

Am preparing to land a reconnaissance group on Ie [Sh]ima. The eastern islands are being reconnoitered today by the Marine Recon Bn.

April 6

The Japanese cabinet fell today.

The northern flank continued to advance without opposition and the southern force [began] to [encounter] a strong Jap position.

During the morning Adm. Spruance came aboard and with Adm. Turner and myself conferred on the next phase of the campaign. We all were in agreement. Adm. Spruance's flagship had recently been hit by a suicide plane whose bombs went completely through the ship, broke a propeller shaft and exploded on the other side of the vessel. He is now on the *New Mexico*.[57]

From 3:30 P.M. on we were under constant air attack largely by suicide planes. Six or seven ships were hit, mostly destroyers in our picket screens. Also an ammunition ship which was abandoned

Very few planes got to the transport area. I saw only four hit the water near our ship.[58]

An ammunition dump blew up on Kadena airfield and a gasoline barge burned on shore—possibly from falling anti-aircraft shells that shot down a friendly plane and caused 41 casualties in shore parties.

April 7

Went ashore in barges *Annabelle the Whore* and *Bertha the Vicious Virgin*.

Yesterday's reports indicate that between 3:30 P.M. and dark our shipping was attacked by 182 planes of which 116 were either shot down by our planes and AA, or dived at or into ships. There were 22 separate groups attacking. Twenty-two got in far enough for suicide dives and 14 ships were hit by 18 planes. Most hits were on destroyers. Two ammunition ships were hit and blew up at Kerama Retto.[59]

This morning at 7:30 I made (reluctantly) a 2-minute Army Day talk over the radio.

News came of Gen. MacArthur being put in command of all Army troops in the Pacific. Adm. Nimitz will retain naval command.[60]

From 10:00 A.M. to 5:00 I was ashore visiting the CPs of the XXIV Corps, the 7th Div and the 96th Div. From a hill watched the Div Bn attack a hill. Had lunch at Arnold's CP. Saw Bradley in his CP at the agricultural school. Very luxuriously furnished.

Visited Kadena airfield—it is ready for planes except for gas and ground crew which should arrive in a day or so. Saw some suicide rocket planes with 2,000 lb. warheads. Four Marine fighter squadrons occupied the Yomitan field today. There was little enemy air activity today.

Adm. Spruance carrier planes sank BB *Yamato,* 1 cruiser and 3 destroyers and damaged other destroyer near Kyushu today.

Planes from Fast Carrier Force (Task Force 58), under the command of Adm. Marc Mitscher attacked the Yamato *as its task force approached Okinawa. Had the* Yamato, *the largest warship ever built at that time, reached the Okinawa area, it could have done considerable damage since its main guns had a longer range than those of any American battleship. However, most of the sailors aboard the* Yamato *realized they were on a one-way mission. The intent of the mission was to distract the U.S. Navy and give kamikaze attack planes an opportunity to break through American defenses. The overwhelming airpower of the U.S. Navy made even this mission next to impossible. The* Yamato *was strong and took the beating of ten torpedoes and five bombs before it sank. American fighters also sank the destroyer* Hamakaze *and cruiser* Yahagi.[61]

April 8

Very little air attack today. Adm. Mitschner's carriers finished off a light cruiser and two or more destroyers of the fleet hit yesterday.[62]

Went ashore and spent day visiting III Phibcorps, 1st Marine Div and 6th Mardiv. Had lunch with Gen. Del Valle who had fresh pork for which I took him to task.[63]

Sixth Mardiv advancing rapidly into Motobu Peninsula, killing about 50 Japs a day. Slight resistance against disorganized groups, some from Navy.

Some sniper fire against 1st Mardiv HQ at night.

Okinawa civilians a pathetic lot[;] coming of holes carrying children, old people, and few belongings. Many seem docile and often smile and wave as we pass. They seem to dislike the Japs. Many of their villages are destroyed but they accept it stoically. Some say they are glad we are here and give us information about the Japs.

The XXIV Corps advanced about 1,000 yds against increasing resistance. I am going to land the 27th Div to give impetus to its attack and use the 77th to take Ie [Sh]ima after the 27th lands. Part of the 27th, meanwhile I shall use to secure the eastern islands.

Buckner to Adele Buckner, April 8

While my HQ is still afloat, where I am in better communications than I could be on shore at present, I have spent the past two days ashore visiting all Div and Corps Headquarters and watching the progress of the fighting. All units are doing splendidly but heavy resistance is developing in the south as I anticipated. We have a deep area of concrete and steel to break, but we can break it. Casualties so far have been light, but will be heavier from now on. The Okinawan civilians are coming out of their holes and being taken over by the civil government section of my command. They are a pathetic lot, small, dark and heavily bearded. It is pitiful to see what modern weapons do to civilian communities harboring enemy defenses, but is necessary to shoot the enemy out of whatever positions they hold. If we were not doing it here they would be doing it in our country and with their characteristic barbarous savagery.

The Jap soldiers told the Okinawans to kill their women rather than let us take them. A few of them did so and, after finding that we treated civilians well, they are most hostile to the Japs. The Okinawans are a docile people who have always been looked down upon and mistreated by the Japs. I passed streams of them on the road today carrying their babies and their few household possessions. Many of them smiled and waved at us. In contrast, a good many Jap women have infiltrated into our lines at night with weapons and explosives and tried to blow up our equipment.

This morning I saw an old man toddling down the road with a heavy sack on his shoulders. He looked scared to death and was passing a halted line of trucks and jeeps. As he passed each he would hold his free hand high above his head to show that he was unarmed. When he got opposite the jeep in front of mine, the soldier in it made a quick move and reached in his pocket. The old man thought his last moment had come and stood petrified with terror as the soldier whipped out a large cigar and presented it to him. He dropped his bundle and began to smile and bow. When I last saw him he was still smiling and bowing himself into a state of utter exhaustion.

We have had intermittent dawn and sundown air attacks daily against our large fleet offshore in process of unloading but two days ago we were under constant attack from shortly after 3:00 P.M. until after dark. In all, twenty-two groups of planes totaling about 182 in all came after us. Some ships were hit but our planes and anti-aircraft shot down 116 that we counted, and a good many others may not have gotten back to Japan. I have had thrills in duck blinds but none comparable to that of seeing an enemy plane shot down when it was heading directly at our ship.

The success of our operation here has overthrown the Japanese cabinet and, considering their recent sea and air losses, it will be difficult for them to find another militant cabinet willing to take the responsibility for conducting a losing war. Nobody wants to take command of a sinking ship. Consequently, unless the whole nation becomes fanatical, it is not unlikely that the next cabinet may be made up of a conservative group that will try to salvage what they can by making peace feelers before long. However, the Japanese mind seems to work in an unpredictable manner. We can only fight and see.

★ ★ ★

April 9

Gen. Griner came aboard after breakfast and conferred regarding his landing.[64] He was attached to the XXIV Corps and landed on western beaches this afternoon except 1 reinforced regiment that is to capture the eastern islands tomorrow.

I spent the afternoon visiting the wounded in the hospital ships: comfort and solace: sailors badly burned by suicide planes.

Our first mail arrived but none from home.

Heavy resistance with increasing arty, mortar and rocket bomb fire encountered on the southern front. Our advance slow.

April 10

Spent the day ashore. The enemy in front of the XXIV Corps is superbly fortified and probably outnumbers our 2 attacking Divs.

Buckner's estimate of Japanese strength was incorrect. The defenders were outnumbered by about two to one. However, the general's assessment of Japanese fortifications was correct. The XXIV Corps had encountered the first of three lines of defense the Japanese had established using an interconnected system of tunnels, trenches, caves, blockhouses, pillboxes, and islanders' tombs on both the reverse and forward slopes of hills. These fortifications neutralized American artillery fire and channeled attacking units into prepared fire zones that often overlapped one another. The Thirty-second Army also had more artillery support than any other Japanese force the Americans had encountered in the war, and it had a six-month supply of ammunition.[65]

Our 96th is receiving a considerable number of casualties. The 27th Div landed today but rains have bogged it down and held up arty ammunition which is now short on our southern front. I told Hodge that a heavy attack would not be profitable until the 27th reached his front line at which time he should make it. I also told him of my plan to turn over the 77th to him after it took Ie [Sh]ima about April 16. I am trying to arrange with Adm. Turner to make a demonstration against southern part of the island at the time of Hodge's attack so as to contain or divert resources of the enemy.[66]

Went to 96th Div CP and took Bradley up to Col. Dill's Regt where an OP overlooked the enemy position but it was too rainy and foggy to see anything.[67] Coming back the roads were so bad we had to substitute a weasel for our jeep. Hubbard was with me.[68]

More mail came today with a letter from Adele mailed March 24.

Sent a message to Gen. MacArthur by way of greeting our new over-all commander.

April 11

Received a gracious reply to my message to Gen. MacArthur.

A Bn of the 27th Div took the eastern islands of Nagokasuko Wan yesterday. They were lightly held. Only 150 Japs killed. One of our destroyers was hit 6 times by a 75mm gun during the landing.[69]

Weather again prevented unloading on western beaches today. Slight resistance found in northern part of Motobu Peninsula but 6th Mardiv continues to advance.

The XXIV Corps continues to consolidate preparatory to an attack after the 27th Div gets on the line.

Bruce came aboard to arrange details of his attack on Ie [Sh]ima. As usual, he is rarin' to try a landing behind the Jap main position in southern Okinawa.[70]

Adm. Sherman came aboard representing Adm. Nimitz to confer regarding airfield development here; the rehabilitation of divisions here and Phase III of this operation. He agreed with our recommendation on the last 2 items. We must await further reconnaissance before we are ready to make final airfield recommendations.

Nine–9:15 P.M.: Watched plotting of a bogie's course, the vectoring of our angel until the latter reported visual contact and then the report: "one bogy splashed."

April 12

Several plane attacks about 4:30 A.M. Flack fell on our deck wounding 1 man: 7 planes shot down near us.

Spent entire day on board the *Eldorado.*

Conferred with Adm. Cobb in the morning regarding his future duties and with Hodge in afternoon regarding his coordinated attack to be made in conjunction with a demonstration.[71] Arty ammunition shortage due to bad unloading, weather and muddy roads; makes it desirable to have him attack after Ie [Sh]ima is captured.

We were under constant air attack from about 1:45 P.M. until dark, mostly by suicide planes. Some battleships (2) and (7) radar pickets were hit. Apparently one sinking.[72] I saw only one get to the transport area and it splashed. Another fell in flames over the island opposite our anchorage from so high a point that we couldn't see it start down. Preliminary reports indicate over 100 planes shot down (Final score: 128).

Some small counter-attacks against 6th Mardiv in Motobu Peninsula. No appreciable gains in the south. Japs bombed Yomitan and shelled Kadena fields without serious injury.

Forty tons of ammunition blew up in the XXIV Corps sector as the result of enemy shelling.

April 13

Press asked me to make a statement regarding the President's death, which I did, chiefly to get rid of them.[73]

Spent most of the day ashore visiting the III Phibcorps and 6th Mardiv. The latter has reached the extreme north of the Motubu Peninsula but must still reduce a center of resistance in the center estimated variously as from 1,000 to 2,500 Japs.[74]

Civilians are pouring in by the thousand and being taken over by the civil government. Had a talk with Crist who has started them to harvesting the ripe barley at my suggestion.[75] The women seem to be doing all the work. It is almost incredible to see what burdens they carry on their heads. In addition most of them have babies strapped to their backs.

Visited Mulcahy and Dillon at the Yomitan airfield.[76] The latter is on crutches from a sprained knee damaged by his jumping into a foxhole when a 20mm shell went through his tent.

Cargo is going ashore rapidly again and the roads have dried out.

No appreciable progress in the south.

Post woke me up at about midnight with news that the war in Europe was over. This misinformation resulted from a garbled message to prepare speeches to be broadcast "*when*" V-E Day came. The "*when*" was garbled. [Emphasis in original.]

About a dozen planes shot down today.

April 14

Spent day ashore. Visited new CP site, went to see Iscom and Talley to speed up ammunition unloading. Saw Hodge and Griner at XXIV Corps HQ. Also went to the 7th and 96th Div CPs. Bradley was sick in bed, apparently with nervous indigestion from his long strain. Easley thought that all he needed was a rest.[77]

Sixth Mardiv reached north end of island with patrols. Twenty-fourth Corps still preparing for attack. Twenty-seventh Div partly in line on the right.

Bradley reported killing about 600 out of 900 counter-attacking him two days ago. No counter-attack against Arnold.

Only 6 or 8 planes shot down today. One picket boat hit by suicides.[78]

Buckner to Adele Buckner, April 14

★ ★ ★

We have now finished our second week of battle and have all the northern part of Okinawa plus some outlying islands both east and west. In the south, we are up against the most formidable defenses yet encountered in the Pacific, well backed up by artillery and navy mortars. I am not hurrying the attack on the south, but am greatly reducing casualties by a gradual and systematic destruction of their works. This we are doing successfully and can, I feel confident, break their line in ample time for our purposes.

While I go ashore every day and visit the front, my headquarters is still afloat so as to work with the Navy which is giving us splendid support and protecting our beaches and ship unloading.

We are constantly under air attack but our carrier planes and my own operating from captured fields have down a splendid piece of work and shot down several hundred of the attacking planes. The quality of Jap pilots is deteriorating and those recently encountered show evidence of hasty and inadequate training.

We were all grieved over the President's death and still feel some concern over his successor's lack of diplomatic experience. We are relieved, however, that Wallace was not Vice-President.

In spite of the bad name given to Okinawa as a snake-infested, malaria ridden pest hole, everyone here finds it the best island we have yet taken from the Japs. The climate has been delightful, the island picturesquely beautiful, the flies, snakes and mosquitoes almost non-existent and the country fertile, well drained and healthy.

Evidently there are occasional typhoons, since the houses are built to resist high winds. They are in small groups surrounded by stone walls about five feet height. Planted along the walls are hedges of topped banyan trees, so trained as to make the pendant roots grow along the wall and for a palisade of trunks close together and surrounding the compound. The houses are mostly of coral rock with roofs of thatch or tiles. There are almost no doors or glass windows, sliding panels instead.

★ ★ ★

So far, everything is progressing well, the men are in good spirits and the fight is past its most critical stage. We will have some tough going but it is getting progressively tougher for our enemies. Incidentally, Jap claims of ship sinkings are absurdly extravagant as usual.

April 15

Spent the day ashore visiting the III Phibcorps. The 6th Mardiv and a civil affairs unit. Saw too much wanton destruction by Marines and told Shepherd and Geiger so.[79]

Went to front-line OP in 6th Mardiv with Shepherd and looked at enemy positions in center of Motobu Peninsula. Remnants of Jap forces seem to be digging in on a hill there. Six Bns will attack tomorrow.

Saw two Marines holding a goat, a third trying ineffectually to milk her and a small kid nearby squalling for its lost dinner.

Saw my first two snakes. Birds seem few in number and species. Have seen 2 small Japanese quail, 2 white herons, half a dozen crows; some swallows, 3 doves, a few English (?) sparrows and a dozen slate-colored birds with black wings and tails about the size of shrikes. Also a beautiful small deep blue Kingfisher.

Air raid against Yomitan field at sunset and at dark. Not much damage done by Jap raid but a good many casualties and damaged planes by our own AA fire. The ships fire low and toward shore. They also burned two gasoline dumps.

A few hostile planes were shot down.

April 16

Spent day visiting CPs of XXIV Corps, 27th Div and 96th Div. Also went to 2 forward OPs in 96th area to look over enemy positions.

Saw Bradley who appears in better health and spirits than he did two days ago.

The general situation on the north and south fronts remains unchanged. Attacks being prepared.

The 77th Div was landed on Ie [Sh]ima at about 8:00 A.M. after having put arty ashore on Minna Jimma. Very little opposition on beaches. Airfields taken and garrison retired to the hill at east end of island. Numbers estimated from 200 to 1,000. Attack will continue against them tomorrow. Only 2 RCTs of 77th Div were landed.

Our new CP ashore is partly occupied and will be ready in a couple of days.

I told Griner to seal up any tombs in his area.

TF 58 reported shooting down 166 planes.

April 17

Very little change in general situation. TF 58 reported "another good day" after saying they were under attack. Saw a picket boat with a suicide plane stuck into the bridge—Captain and 30 of crew killed.[80]

Visited 1st Mardiv and spent rest of day in civil government camps. Lt. Cmdr. Fraser (Mass[achusetts] lawyer) has Shimubau camp well organized and doing useful work.[81]

Watched civilians also on Peninsula between Chimu and Nakagusuku Wan where about 40,000 of them are left practically to their own devices.

Buckner to Adele Buckner, April 17

Heretofore I have been spending most of my days ashore, but sleeping on the command ship with Adm. Turner. Tomorrow I will move permanently ashore, now that I have all my wire lines and other communications installed. I was in my command post today and it is a pleasant spot with a lovely view except on occasions when unpleasant things are dropping into it from guns and planes, at which time I have a dug-out to retire into.

I spent the day visiting and inspecting my civil government camps. Our men are doing a good job in handling the natives and making them as self-sufficient and healthy as possible. They have been living in caves and dugouts for some time and need a lot of cleaning up. They say that we give them more and better food than they have gotten since the war started.

The general situation here is little changed except that we took the air field on Ie Shima yesterday and expect to clean up the rest of the garrison by tomorrow or next day. They are well dug in on a hill, but I landed enough troops to handle them without difficulty.

Everyone here considers Okinawa the best island they have seen in the Pacific. Strategically it [is] highly important to our air and naval forces as a base to prevent further trouble from starting in the Orient. I hope we are sensible enough to keep it.

★ ★ ★

April 18

Adm. Turner came aboard. Says his carrier flyers are carrying a heavy load in defending themselves and helping us and are showing fatigue.

Moved my CP ashore after lunch. Got settled and visited XXIV Corps CP.

All set for tomorrow's attack.

Took Hubbard forward to 7th Div CP to spend night so as to watch jump off tomorrow from forward OP in that Div. One of our 155mm gun batteries fired over our tent all night but after a couple of hours I got used to it and it ceased to keep me awake.

April 19

A system of extremely narrow bad roads allowed only one-way travel and produced thick clouds of dust when used, making it difficult to resupply combat units and holding up the XXIV Corps's advance. From April 14–19 the American and Japanese lines remained static. During the night of April 18–19, the corps fired a heavy artillery barrage that did little damage to the fortified Japanese positions.[82]

Got up at 4:35 and went to forward OP with Arnold. Arty preparation and . . . use was beautiful. Very little Jap counter fire. Watched flame thrower tanks which seem very effective.

Very little resistance to start with. Men did not advance quite fast enough at first.

At about 9:50 left Arnold and went via 96th Div CP to OP of Col. Dillon['s] 96th zone. Resistance much stiffer there. Returned via 27th Div CP to my own.

Result of day's operations: a gain of about 800 to 1,200 yds on right and left leaving a salient in the heavily fortified escarpment area in the center. Expect to work on flanks of Jap salient tomorrow. Progress not quite satisfactory.

Heavy thunderstorms during afternoon.

Visited Hodge before supper and told him to speed up advance. Seventh Div too cautious.[83]

April 20

Visited 27th Div in the morning. Saw Col. Stebbins of 105th.[84] He was slow in getting his attack off this morning—Jap arty. Concentration and shot out bridges given as reason: Too many reasons and not enough advance. Told him so. Also saw Col. Kelly of 165th Inf and urged him toward a faster pace.[85] To go where the going is good and pinch out pockets of resistance.[86]

The Kadena airfield was strafed and bombed about 8:30 or nine in the evening. One plane was injured by falling AA shells. A bomb hit one shelter and killed 8 men and wounded 17.

Later in the night, about 4:30 A.M. I think, seven or eight shells, about 155mm size, fell not far from our CP.

April 21

Visited Bn OP in [large blank space in original text] Inf Regt of Col. Halloran.[87] His right Bn Commander thinks 27th Div on his right is not helping him as much as contemplated. I then went to 27th Div CP and found that the left Bn of that Div had been driven back, inexcusably I think, by a counter attack. There was also some mystery about loss of tanks that I could not fully get explained. The right of the 27th had progressed fairly well.

In the afternoon I went out to the *Eldorado* to see Turner and discussed the general situation and the coming of Adm. Nimitz tomorrow.

Communications with the 77th Div on Ie Shima have not been good but today Bruce sent a staff officer over to say that all organized resistance was over and that he had killed over 1,900 Japs. Probably 500 more to kill. His total killed and wounded over 800.[88]

After dark a number of Jap planes came in[; air raids continued] off and on until midnight with lots of anti-aircraft firing and some bombing and strafing.

April 22

Hodge called up early and confirmed my observations regarding the left of the 27th Div and their poor use of tanks. He had sent BG Bradford to coordinate between the 96th and 27th Divs.[89]

Adm. Nimitz, Gen. Vandergrift,[90] Adm. Spruance, Adm. Sherman and others arrived by air at noon. I took them sight seeing. Adm. Nimitz discussed Phase 3, the rehabilitation of units here, the transfer of Okinawans from the Marianas back here, the future of this island and succeeding operations against Japan. Phase 3 may be abandoned if sufficient fields can be found here to fulfill air support requirements. Arranged for further trips tomorrow to the northward. Adm. Nimitz presented me with a bottle of liquor which I told him I would open when all organized resistance here had ended.

During the night our land based planes have shot down 32 attacking "Vals," losing only 1 plane and no pilots. Most of the Vals were shot down just before dark.

Buckner to Adele Buckner, April 22

> Eddie Post and I are now established a pyramidal tent at our new command post ashore. We have a convenient dug-out nearby into which we slide when Jap planes are overhead and fragments from anti-aircraft shells are raining scrap iron.

Practically every day I get to some part of the forward regiment and watch the fighting. In this way I get a good idea of the situation at first hand and am in a position to make necessary decisions. The Japs here seem to have the strongest position yet encountered in the Pacific and it will be a slow tedious grind with flame throwers, explosives placed by hand and the closest of teamwork to dislodge them without very heavy losses. In the meanwhile, however, we are making great headway with the part of the island we have and are developing splendid air facilities that we are already using. We will be wise to hold this island after the war under conditions that will permit us to have military control without incorporating the Okinawans into our population as civilians free to enter the U.S.

★ ★ ★

We have not taken Ie Shima with a splendid airfield somewhat and ditched at present by the late garrison. We killed over 2,100 Japs on the island and there are probably 500 snipers still hiding in caves that will have to be accounted for. They won't surrender but they skulk around at night and shoot, throw grenades and try to blow up ammunition dumps, weapons and supplies. They expect to die but try to do as much damage as possible first. They present a considerable problem.

Today we had a very distinguished visitor so I spent a good deal of the time taking him sight seeing and discussing the local and future situation, all of which was very satisfactory.

★ ★ ★

The artillery is beginning to roar down at the front and parachute flares are lighting up the whole sky. This probably means that the Japs are putting on a night counter-attack. I hope so since this will bring them out of their caves and pill boxes where we can use our artillery on them with good effect.

I have twice had to stop writing this letter due to Jap planes that made it necessary to turn out the light. Their raids seem now to be over for the time being, so I will try to catch some rest.

April 23

Spent the day taking Adm. Nimitz to the north to see air field sites and visit III Phibcorps and 1st Mardiv. Had lunch with Geiger.

Told Adm. Nimitz that Okinawa should be retained by us as a means of access to the China sea, a flanking position against north and south movements along the China coast; a check against further aggression by Japan and as an outpost to prevent Russia from expansion into the Pacific from Chinese ports that she might acquire at the end of the war by occupying them under the pretext of helping us against Japan. I made this suggestion with the proviso that we should control this island as a "protectorate," "mandate" or some other name that would leave the Okinawans as aliens not permitted to enter our country as citizens and add to our already complex race problems.[91]

April 24

During the night of April 23–24, the Japanese artillery increased its rate of fire to cover the withdrawal of troops from the first Shuri line. Tenth Army surged forward the next day.[92]

Some progress on southern front—Hill 178 taken and a foothold gained on the escarpment. Japs apparently retiring to another strong position. Heavy Jap artillery fire.

Very little air attack last night and anti-aircraft rain today.

Inspected unloading at beaches. Labor crews at the dumps appear to be the bottle neck.

Adm. Nimitz left this morning, apparently well pleased.[93]

Richardson published a "newsmap" on Okinawa without mentioning anything but major *Army* units and their commanders. Wrote him an official letter urging him to give due credit to my *Marines* [emphasis in original]. Richardson is always a menace to good relations between the services in the Pacific. Adm. Nimitz knows it.

In the Pacific theater, marine units normally got better press coverage than army units. Captain Harold "Min" Miller organized press coverage for the navy and Marine Corps out of Nimitz's headquarters at the insistence of Navy Secretary James V. Forrestal. Miller worked to get big-name writers to cover the Pacific by offering reporters greater access to frontline units than the army, giving them combat film footage, and allowing them to use naval communication channels to get their reports back to their news organizations. The Marine Corps's domination of press accounts became an issue among army generals toward the end of the campaign.[94]

April 25

Flew to Ie Shima in a cub plane and saw Bruce. Island about cleaned up and 77th Div will be completely loaded by April 27 to move to Okinawa and be attached to the XXIV Corps. Unfortunately, Bruce blew up all tombs on the island as a precaution against their use by snipers, a most unnecessary piece of vandalism committed with pious intentions.

Slight progress on southern front and preparation for another coordinated attack tomorrow. Visited XXIVth Corps, 96th Div and 27th Div CPs in the afternoon.

After supper, assembled my staff and started them to work on my tentative plans to be put into effect when and if Phase 3-C is called off. Adm. Nimitz has recommended against 3-C as unnecessary since adequate air fields sites are available here without it.[95]

April 26

On this date, XXIV Corps launched an assault on the Maeda escarpment, a cliff wall on the line just west of the center.

Adm. Spruance and Adm. Halsey came to my CP just after lunch and went off on a sight seeing expedition.[96]

The rest of the afternoon I spent with Arnold on Hill 178 which gave me a beautiful panoramic view of most of the battlefront. Our troops made considerable advances and broke the enemy's hold on one end of the escarpment.

From 3:45 to 4:00 this morning about eight 155mm shells fell near our CP but did no damage.

Buckner to Adele Buckner, April 26

> Yesterday I flew over to our newly captured island of Ie Shima in a cub plane and landed on a small strip of the Jap air field that had not been heavily mined, dug up and booby trapped. This island has great potentialities for air development and my engineers are working like beavers behind the bomb disposal squad, a small unit, all got blown up themselves but we have had no fatalities yet in the second group. In taking the island, we killed about 3,200 Japs and interned over 1,500 civilians. There are probably about 100 Japs still concealed in camouflaged caves but it always takes time to clean these out. They are still finding them on Guam, Saipan and Taiwan in large numbers.
>
> This morning we made another coordinated attack in the south against the enemy's second position. We have broken their first position but they have many heavily fortified lines for us to contend with.
>
> All the northern part of Okinawa and the neighboring small islands are now ours and we have counted over 20,000 good Japs. Many others, have no doubt been killed behind enemy lines by artillery and air bombardment.
>
> For several mornings, a long range Jap gun has been dropping shells near our CP between 3:45 and 4:00. We can hear the whine of the projectile on its way toward us followed by the "crump" of the

explosion and whistle of fragments and several seconds later by the distant report of the gun. So far he hasn't hit anything or anybody. We are sound-ranging on this battery and have him about located, so our counter-battery will probably get him before long. Apparently he is firing from the mouth of a cave.

We have had a couple of rainy days that have discouraged Jap air attacks but it is now clearing so we can expect more of it. One advantage in establishing ourselves here consists in forcing the enemy to expend his aircraft on us. His air losses are far beyond ours[;] so we are wearing him down. For instance, two days ago our planes based on captured Jap fields here shot down 32 enemy planes in a couple of hours with the loss of only one plane and the pilot of the lost plane was rescued by a seaplane. The Jap seems to be getting low on trained pilots and constant attrition keeps him from getting caught up.

Due to the publicity given to the Okinawa campaign, I am getting a deluge of trash mail from cranks, collectors and chiselers. Many ask "Please write me a letter for my collection." Some run about like this "Ever since I read about the brilliant exploits of your Tenth Air Force in New Guinea I have been an ardent admirer of yours and prayed for you every night. Wont you answer my prayers by sending me your insignia, an autographed photograph and a few little battlefield souvenirs such as Japanese flags or perhaps a light machine gun. Congratulations on your brilliant strategy which I think is swell. They say generals aren't human but I know *you* are" [emphasis in original].

"May God bless you and don't forget to send the trophies. We need people just like you." etc. etc. This is no exaggeration.

* * *

April 27

At a staff meeting in the morning I announced my decision regarding the use of the III Phibcorps immediately after receipt of word that Phase 3-C had been called off. My decision was at variance with my staff recommendation.[97]

Adm. Halsey left in the afternoon.

Still very little progress in the center of the line but some gain on both flanks. [The units attacking the Maeda escarpment had stalled.] Part of 77th Div has arrived behind the 96th.

I visited Iscom and the 1st Mardiv.

Two snipers with telescopic sights killed last night on the Yomitan air field. Infiltrators also caught in rear of 7th Div with orders to look for CPs and kill senior commanders. A prisoner said that his CO drew lots and the half who "won" were privileged to *have* to do this [emphasis in original].

BUCKNER TO ADELE BUCKNER, APRIL 27

★ ★ ★

Adm. Nimitz seemed well pleased with his visit here a couple of days ago. He left me a bottle of liquor that I promised to open on the day that all organized resistance here was over. I am getting thirsty.

We are now picking up numerous snipers behind our lines but so far they have done little damage. We wounded and captured one yesterday who said that his company had drawn lots and the half who "won" were privileged to *have* to infiltrate into our lines, look for command posts and kill senior officers. I think we have killed all those who "won." [Emphasis in original.] Two were shot last night way back on the Yomitan air field with telescopic sights. They never got to use them. Our rear elements are no longer alarmed when they hear firing behind them; they merely feel satisfaction in the thought that our "anti-termite" patrols have shot another Jap.

Yesterday I had the rare experience of finding an observation point that permitted me to observe the entire battle front. Action was lively all along the line since we were putting on a heavy attack and the whole thing was visible. It was really a superb spectacle, plane strikes, artillery concentration, smoke screens, flame throwers, tanks and the steady determined advance of the infantry closing with the enemy. Along with this were the crash of bombs, the screech of projectiles, the whistle of shell fragments, the sputter of machine guns and the sharp crack of rifles. I shall never forget it. It was really stirring.

I could be taking some wonderful pictures but somehow I don't. I[t] simply doesn't seem appropriate to be snapping a camera when things like this are going on.

I was glad to see Courtney and Patton get their fourth stars.[98] Our fickle public has forgotten that only recently they were trying to hound George out of the service.[99]

Our reorganization in the Pacific so far made no difference in my immediate chain of command. I still operate under Adm. Nimitz. However, I had a pleasant exchange of radiograms with Gen. MacArthur, each of us given birth to a copious litter of adjectives.

My social news here may be briefly summarized as "No women, no liquor."

April 28

Last night began with a romantically beautiful moonrise but there the romance ended. Jap suckers were around in the air all night. At midnight they buzzed over our CP at very low altitude and bombed the airfield. Later at about 3:00 they did it again. AAA was spectacular but inaccurate. Searchlight work was poor. Night fighters got 2 Jap planes.

Looked over road net to the north and dropped in on III Phibcorps and 6th Mardiv CP.

4:00 P.M.—conferred DSM cluster at a small ceremony to Hodge for his Leyte campaign prowess.

After moonrise heavy air attacks began again. Post and I moved our bunks into the dugout. During the afternoon and night the shore based fighters got 35 planes[,] and the shore and ship AAA an equal number (counting 22 suicide planes). The local carrier based planes also got 35. Yesterday 1 ammunition ship was sunk[,] and another [ammunition ship] and a destroyer [were] hit. A hospital ship is also reported struck.[100]

April 29

During the morning I went via XXIV Corps HQ to the 27th Div to assure Griner that his being taken out of the line and moved north as the island garrison was no indication that I was not completely satisfied with the Div's performance. He was obviously relieved.

I spent the afternoon visiting the wounded in the 69th Field Hospital. I saw a man's brains through a hole in his temple. The doctors said he had an even chance of recovery.

April 30

More air raids after moonrise last night. The Yomitan airfield was shelled from near Naha. One plane destroyed and several badly damaged.

In the morning went aboard the *Eldorado* to see Adm. Turner. Had lunch there. Adm. Oldendorf was there and brought a letter from Adm. Nimitz saying the 24 Okinawan pine trees I had sent him at Guam had arrived in good condition.

Bruce took over from the 96th Div. A Regt of the 1st Mardiv moved into the line relieving the 27th Div. Small counterattacks in the center from 1 Co to 1 Bn.

At 4:00 P.M. attended at XXIV Corps HQ the wedding of the Jap captured Capt. and the Okinawan girl. Chaplain read civil service. Interpreted. Lost ring made from quarter. Bride delayed ceremony to fix her obi. MP present with shotgun. First sergeant said "Bring 'um in" and "Take 'um home."

Groom made speech. Photographer present. (I explained to press people the propaganda purpose of the ceremony.) Accordion and torri added color.

May 1

Accompanied Bruce to two front line Bn OPs. Got splendid view of fighting on the front of the 77th Div.

Had 2-hour press conference at 3:00 P.M. Some of the correspondents sought to make a scandal out of the "Hollywood wedding" yesterday of the Japs. I explained its purpose to get information out of them and let Japs know they would be well treated if they surrendered. Most of them accepted it but a few will want to raise controversial bad feeling for sensational purposes.

May 2

After breakfast visited Arnold in Hospital. Had his appendix out last night. Doing well. I wrote Marg, his wife.

Adm. Oldendorf and Adm. Deyo arrive at 10:00 A.M.[101] I met them at the dock, had them to lunch, showed them the Jap buzz bomb and sent them off to see Hodge and Bradley about naval gunfire support.

I have visited the 1st Mardiv CP. They had great assurance and expected to make large gains at once.

May 3

It was apparent to me that the 77th Div and the 1st Mardiv entered the line expecting to show their superiority over their predecessors by a rapid breakthrough of the enemy position.[102] They were promptly stopped and learned some valuable lessons today. From now on they will be more valuable as all-around fighters.

Spent the morning at the 31st Field Hospital (Col. Rogan Commanding[103]) and visited the 77th and 1st Mardiv CPs in the afternoon. Del Valle was feeling a little off his feed since faced with a cold.

Buckner to Adele Buckner, May 3

> This morning I spend visiting the wounded in hospitals and this afternoon went up to two of the divisions in line, one army and one marine. Our surgeons are doing wonders. I talked to several men that had been shot in the brain several days ago and they are getting well. There are almost no infected wounds and the blood donations save hundreds who would otherwise die of shock and bleeding. On the whole, the wounded are cheerful and optimistic. It is remarkable how badly a man can be shot up and still recover.

The news that Hitler and Mussolini are both dead is most cheering.[104] Two serious post-war problems are solved and a good precedent set for disposing of some of their ilk.

We continue to move slowly but are killing the Japs steadily. We have already killed 30,000 Japs that we know of. This is more than the total killed on Iwo Jima and our losses have been less than half those suffered in taking that island, although I consider the Jap defenses here far more formidable than those on Iwo Jima. When we finally break through the percentage of Jap losses to ours will greatly increase in all probability.

For two nights we have had no air attacks due to rain but tonight it is clear so we can expect a reoccurrence of moonlight raids. However[,] the moon rises later every night so we will probably not be visited before midnight. I usually sleep in a hole during raids. Eddie and I have a good one near at hand and now manage to sleep through all the noise so as to give the raiders no satisfaction over keeping us awake.

The thunder of artillery continues all day and all night. After dark the sky over the enemy is illuminated by parachute flares and the constant flash of the big guns and shell explosions keeps flickering like distant lightening. This drives the enemy into the ground and gives him very little rest.

★ ★ ★

Our tanks have been invaluable in reducing Jap pill boxes and fortified caves. They fire into the entrances while the infantry closes with explosive charges or else uses incendiaries. The flame thrower tanks have long range and have been very effective. The main problem is to find a place where we can cover and neutralize all the numerous caves that bring cross-fire on our infantry in a particular place. We look for soft spots, take them and then surround the stronger hills and reduce them after our front line has passed them. Often Japs will bob up out of concealed tunnels with machine guns and mortars a mile behind our lines at night. They also slip in after dark with explosives and try to blow up tanks[,] artillery and command posts. W[e] have been very successful in stopping infiltration but it keeps us constantly on guard. Japanese infiltration tactics defeated the British on the Malay Peninsula when the Japs had fewer troops than they had. The Singapore garrison that surrendered exceeded their captors in numbers.

I feel well satisfied with my troops and confident of the outcome but I must avoid a spectacular hurry in order to save lives.

While the European war seems about over it will be six to nine months after its close before we can profit here by the transfer of troops to this theater. Meanwhile we will continue to press our enemies and have them in a good position for the kill.

May 4

In a power struggle within the Japanese Thirty-second Army, unit commanders and Cho, the chief of staff, convinced Ushijima to reject the defensive tactics they were currently employing and stage a counteroffensive. A heavy artillery barrage and kamikaze attacks on the U.S. fleet the night before preceded the attack at dawn on May 4. A Japanese regiment also attempted to stage an amphibious landing on the west coast that evening.[105]

Last night heavy air attacks struck Yomitan field and the fleet. Eight men were killed in a Hospital. Our CP and the field were shelled again. In the south the Japs tried to envelop both our flanks in barges and penetrate the center at the same time during the night that the air attacks came (about midnight). Each attacking force was a Bn. Naval gunfire sank the eastern Bn, the center was stopped but the western group got ashore opposite the 1st Mardiv. About 200 in one group were killed but part of another group got inland with about 80 Jap infiltrators that are still at large.

After breakfast I had a staff meeting and gave out decision regarding the capture of neighboring islands for radar stations to control planes. Adm. Turner is impatient about this, so the 2nd Mardiv will have to be used if speed is important.

Spent the day at Ie Shima. Thomas (Iscom) recovering from pneumonia.[106] Interviewed his staff to see how I could help their project. They predict readiness of field for fighter group; May 12. Adm. Spruance sent staff officers to find out date. Our land based planes shot down 45 Jap planes today. I sent congratulatory message to Mulcahy—my third.

May 5

Met Adm. Spruance and Adm. Hill at dock and took them to XXIV Corps CP. After reviewing situation, sent them on a tour of the Div CPs and Shimabaru. They left via my CP in the afternoon.

After lunch conferred with G-3 section and gave decision upon which to issue Army order for attacking with both corps.

Dougherty came ashore from Adm. Turner to discuss securing radar picket islands.[107] Turner seems less in a rush now that I have pointed out the necessity for bringing up the 2nd Mardiv if speed is essential.

Later and more complete information, including a captured enemy order, indicates that the counterattack was by the entire 24th Div. It continued sporadically today in our center. Over 3,000 Japs were killed yesterday, last night, and today.

Ushijima called off the counteroffensive on May 5. His units suffered horrendous casualties in attacks launched primarily against the XXIV Corps, and made no progress, except for a small penetration in the 77th Infantry Division sector. The attacks are considered by observers to have been a disastrous turning point in the campaign for the Japanese. Historians James and William Belote called the attacks on May 4–5 the "only serious Japanese mistakes of the Okinawa campaign." The authors of the official army account of the campaign called the counteroffensive "a colossal blunder." Buckner was impressed with the effort, describing it as "one of the best coordinated attacks I have ever seen." He also added: "The enemy means business, but he had waited too long and he didn't have what it took."[108]

May 6

More air attacks last night but no great damage.

Called at CPs of XXIV Corps, 1st Mardiv, 77th Div and 7th Div. Also watched fighting from 1st Mardiv OP. Saw Arnold in Hospital Not much gain today but resistance seems slightly weaker.

Conferred with Geiger regarding details of his going into the line as a corps.

Turner has new ideas on radio picket islands—the third change in three days.

Adm. Spruance wants 1st priority given to getting fighters to operate from here. This I have ordered.

During the night the cases of about 8 of our 5-in naval star shells fell in our CP. One near the corner of Roney's tent went 7 feet into the ground.[109] We were not bothered by enemy shells.

May 7

Conferred with Admirals Turner and Hill (the latter will soon succeed Turner) on the *Eldorado* regarding radar islands. Decided to take small ones with local troops. To get a reinforced Regt of the 2nd Mardiv, now on Saipan, to take those with slightly larger garrisons and to take Kume with local troops 30 days after resistance here was over.

Later a message from CINCPOA arrived for 3rd [Marine Division] July 15. 2nd Mardiv was recommended for this and a RCT of the 3rd Mardiv to substitute for the 2nd in taking radar islands. (This latter was disapproved. Third Mardiv held for another operation.)

Buckner to Adele Buckner, May 7

Tonight it is raining so we will probably be free from the air attacks that come on every clear moonlit night. A couple of nights ago, a bomb hit the dug-out housing the wounded awaiting air evacuation and killed a dozen or more. Ordinarily bombing is directed at the shipping and air fields, but we have to take cover from the falling projectiles from our anti-aircraft guns. Several days ago one man in our HQ, was killed and another shot through the leg by falling .50 cal. bullets. The Japs tried a counter-offensive several days ago, but we stopped it easily and with great loss to the enemy. We have killed over 33,000 so far.

Now that the northern part of the island has been mopped up, I have a re-grouping of my division that should give impetus to our attack. However, we have to be somewhat deliberate in attacking stone hills honeycombed with connecting galleries and bristling with machine guns.

Our civil government now cares for about 130,000 Okinawan civilians. Although most of their homes and villages have been destroyed, their crops overrun and their young men killed, they seem stoical, docile and actually cheerful. One of our interpreters, an Okinawan from Honolulu, told me that he had talked informally with hundreds of them and that they had said that they were happy that we were here to drive out the Japs who treated them brutally, confiscated 2/3 of all their crops, forced them to labor hard without compensation, [and] looked down upon them as degenerates. They trust us and feel that we will relieve them from their long period of suffering. Most of our civilians are old men, women and children. Men of military age have been drafted and taken away where they either fight or work in labor battalions. Some of them fight very well if thoroughly indoctrinated by the Japs concerning our cruelty and torture of prisoners. All are surprised at the good treatment they are receiving.

We are collecting them from tunnels, caves and dugouts where they have been hiding in the hills and putting them into concentration camps wherever shelter can be found. We found 300 in one cave that had a spring in it. Their pigs, chickens, goats and lice were all living with them. Many were wounded. They are dirty but remarkably free from disease, except for scabies (mange) resulting from dirt. Most of them were fairly well provided with food or foraged in nearby fields of cabbage, radishes, barley, potatoes and soy beans.

We have organized these camps, using natives as foremen and, with the captured Jap rice and fish, have made them self supporting. They harvest crops under supervision[,] build shelters, thresh and grind grain, make fishing nets and boats[,] keep their premises and themselves clean. They get regular medical service and are kept busy. They seem cheerful, trusting and apparently without resentment over their losses. However, there is no telling what an Oriental is thinking about. When we moved the peaceful old men of one district we ceased to be bothered by sniping there.

Our best civil government men are practical man-handlers who would make good 1st sergeants or Alaskan chiefs of police like Bob Huttle of Anchorage. The academic experts, lecturers on "Oriental Peoples and their Psychology" and *Bell for Adano* apostles of democracy are worse than useless.[110]

⋆ ⋆ ⋆

May 8

Official word came of Germany's complete surrender. At noon every gun of our land and ship support batteries fired one round at the enemy. We then tuned into the Jap radio frequency and announced in Japanese that the volley was in celebration of the victory. Tomorrow we are dropping an extra of our Jap newspaper with elaboration of this news.

Heavy rain bogged down our tanks and slowed our advance.

Visited III Phibcorps CP but got stuck in the mud trying to visit the 6th Mardiv.

May 9

Spent day driving in jeep to extreme north end of island. Saw plane picked up by station 180 miles away and followed to 134 mi when I left.

Heavy rains bogged down tanks and prevented substantial gain.

May 10

Vice Adm. Wilkinson came ashore for a visit with some of his staff.[111] Vice Adm. McMorris arrived by air and went out to see Adms. Spruance and Turner.

Hodge came to my CP regarding slow progress. Thought army attack tomorrow should be postponed until more ground was gained. I told him to gain the ground today. I visited Geiger and told him the same.

At 3:00 P.M. I held a press conference regarding tomorrow's attack. Told them not to expect anything spectacular but expressed confidence in a steady and successful advance. No heckling today. My great display of patience with hecklers at the last meeting had a good effect.[112]

May 11

Buckner launched a coordinated assault on the Shuri defensive line with III Amphibious Corps's marines in the west and XXIV Corps's soldiers in the east. This organized American attack soon broke down into small battles for specific points. On the whole, the Japanese held their positions during this offensive.[113]

Attack started at 7:00 A.M. Progress all along the line. Visited both corps CPs and put a little pressure on corps Commanders. Pocket on right of 77th Div cleared out. Has held us up for some time.

Adm. McMorris came ashore and discussed future plans. Nothing definite yet since Joint Chiefs of Staff have handed down no decision. With MacArthur in command of troops, Kruger's army will have the edge on us in important assignments.[114]

Considerable Jap air activity today primarily against carriers and picket boats. Over 150 Jap planes reported shot down.

Yesterday [large blank space appears here in original text] encountered a Jap fighter at 38,000 ft. His guns froze but he brought down the plane by ramming its tail three times with his propeller and cutting it off.

May 12

Adm. McMorris left early in the morning for Guam and I spent the day visiting both corps CP[s], all four Div CPs and three forward OPs giving me a view of the entire front. Progress being made on both flanks but not much in the middle. This was expected.[115] Right of 6th Mardiv reached edge of northern part of Naha and left of 96th Div got started well up the NW slope of this "Conical Hill."[116]

May 13

After breakfast went to III Phibcorps and 96th Div. CPs and then joined Col. May in 383rd Inf OP overlooking attack on "Conical Hill."[117] His handling of the Regt was a beautiful piece of troop leading. I could watch the Bn and Co movements easily from the OP and even see Japs, effect of fire, etc. I was there over four hours. May should be promoted to BG.

Buckner to Adele Buckner, May 13

★ ★ ★

> Today I spent five hours in a forward observation post watching a regiment take a hill, all in plain view. It was a most inspiring sight. Yesterday I visited both corps and four front line command posts and

three observation points overlooking the entire battle front. By gaining intimate familiarity with the problems of front line troops and of the terrain features, I find it much easier to direct the battle than I could possibly do otherwise.

We are making slow but steady progress and killing lots of Japs. It is tough going and will continue to be for some time, but I feel that we have control of the situation and are ready for any counter-attack. We repulsed the last large one with heavy losses to the enemy and light losses to our men.

The Japs are fighting desperately and are pouring in their air power as fast as they can bring it down. While our shipping is not unscathed, our unloading of equipment and supplies continues to progress smoothly and the drain on Japanese planes has been very heavy. Their pilots show the result of short and hasty training.

Okinawa is barely recognizable with its new network of coral surface, four-lane roads and its air field and base facilities. It is remarkable what has been done in so short a time.

Naturally I am eager to get this island completely cleaned up so as to move on to other battlefields, but it can't be hurried without heavy losses. With Gen. MacArthur now taking over the Army forces it is difficult to predict my future assignments since he has his own group of generals that he has been working with and my chances can scarcely be as good as those of Krueger and Eichelberger as the result. However, the[re] appears to be plenty of fighting in prospect to satisfy the most ravenous appetite.

Buckner had good reason to worry about his future. MacArthur was quite open about his low opinion of Buckner. On March 4, Eighth Army commander Robert Eichelberger wrote his wife: "Big Chief says if Buck ever comes under him he would bust him because he has sold out to one of our sister services." Just before the landing on Okinawa, Col. Weldon Rhoades witnessed another conversation between MacArthur and Eichelberger. MacArthur was agitated because a field army was serving under naval command, but he was also grateful that he would not be responsible for the operation. He expected the Japanese would fight to the last man, and American forces would suffer extremely heavy casualties.[118]

★ ★ ★

May 14

Went to forward OP in 6th Mardiv with Shepherd. Two adjoining Regts each apparently waiting for the other to move forward. Told Shepherd to keep them going. Returned via III Phibcorps.

After lunch had G-3 conference and gave out decision on ICEBERG 3-E.

Dougherty came in with message of impatience from Adm. Turner Re: unloading. I conferred with G-4 and later had Wallace in. He felt somewhat harassed and I don't blame him since priorities are constantly changing and requirements mounting without his being given more means of speeding things up.

On our left, Col. May advanced his Regt along the coastal flat 2,400 yds and took the Yonabaru air strip. The Japs still hold the far side of "Conical Hill."

May 15

Visited both Corps CPs in the morning. Very little gains during the day due to rain which impeded tanks and a Bn counter-attack against the 6th Mardiv. Had conference with G-3 section and approved plan for Plan 3-E.

May 16

Considerable air bombing this morning at about 3:00 A.M. Yomitan and Purple Beach areas struck by bombs: a few killed and 1 plane burned.

Adm. Spruance came ashore. Also 2nd Mardiv and 3-E Iscom and staff arrived to discuss plans.

Adm. Hill came ashore. He takes over from Turner tomorrow but the Tenth Army will be directly under Adm. Spruance

Had a G-4 conference regarding an army service area. Deferred decision pending further information from Iscom.

Visited XXIV Corps CP.

During the bombing this morning a 3-in shell fragment from an AA shell went through my tent near the foot of my bed.

Jap guerrillas starting a terroristic campaign in the north. Okinawan local headman beheaded and about 50 women and children murdered by them. This calls for more aggressive patrolling by the 27th Div.

May 17

Adm. Turner turned over today to Adm. Hill and I now report directly to Adm. Spruance. Hill is in charge of the combined air forces, ship and shore based, if I interpret the obscure directive properly. I also control all unloading.

Turner, who has just been nominated as a full admiral (4-star) came ashore and I took him on a tour of the island. He said he had recommended to Adm. Nimitz that I be given command of the troops making the initial landing in Japan proper.

May 18

Turned down my staff's recommendation to establish an army service area by using service troops now assigned to Iscom. Too complicated and productive of dispute.

Visited III Phibcorps where I also saw Hodge and then went to all four front-line Div CPs. Also went to a 1st Mardiv OP. Not much progress today but some movement almost everywhere and a good many Japs killed. A great deal of hand-to-hand fighting.

After dark Yomitan airfield was bombed by planes with incendiaries, destroying 1 plane, injuring 16 others and setting off a napalm mixing point with a tremendously spectacular explosion. There was no AA firing due to the restriction of a "control green" alert in spite of AA requests for permission to fire. Will investigate.

(The explosion subsequently turned out to be a naval bomber with 2 1/2 tons of bombs. Only two men wounded. Investigation showed green control due to CAP planes. The night CAP splashed the Jap who set off the explosion).

May 19

No material change in situation.

Visited new CP and gave instructions regarding new mess Bldg.

Went to see Mulchay regarding air control. I also saw Iscom.

May 20

At noon made a broadcast dedicating the new "Radio Okinawa" station. Knowing that the enemy would listen and translate what I said, a good deal of it was directed at them in a round-about way.[119]

Visited 6th and 1st Mardiv and 96th Div CPs. An air of optimism exits in the front line Divs who seem to feel a slight weakening in the Japs before them, in spite of the fact that the most savage of hand-to-hand fighting is going on all along the line. Some progress made today, most of it by the 1st Mardiv.

Maj. Gen. Casey,[120] engineer, from Gen. MacArthur's command came up to explore air base possibilities to support future operations against Japan by his forces. He brought an oral message to me from MacArthur which, if quoted correctly by him was anything but complimentary. In effect, he said "Keep your chin up and don't be discouraged even though it may seem hard, because if you keep on pushing you will be surprised to find that the enemy forces will suddenly break and it will be all over"—a somewhat belittling message if correctly delivered, which I doubt.

May 21

From May 21–29, the Japanese withdrew forces from the Shuri line using a plan calling for "retreat and attack." Colonel Yahara Hiromichi, the Thirty-second Army operations officer, was responsible for developing the plan. He drew his operational inspiration from Napoleon's decisions at the battle of Marengo and the French counterattack on the Marne in World War I. "Our general retreat policy . . . was aimed at a total retreat toward fortifications." He counted on the rain and mud to slow down the American advance. The plan required an attack before U.S. troops went on the offensive. When the Japanese 62nd Division failed to achieve the desired results, Yahara suspected there was a lack of will in the unit. Nevertheless, the successful Japanese withdrawal thwarted Buckner's plans to destroy the forces defending Shuri.[121]

Last night about 9:20 a well prepared Bn counterattacked against the 6th Mardiv was driven back. About 300 Japs killed and a barge sunk.

Visited both corps and all four Div CPs and went to forward OPs of all but the 1st Mardiv. Got a good view of the left from "Conical Hill." Our front line troops are showing a gradually increasing feeling of optimism, particularly in the 96th Div. Jap resistance on our left appears to be less determined but they still see strong opposite our right. The 6th Mardiv is less optimistic and its progress a trifle slower than I had hoped. It now looks as though an envelopment of the enemy's left will bring fruitful results.

A captured Jap document shows concern over our methods of reducing their defenses.

May 22

I wasted today getting caught up on paperwork. It rained most of the day and made tank operations impossible. Nevertheless, the 6th Mardiv made substantial gains on the right and one Regt of the 7th Div established a left flank guard in the foothills southeast of Yonabaru against light resistance and very little artillery fire. This paves the way for an envelopment of the Shuri position from the east.

Had Gen. Casey and some of his group in for old fashioned cocktails before supper. We used Okinawan raspberries for cherries and Adm. Halsey's liquor.

Turned down a G-1—G-2 recommendation to offer a truce to the Japs while we took civilians into our lines. Let the Japs feed them as long as possible. They would let us have the useless ones to feed while they kept all capable of work for strengthening their defenses.

Buckner to Adele Buckner, May 22

We are having a deluge of rain today which is hard on our attack since it bogs down our tanks in the sticky clay and without them it was suicidal for our troops to rush the pill boxes and cave openings that bristle with machine guns. A constant dribble is coming into my tent through a hole made by a shell fragment a couple of nights ago which does not improve my attitude toward the individual who did it.

Yesterday I spent inspecting the front and looking over the Jap position in front of all our divisions on this line. The defenses are still formidable but an increasing air of optimism is evident among our men all along the line. Jap casualties are mounting, their weapons are being knocked out and no replacements are in sight, yet the enemy can see our ships discharging thousands of tons of cargo every day before their very eyes. Jap air attacks continue almost daily but they are gradually weakening and the quality of their pilots is deteriorating. We had hoped that one of the results of our campaign here would be to make a deep cut into Japanese air power and we seem to be succeeding. Two days after I sent the enclosed message to Mulcahy his boys shot down 45 planes. The outstanding performance among his pilots was when one of them was in a dog fight with a Jap at 28,000 feet and his machine guns [strike through in original] jammed. Being unable to shoot he cut the Jap's rudder off with his propeller causing the enemy plane to crash. Our pilot then landed safely with a bent propeller and a plane full of holes.

To give you an idea of the ferocity of the hand to hand fighting on the ground, one hill changed hands 9 times before we finally secured it. A wounded officer who could not be brought out when the Japs drove our men out of their positions, lay in a pile of corpses and played possum twice while the enemy were going through his pockets. When we retook the hill he felt much better.

On another occasion three of our men were driven into a cave by machine gun fire and found the cave to be part of a gallery filled with Japs. They kept quiet for three days while the hill was in Jap hands. A Jap water detail brought them water in the dark which they accepted without expressing gratitude in English. When we recapture the hill they had some interesting tales to tell after a three-day period of considerable nervousness.

* * *

Naha is a deserted ruin and of no value except as a port. Most of it is burned out and we now have heights controlling it but can't occupy it because the Japs have hills on the other side. Shuri Castle and the neighboring heights are the key to the present enemy line. When we break this, things should move more rapidly. The Japs are defending this with desperation. Today a captured document indicated that they were greatly worried over our methods of warfare and were somewhat at a loss in attempting to stop our slow but steady mopping up of their powerful cave defenses. Our system is working well and our losses in proportion the Japs killed are far less than at Iwo Jima although the Jap defenses are much stronger. We have killed about 50,000 and probably have in the neighborhood of 30,000 still to improve.

★ ★ ★

May 23

Saw a demonstration, in the morning, of the new recoilless weapons. They look good due to lightness. Directed that they be given to 77th Div for trial against Japs.

Last night at 4:00 A.M. attack of about 250 Japs against the 96th Div was exterminated. It was apparently part of a Bn attack.

Admirals Wright and Connolly came after lunch to discuss future operations.[122]

Squeaky Anderson also called during the afternoon and we had a good Alaska discussion.[123] Steady rain all afternoon—bad on tank action.

Small counter-attack took place pretty much all across the front possibly in response to an order for a general counter-attack that didn't reach units in time. The 7th Div got past Yonabaru and is turning west. Heavy rain has stopped our tanks and is impeding supply just at a time when rapid progress by the 7th Div is most desirable.

May 24

Seventh Div made about 1,000 yds in enveloping movement. I visited 7th and 6th Marine Divs.

Clear weather and bright moonlight brought many air attacks on all 3 fields. At about 9:30 P.M. four twin-engined bombers, each with 14 men armed with incendiary grenades tried to land on Yontan field. They were shot down, two in flames which I saw. The fifth made a belly landing on the field and the men set fire to two 600-drum gasoline dumps and destroyed 8 planes, mostly transports. About 8 of the Japs were shot. They had maps and photographs of the field with arrows and circles marking points to be attacked. Ie Shima and Kadena fields were bombed without serious effect. About 75 Jap planes were shot down, 23 of them by AA. Some bombs dropped in the naval area of Ie Shima killing 30 and wounding 30.

A bridge was established by the 6th Mardiv into Naha and tanks gotten across but the mud prevents their effective use there or elsewhere.[124]

(Two days later 70 Japs were buried from the five planes that attacked Yomitan. All 14 from the one that landed were eventually killed. One wounded Jap played possum and threw a grenade, killing one man and maiming two.)

May 25

On the way to Yomitan Field this morning, saw a mongoose cross the road. Yesterday I saw a flock of 25 white heron feeding. No dogs and only 3 cats seen on the island. Two of the latter were bobtails. Wild white lilies are in bloom, also some very pretty red gladioli. It appears that this place would blossom like Hawaii if flowers were planted but the Okinawans can't spare the land. They can scarcely live off of 2 acres per family if they use any of the land for flower gardens. They eat bread and die and seem to have no pleasures other than building tombs.

Deluges of rain came down all day, completely immobilizing all tanks. Despite this, the 7th Div made several hundred yards to the south. Japs are appearing in the open more often, which keeps up the killing rate despite slow progress.

May 26

Rain continued all day with a short break in the afternoon marked by an air raid on shipping. One ship reported hit by 2 suicide planes.[125]

The 7th Div made slight progress. Adm. Halsey and some of his staff came ashore the afternoon to ask what I thought about withdrawing the fast carriers from protecting Okinawa and giving them an offensive mission. I told him that Mr. Scipio Africanus had acquired an enviable reputation by displaying similar sentiments.

Had supper with John DeWitt in an embellished Okinawan house with 3 Navy nurses and danced after supper to the accompaniment of Radio Tokyo and artillery fire.[126]

May 27

Still bogged down in the mud with no advance, tanks unable to move and supply difficult. About 6 inches of rain in 48 hours.

Post and I had dinner with Mulcahy followed by a poor 16mm movie that was stopped in the middle by a considerate air raid.

May 28

Still wet and sprinkling all day. Heavy air attacks continue nevertheless. Stubborn resistance against all advances except on the extreme flanks where some progress was made.

I sloshed my way in a jeep to the 27th Div CP. Griner is moving northward and combing the island for Japs. Thinks he has over 100 with 10 heavy machine guns cornered in the mountains. He says the Okinawan civilians are stealing our food and giving it to the Japs.

Suicides hit 3 ships in Nagakusuku Wan. None sunk.[127]

Buckner to Adele Buckner, May 28

We continue to be deluged with rain, about seven inches having come down during the past four days. This came at an unfortunate time, since I had caught the Japs napping and shoved a division past their right flank. The mud slowed down the movement of our heavy weapons to such an extend that I was unable to take full advantage of the initial success, thus giving the enemy a chance to man previously constructed, but at the time, unoccupied defensive positions. However, the move has considerably extended the Jap line, thus weakening it for his depleted force. The Jap garrison appears to have considerably exceeded our initial estimate, but we have killed over 55,000 and we will still have the privilege of exterminating a lot more.

While our progress is still slow the Jap casualties continue to be high. Bradley, who commands the 96th Div, was on a particularly slippery range of clay hills when the heaviest of the rain struck him. In his daily report of movement he reported: "Considerable movement by my front lines. Those on forward slopes slid forward and those on reverse slopes slide back."

Jap air attacks continue with great desperation. In fact, one is going on now against our shipping which is unloading. The Jap planes are coming in under the clouds at very low level. Occasionally they get a ship this way. Night attacks are usually directed at our airfields and come practically every night when it isn't raining. Last night fighters went up and got several of the attackers. In all, this campaign has cost Japan about 4,000 planes.

The roar of the anti-aircraft from the shore is increasing and 5-in shells are beginning to whistle uncomfortably near to the top of my tent, so I shall repair to my fox-hole until the shooting subsides.

Out of my hole again. Too cloudy to see the shooting but the raid sounded like a heavy one, the second this morning. Reports will soon come in. Both sides of the island were attacked at once this time and were in the cross-fire of the anti-aircraft, thus making foxholes popular. One shell hit just outside of my CP but did nothing other than to blow up a lot of mud and cause a certain about of merriment among those who watched the others trying to dodge it after it had already landed.

★ ★ ★

May 29

Strong enemy resistance still confronts the 77th and 96th Divs and the right of the 7th. However, the 7th has now advanced 3,000 yds south of and 2,000 yds to the west of Yonabaru. The Naha and Shuri fronts have apparently been deserted permitting the 6th and 1st Mardivs to advance from 1,000 to 1,800 yds, giving most of Naha to the 6th and Shuri Castle to the 1st with almost no opposition.[128]

I ordered a rapid drive to the southeast by the III Phibcorps, changing the corps boundary so as to pinch out the 77th Div. The XXIV Corps was ordered to drive west with the 7th Div and meet the III Phibcorps, thus cutting off the Japs still holding the line. The 7th also to be prepared to make a turn later to the south so as to outflank the next fortified line to the south if the enemy gets back to it.[129]

It looks as though the envelopment by the 7th had forced a withdrawal but the Japs made the decision to withdraw after it was too late. Developments will show.[130]

May 30

At 9:00 A.M., I went to the 7th Div cemetery and made a Memorial Day address to the assembled Army chaplains, after which they dispersed to hold services at their respective Div cemeteries.

Some progress along the line, with evident enemy weakening. If our estimate of enemy casualties are approximately correct, the Japs will be unable to reorganize another line. I have directed unremitting pressure. Supply and evacuation are our main problems. I am a little disappointed in the progress of the 6th Mardiv on our right. The 7th on the left has done remarkably well. We have had about a foot of rain in one week. Some troops have been taken from airfield construction and put on roads. I shall probably be taken to task for this by higher HQ but it is the right thing to do.

Airfield construction on Okinawa began within days of the American landing. Engineer and construction units began building or enhancing airfields that could support B-29 bombers, which could then strike Japan proper. The rains of late May and Buckner's transfer to road maintenance slowed down work on these fields. The rain that turned the roads into massive mud slicks was a critical factor that constrained the Tenth Army's advance. Many routes broke down from

heavy use or became impassable from the rain, making maintenance work critical. In addition to slowing down airfield construction, the 14.68 inches of rain that fell on the island also slowed down unloading operations on the beaches.[131]

May 31

The entire enemy line appears to be crumbling. The two enveloping prongs were directed to join south of the Shuri position. The XXIV Corps to drive southeast to the coast and prevent the enemy from retiring to the [large blank space appears here in original text] peninsula and the III Phibcorps to secure the port and airfield of Naha. Supplies being pressed southward by water to new beaches.[132]

Iheya landing was to have been made but Adm. Hill notified us it had been postponed due to local conditions.[133]

June 1

Bad roads precluded my going to the front. Progress continues against weak resistance.

Iheya attack force anchored off Hagushi beaches awaiting orders.

June 2

Seventh Div still advancing. With 96th pinching out 77th.

First Mardiv seems stuck for no apparent reason. Told Geiger to start things moving (through his Chief of Staff whom I found at his CP in his absence).

Iheya attack scheduled for 10:30 tomorrow.

Buckner to Adele Buckner, June 2

The rain is still checking our pursuit and slowing down our drive for the kill. But for the deluge, I feel that the enemy would by this time have been destroyed. As it is, we will have a little time to reorganize, but he is leaving his own tanks and artillery stuck in the mud as he retires, and will never regain his former resisting power. We are pressing him as relentless as possible and are supplying our troops near the shores by water and those in the center by air.

The Japs felt that the desperate air attacks aimed at out ships would starve out our expedition but we are still well supplied and the Jap air power is being steadily beaten down.

I am delighted to hear that Courtney Hodges is coming over. However, I hope that too many of the senior officers from Europe don't supersede us here in commands. We hope to be permitted to finish what we started on a shoe string.

When Adm. Nimitz was here he gave me a quart of rare old liquor which I told him I would open on the day when organized resistance in Okinawa was declared over. I am getting thirsty. Over 60,000 Japs have been purified.

★ ★ ★

"Storming" the Beach: Tenth Army units land on Okinawa's Higashi Beach, April 1, 1945. The Japanese Thirty-second Army allowed the Americans to land unopposed, conserving its strength for the relentless defense of the southern half of the island. U.S. Army Signal Corps photo.

The Commanding General: Simon Bolivar Buckner, Jr., was the son of a Confederate general turned politician. His father got Theodore Roosevelt, then president of the United States, to appoint him to West Point. Buckner, who had seen no combat in World War I and spent most of World War II in areas that had little impact on the outcome of the conflict, was looking forward to leading the Tenth Army into action. U.S. Army Signal Corps photo.

Slow Advance: Infantry elements of the XXIV Corps carefully move south. On April 4, the corps made contact with the first line of Japanese defensive fortifications. During the early days of the campaign, the Japanese succeeded in actually turning back American soldiers. U.S. Army Signal Corps photo.

Artillery Strike: Southern Okinawa's hilly terrain aided Japanese troops defending the island. The U.S. Army relied on artillery to destroy Japanese positions, which were heavily fortified to withstand American shelling. U.S. Army Signal Corps photo.

Tank Warfare: Confronted with strong Japanese fortifications, Tenth Army found American armor a valuable asset, relying heavily on tanks to provide powerful and accurate heavy firepower at the excellent Japanese defensive positions. Tanks equipped with flamethrowers were particularly effective in close combat with dug-in Japanese. U.S. Army Signal Corps photo.

Infantry Support: Tanks were vulnerable to Japanese suicide squads that would throw themselves and explosive charges under the lightly armored carriage. Although tank units tried using a cluster of antipersonnel mines affixed to their turrets to thwart such attacks, most tankers preferred to work as part of infantry-tank teams when they assaulted the Japanese lines. U.S. Army Signal Corps photo.

Radio General: Buckner made time during the battle to give some talks over the radio. He had little love for the media and saw speaking duties as an obligation—one he performed rather reluctantly. On May 20, to mark the American radio station's first day on the air, he discussed Tenth Army's progress in the campaign. He expected the Japanese defenders to be listening in, so he directed some of his remarks toward them. U.S. Army Signal Corps photo.

Quagmire: In May, heavy rains turned trenches, foxholes, and roads into mud slicks. The cold, clammy weather slowed Tenth Army's advance, allowing the Thirty-second Army to escape after the Americans breached its last established line. U.S. Army Signal Corps photo.

Seven Stars: Lieutenant General Buckner and Gen. Joseph Stilwell confer in early June. Buckner, at the time commanding the Tenth Army, an amalgamation of marine and army units, never appreciated the differences in tactics between the two services. Stilwell, who was harshly critical of Buckner during this inspection trip, discussed with Gen. of the Army Douglas MacArthur the possibility of removing him from command of Tenth Army before the invasion of Japan. It proved to be a moot point. Buckner was visiting a frontline marine unit when shell fragments killed him during a Japanese artillery barrage as the campaign neared its end. Stilwell was sent to replace him. U.S. Army Signal Corps photo.

Stilwell on Okinawa: Stilwell visited a number of frontline units during his inspection trip. Here he examines the 7th Infantry Division's progress during a stop at a regimental command post. The "Seventh has no respect for the Japs," the general observed in his diary. His guide during much of his inspection was Maj. Gen. Archibald Arnold, the 7th Division commander (left of map). *This was a homecoming of sorts for Stilwell, who had commanded the 7th Division at the start of the war. In his diary he noted: "Recognized everywhere and got friendly greeting." U.S. Army Signal Corps photo.*

Two Generals in the Mud: Stilwell often had to travel on foot because the thick mud immobilized most vehicles. He told the soldiers of the 96th Infantry Division that the mud on Okinawa was the worst he had ever seen: "Mud is bad anyplace, but where caterpillars sink and spin their tracks, it's damn bad." U.S. Army Signal Corps photo.

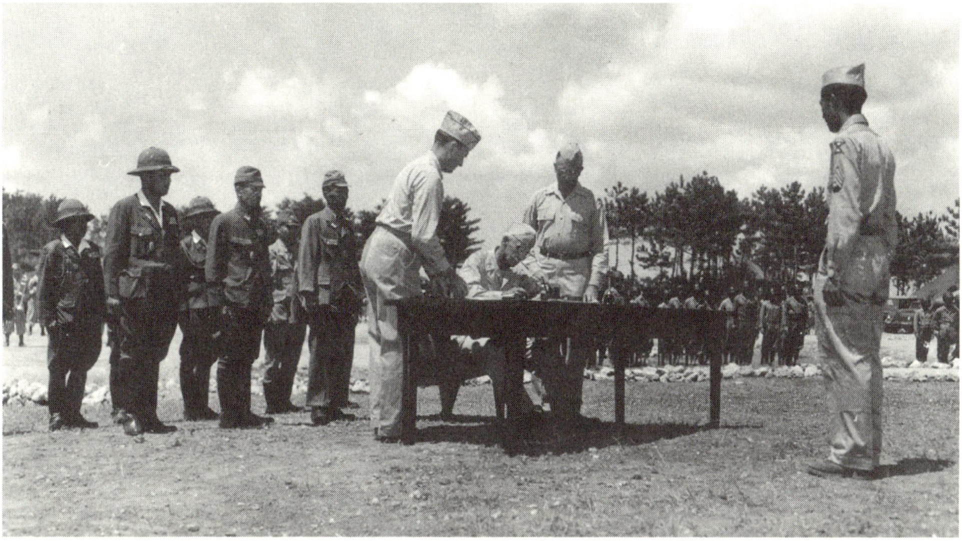

The Last Surrender: The Japanese garrison in the Ryukyus Islands surrendered to Stilwell and the Tenth Army on September 7. Japan's formal capitulation took place aboard the USS Missouri *five days earlier. The Japanese in the Ryukyus were the last element of the emperor's military to end their resistance. U.S. Army Signal Corps photo.*

"Sign Here, Sir": There were few recreational activities on Okinawa for either soldiers or their commanding general in the early days of the American occupation. Stilwell's diary indicates that letters from home and visiting entertainers were the only breaks from the monotony of life on the island. Stilwell is shown here adding his signature to the collection on the band's drum after a USO show in August, 1945. U.S. Army Signal Corps photo.

Part II

Buckner and Stilwell

As Tenth Army slowly advanced against the Japanese, Buckner had an important visitor. Joseph W. "Vinegar Joe" Stilwell, the commander of Army Ground Forces, arrived on an inspection trip. On May 10, after four months in Washington, Stilwell convinced Gen. of the Army George C. Marshall, the army chief of staff, to allow him to travel to the Pacific to secure a command in the coming invasion of Japan. Stilwell noted that Marshall "had nothing to offer except that I could go and make my own arrangements. . . . Doug obviously out of control; WD afraid of him." Stilwell spent a month inspecting units, including Tenth Army.[1]

The Stilwell portions of this section are a record of observations from the front. In a manner that was typical of him, Stilwell went directly to the units engaged in combat, including the 7th Infantry Division, which he had once commanded as a major general. Another unit he visited was the 77th Infantry Division. Like Buckner, Stilwell was particularly impressed with the combat leadership of Maj. Gen. Andrew D. Bruce, the 77th Division's commander. Stilwell also saw that the Japanese were putting up a fierce resistance, but he was quite critical of Buckner's combat leadership.

The momentum of victory is Buckner's theme in this portion of his diary. However, he was forced to respond to negative comments about his leadership when journalists published articles critical about the conduct of the campaign. He was less interested in rethinking his tactics than in pushing his subordinate commanders forward. He constantly recorded his stern and demanding conferences with officers, which were designed to motivate them. Nevertheless, he had strong critics within the U.S. Army. On June 18, the day Buckner died, Stilwell met with MacArthur to discuss replacing Buckner as Tenth Army commander for the invasion of Japan. As circumstances developed, he would do just that.

Buckner, June 3

Went to church. Flowers in arty shells.

Talked to Geiger after breakfast and told him to get the 1st Mardiv off its tail. Told him I was dissatisfied with its progress. Sent O. P. Smith down to investigate.[2]

Seventh Div cut through to southern coast and started with 1 Regt out [to] the Chinen Peninsula. Arnold had delivered to me a bottle of sea water and beach sand and a picture of two soldiers bathing their feet on the southern shore.

Joe Stilwell arrived by air from Manila unannounced at 3:00 P.M. With him were Maj. Gen. Heileman, Maj. Gen. Dorn and Brig. Gen. Bergin.[3]

Regiment [from] 2nd Mardiv landed on Iheya without opposition. No Japs found. Radio station captured intact.

Stilwell, June 3

Up at 5:30. Left at 7:05 in a B-17. Seven hundred forty-nine knots. In at 1:15 at Yontan. Lot of ships in Keramas, and at Okinawa. Big doings—roads, dumps, etc. No notice received here of our visit. A Commodore took us to Tenth Army in his jeep. Road layout is ambitious, but the muck is terrible.[4] Okinawa tombs. Surprise to staff, who were unprepared for us, Buckner, Post chief of staff, Schick, deputy chief of staff, Ely, G-2, Dumas, G-3, etc. Had long talk with Buckner. After supper, met special staff. Then long session with the GS. (Jap suicide boats at Keramas, and crews at Naha being briefed when landing came.) Twenty-nine Jap planes today, just after we got in.

Buckner, June 4

Sixth Mardiv made amphibious landing just south of Naha, met little resistance and advanced about 1,000 yds.[5]

Regiment from 2nd Mardiv reported that landing yesterday on Iheya was successful. No Jap troops found there. Radio station undamaged.

Stilwell party went to visit XXIV Corps, 96th Div and 7th Div CPs and spent the night presumably with the 7th.

Seventh Div moving southwest and 96th south against light resistance. Corps boundary changed to give XXIV practically all the enemy positions due to slow progress of III Phibcorps. First Mardiv moving slowly but is still so far behind that the 96th Div right flank has to be protected by troops that could be used profitably elsewhere.

Supplies now land at Yonabaru.

Heavy rain today. Typhoon reported passing east of us.

Stilwell, June 4

Heavy bombardment last night. Shoved off at 8:30 for Hodge's Headquarters. Deep mud. Got there at 9:30. Old fort (1457) on peak. Local boy protecting against encroachment from south. ("One of 8 views of Okinawa.") Monument to the "Loyal Dead." Chinese inscription. Seventh Division took it; [with] grenades. Left Hodge at 10:30 and poked on towards 7th Division. Stuck on cross-road. Rescued by Capt. Miller of Houston in an M-5 tractor with 2 trailers of artillery ammunition.[6] Abandoned the 3/4 ton and got to 7th Division CP. [Major General Archibald V.] Arnold [division commander], Booth, chief of staff, Ready, assistant division commander.[7] Had chow and shoved off for beach in 2 1/2 tonner. Roads impassable. LVT along beach to Yonabaru. Then a 3/4 tonner, to Shimazato and up the hill to 32nd CP. Keller (executive officer) there.[8] Finn out.[9] On to 184th and saw Green and Bjork.[10] On to 17th and Pachler.[11] Then to OP and got a look at south side. Cleared after steady rain. Good view of port and whole lay-out, nice escarpment. Looks tough, but good approach near shore. Troops close to phase line. Back to 32nd and saw Finn. Recognized everywhere and got friendly greeting. Yonabaru at dark. LVT up the coast again and back at CP by truck at 9:00. Chow and turned in at 10:30 in Arnold's tent. CP is a sea of mud. Seventh [Division] has no respect for the Japs. (Eight hundred fifty killed, 3,500 wounded in this operation). Bn. commander loss heavy.

Buckner, June 5

Rear Adm. Cotter, in charge yds and docks for Adm. Nimitz arrived to examine into airfield and base construction by CBs.[12]

Stilwell's party came back and looked the island over from cub planes. ~~Went too close to the Jap lines and got shot at by AAA.~~ [Strike through in original.]

Hodge called up and said that Col. May, 383rd Inf had been killed near Ewa. I regarded him as the best Regtl commander in the Tenth Army and outstanding General officer material. Had just recommended his promotion.

First Mardiv still trailing behind the 96th Div.

Stilwell, June 5

Showery. Breakfast at 7:00. Off at 8:00 to truck in a weasel [amphibious tracked vehicle] driver De Conter, original 7th driver.[13] Truck to beach. LVT to Navy lay-out and 3/4 tonner due west on main crossroad to CP.

Navy has big anchorage proposition on east side. Protected by islands. (Complained to Finn about a sniper south of Shinzato! Fifteen men in their party!) Four Japs killed last night coming ashore. Estimated 15–20,000 Japs left and two weeks to finish them. They are holing up in S.W. corner.

Buckner's pre-mortar very sanitary. Now further improved by a foreskin at the lower end. (It would not do to see directly into the puddle.)

Tactics all frontal. Sixth Marine landing south of Naha only attempt to go by. No thought of repeating it.

Buckner laughs at Bruce for having crazy ideas. "Two out of 15 are O.K. The rest are impossible." It might be a good thing to listen to him.

One-thirty: Took off in a cub. Down to Naha—across the island to Yonabaru. Looks like Verdun. Escarpment must have been tough. Caves, holes and tombs everywhere. The poor Okinawans have had even their ancestors blown to pieces. Complete destruction in center of island. Naha harbor blocked by sunken ships. Sixth Marines fighting on hill just south of islet. Went around to southeast peninsula on sea side and came in at south port. Seventh behind a smoke screen, apparently having a hard time. Circled close—cruiser and destroyer firing from South. Back up east coast, around the *Nakagusuku* [Stilwell wrote this word in kanji characters] castle and down to Naha again. Howitzer battery let off just as we went over. Back up coast & Ie Shima. One rocky hill, rest of island flat. Fight at the hill and in town just in front. Complete destruction. Three strips to go in on Ie. Are in use now. Sunk Jap cruiser near the leper island. Stacks showing under the water. Back to field. One hour 40 minutes. (Col. Bentley the pilot.[14]) Jap parachute wired shut. Stopped to see the Baka bomb, rocket propelled; one many suicide affair. Seven of them here in crates. Back at 4:30. Report that Col. May of 96th Division is killed. Buckner is tiresome. I tried to tell him what I had seen, but he knew it all. Keeps repeating his wise-cracks. "The Lord said let there be mud," etc. etc.—Sat through number 53 again.

Buckner, June 6

By using a jeep, a command car and three tractors I finally made my way via the III Phibcorps and 1st Mardiv to the 7th Marine Regt CP. My object was to go to Iwa and look over conditions so as to see whether there was any excuse for the 1st Mardiv's being behind the 96th Div. At the 7th CP I met BG Jones, Assistant Div Commander, 1st Marines—who had just heard that the Div had caught up, so I returned to my CP after telling them purpose of my trip.[15]

Stilwell party visited 77th and 96 Div CPs.

A new Jap defensive line being developed behind the escarpment in the south of the island. Sixth Mardiv made a little progress, taking the rest of Naha airfield and putting a pontoon bridge across the inlet.[16]

Stilwell, June 6

"You probably can't reach the 96th or 77th." "May get stuck all night," etc. These boys are CP sitters. We shoved off in a 2 1/2 tonner and got to within 1/2 mile of the 96th before we stuck. Sea of mud there 2 feet deep. Two cats could not dredge us so we wacked it to the CP. Saw Sgt. Meyers, redhead, formerly 7th.[17] Bradley looked well. Saw Charlie White.[18] Lunch. Very modest and efficient atmosphere.[19] The Marines were *following* Bradley's advance, in his zone, till he complained [emphasis in original]. Poor showing by Marines; they don't know how to keep their supply going, and they certainly lagged. Ninety-Sixth has reached the escarpment. We were pulled back by a tractor and then went to the 77th CP without any trouble whatever. Saw Bruce and Hamilton and had long talk.[20] Bruce is only man I've met who remembers his tactics. (Hamilton now regimental commander.) Back at Tenth CP at 5 P.M. Found that the boys had been out at last. Buckner went down to Marine 1st Division to see why they weren't moving. Dumas took a flight in a cub, and saw the most amazing amount of stuff—civilians, tanks, guns, troops, fights, beaches, rockets, etc., etc. Had the nerve to say he had been attacked by a Jap plane. The typical brilliant young staff officer. He and the *nut Ely* put on a daily show at the GS conference, which is a kindergarten affair [emphasis in original]. As Donovan says, this is merely an administrative staff with no influence on the operation.[21]

Buckner is obviously playing the Navy. He recommended Geiger as army commander. Nimitz is perfect. His staff is perfectly balanced. Cooperation is magnificent. The Marine divisions are wonderful. In fact, everything is just dinky. His own staff is perfect—he picked them himself. It is all rather nauseating. There is NO tactical thinking on push [emphasis in original]. No plan was ever discussed at the meetings to hasten the fight or help the divisions. The 96th had the whole escarpment and the 6th Mardiv is to be "pinched out."

Buckner, June 7

Stilwell party left for Manila. At press conference Stilwell said press had under publicized and failed to appreciate this campaign either in hardship overcome[,] ferocity of fighting or colorful events.

Flew over southern part of island in a cub with Bentley. Followed front lines and reconnoitered plateau positions defended by enemy. A tough nut to crack. Stone cliffs full of caves[;] expect a difficult approach from the southeast and somewhat easier one on the west.

First Mardiv broke through to west coast. Tails up again. Geiger also feels better. After riding both somewhat I gave them a little praise today.

Stilwell, June 7

Air alert again twice last night. Nothing happened. Ty had a nightmare. Sunny day. Press conference at 9:00.

According to press accounts, Stilwell warned that Japanese soldiers were fighting with more tenacity than German troops. He added that suggestions the war would soon end were at best overly optimistic. "All that is slop," he told correspondents. " When they are so tenacious individually I don't see how we can expect a crack in morale in the mass." He coyly avoided a question from a New York Times *reporter about the number of troops it would take to invade Japan. The journalist said he thought it would take half-million. "We'd be foolish to try to do it with less, don't you think?" replied Stilwell. He also added that if the Japanese armies in China and Manchuria fought on after the fall of Japan proper, the war would continue for another two years. A* New York Sun *editorial commented: "Everybody will hope, of course, that the general is overconservative, but none can deny that he is qualified to speak from experience."*[22]

(Engineer troops that should have been helping troops were building rear installations. Getting ahead of ourselves as usual.) Lunch, bath and many pictures. Left at 10:15 for field; shoved [off] at 11:15. Not allowed over Kerama.

★ ★ ★

Buckner, June 8

Aguni landing postponed until tomorrow. Gen. Hunt USMC in for lunch today on return from Iheya landing.[23] Returns to his ship today.

Wallace came in feeling downhearted and "sniped at." I was rather severe with him over laxity in permitting unnecessary burning of native houses. I shall have to let stew a couple of days before giving him any encouragement. He is too sensitive and is inclined to feel that he is persecuted. However, he has ability.

Directive came directing future activities of Tenth Army over which I have every reason to be jubilant.

Buckner, June 9

Aguni landing reported without resistance. One Jap jumped off cliff.

Visited III Phibcorps and 1st and 6th Mardiv CPs. All commanders in high spirits.

Sixth Mardiv have now surrounded an estimated 1,500 Jap naval personnel. Fifty committed suicide last night. Their commander, a naval captain is reported to have been among them. First Mardiv now up against main position in the south. About 15,000 troops estimated to be there.[24]

Last night Jap planes tried to drop artillery fuses to them by parachute. Most of them fell in the water and 1 chute within our lines.

Will drop offer of surrender to Japs tomorrow with little hope of results but largely at the behest of psychological "experts."

A reporter for the New York Journal-American *called the gesture "without precedent in the Pacific War." The message, addressed to Lt. Gen. Ushijima Mitsuru, read: "The forces under your command have fought bravely and well, and your infantry tactics have merited the respect of your opponents. Like myself, you are an infantry general long schooled and practiced in infantry warfare. I believe, therefore, that you understand as clearly as I, that the destruction of all Japanese resistance on the island is merely a matter of days." When Ushijima received the note, he said with a smile, "The enemy has made me an expert on infantry warfare."*[25]

Buckner, June 10

Attended morning services. Chap. Hillyer had a photographer there and photographed me as "Exhibit A."[26] When the first services ended, the group for second services were there and he wanted me to pose for a picture with the second group. I declined, saying that I regarded the services as being devoted to the Lord rather than to the photographer.

Adm. Hill dropped in. Wants to speed up radio fighter control stations—(so do we).

Buckner, June 11

Adm. Byrd arriving by plane to see Adm. Hill.[27] Sending him a small can of pemmican in a large basket with the compliments of the Tenth Army.

Mulcay came to say good-bye. He is being replaced by Maj. Gen. Woods.

Ninety-sixth Div got 1 Bn up to the rim of the escarpment. Right of 1st Mardiv made a little progress. Seventh Div took "hill 95" with 60 caves in it.

Buckner, June 12

Adm. Byrd came ashore and, after a very pleasant talk, I sent him on an island tour.

Shick brought in a clipping from the N.Y. *Herald* [*Tribune*] by David Lawrence apparently instigated by Mr. [Homer Bigart] here and saying that the

Okinawa campaign was a monumental fiasco of incompetent bungling and demanding that I be investigated for not using the Marines for an amphibious envelopment.[28] He also announced friction between Army and Marines here. Evidently he is seeking raise a newspaper controversy. The enemy should be pleased by his services for them.

On May 29, the New York Herald Tribune *published an article critical of Buckner's rejection of a second landing. Homer Bigart, the author of the piece, correctly observed that the Japanese were fighting a battle of attrition in the southern half of the island. He also noted that the marines were able to take the northern half of Okinawa quickly because the Japanese made little effort to defend it. Once the III Amphibious Corps finished taking the north, Buckner redeployed it in the south, using what Bigart called "ultra-conservative" tactics. "A landing on southern Okinawa would have hastened the encirclement of Shuri. Instead of an end run, we persisted in frontal attacks," he wrote. "It was hey-diddle-diddle straight down the middle." Syndicated columnist David Lawrence used this dispatch as the basis for two columns, neither of which appeared in the* Herald Tribune, *that were harshly critical of Buckner's strategy and interservice leadership. In the first column, Lawrence claimed an amphibious assault would have saved American lives. He noted that Buckner had no combat experience and wondered why Nimitz had not ordered a second assault landing. A week later, he started another column on Okinawa with a loaded sentence: "Why is the truth about the military fiasco at Okinawa hushed up?" He said the truth was beginning to leak out with the high casualty figures. He called the battle a "fiasco," and blamed Buckner and the army for employing conservative tactics. In a deliberate distortion of the facts, Lawrence wrote that the marines' rapid conquest of the northern half of the island was ample proof of the soundness of their tactics. He demanded an immediate investigation into Buckner's decision.*[29]

The 6th Mardiv expects to clean up their area tomorrow. The 1st Mardiv has at last advanced to the main enemy position. The 7th Div is meeting many counter-attacks near Hill 95 on the left and, along with the 96th on the right have a foothold on the escarpment.

Buckner, June 13

Heavy fighting continues without much gain except on the left of the 7th Div. About 1,000 Japs killed. Dropped 45 plane loads of napalm on reported location of enemy army CP.

Went to visit Adm. Hill and Adm. Byrd on the former's flagship.

Sixth Mardiv subdued all organized resistance on Oroku Peninsula. About 3,500 Japs killed in all on this positions; mostly navy personnel. Over 50 surrendered, including a couple of officers, one accompanied by his wife. A number blew themselves up with grenades.[30]

Buckner, June 14

Spent day visiting Bn OPs in 96th and 7th Divs. Got a good look at the hostile position. On way back stopped at the two Div OPs. Arnold and Bradley in high spirits, having each gotten a Bn and a number of tanks on top of the plateau, and well into the enemy position.

The 383rd Inf had its new Colonel badly wounded and his successor had just arrived when I was at their OP. Last night a Bn advanced into a mine field, lost 3 Co Commanders and a Bn staff officer and fell back. They are clearing out the mine field today.

This is Adele's birthday.

Buckner to Adele Buckner, June 14

★ ★ ★

I spent the day at the front looking over the enemy positions which showed signs of weakening. But for the rain when we broke the position which bogged down our heavy weapons in the pursuit, the Japs would never have reached their present stronghold in a plateau almost surrounded by cliffs. However, we pressed today's attack from a quarter that seemed to surprise the enemy and got two battalions and some tanks on top of the plateau. If we can hold on tonight we can probably break this position tomorrow or next day and the Japs will be forced to a final ridge at the southern tip of the island and soon destroyed. They are likely at any time to try a last desperate counter-attack which I would welcome as a quick way of ending the campaign. It has been a tough one, but we still have a record of ten Japs killed for every one of ours and have broken the strongest defenses yet seen in the Pacific.

We have splendid relations here between the Army, Navy and Marine components of my command in spite of unpatriotic attempts on the part of certain publicity agents at home who are trying to sir up a controversy between the Army and Marines. I saw an article by

David Lawrence saying that I had made a monumental fiasco of the whole campaign by not doing it the "Marine way." By the same mail I got a letter from the Army-Navy Staff College saying that their studies of the campaign indicated that it had been handled beautifully. Take your choice. Incidentally, the count of Japs dead today reached a total of over 75,000 killed since we landed.

We are now attacking Japan every day from our fields here and have already developed our island into a powerful offensive base. When we clean up the Japs here Gen. MacArthur will probably take over our command and I hope he will point us toward Tokyo. It would be great to fight our way all the way through Japan the Kuriles and return via the Aleutians.

★ ★ ★

Buckner, June 15

Investigated the burning of some shacks by Engineers in Machinato. Found it justifiable.

Had press conference at 4:00 P.M. outlining whole campaign. Stressed teamwork rather than spectacular events but gave credit to May and 383rd Inf for taking "Conical Hill," which made envelopment of Shuri position possible, but dwelt on the importance of pressure by other units.

Buckner was not one to take criticism of his second landing decision lightly, and he vigorously defended his approach. The New York Herald Tribune *was one of the few major national publications that covered this conference. According to this account, strategy and American progress on the island were the two topics the general discussed. The purpose of taking the island, Buckner said, was to use its airfields to bomb Japan and build it up as a base for the invasion of the main Japanese islands. This mission and the geography of southern Okinawa ruled against a second landing. Reefs would have made an amphibious assault difficult and the hilly terrain would have made it easy for the Japanese to contain American forces on the beach. "If we'd scattered our forces we might have got licked, or it might have unduly prolonged the campaign; or we might have been forced to call on additional troops, which we did not want to do." He explained that economy of troops was necessary because the congestion of more units would have slowed down construction of the airfields. "We didn't need to rush forward, because we had secured enough airfields to execute our development mission."*

Buckner also had defenders in both the navy and the press. When Admiral

Nimitz read the Lawrence columns, he responded with a statement that attacked the journalist and defended Buckner. "The article, which has been widely reprinted shows that the author has been badly misinformed, so badly as to give the impression that he has been made use of for purposes which are not in the best interest of the United States," Nimitz charged. While the criticism might seem reasonable in the United States, he explained that the invasion of the island had been carefully planned and his staff had considered a number of different options. "During the operation each service took losses and each service inflicted great damage to the enemy. Comparisons between services are out of place and ill-advised." An Associated Press correspondent characterized the admiral's statement as "rare" in its bluntness, while Richard Kluger notes in his history of the New York Herald Tribune *that Nimitz carefully avoided criticizing Bigart's reporting. Bigart and his paper retreated from their earlier criticism of Buckner, denying Lawrence any cover. "This correspondent still believes that a landing on the south coast of Okinawa would have been a better employment of the Marines. But to call the campaign a fiasco is absurd. The writer covered the Italian campaign during the Anzio and Cassino actions and he knows what a fiasco is." The* Herald Tribune*'s editorial board later noted that Bigart's report "did not on its face, warrant the conclusions Mr. Lawrence drew." As a result, Bigart's comments "would seem to leave Mr. Lawrence open to merited rebuke." Buckner never lived to see Nimitz's statement.*[31]

Buckner, June 16

Twenty-fourth Corps has half of the plateau. Japs are beginning to blow themselves up or cut their own throats. A dozen or so did so today. Large attempts at infiltration. Sixth Mardiv and the 8th Marine Regt from 2nd Mardiv to go in line on the right tomorrow. Looks as though the enemy were at the end of their rope so far as organized defense is concerned as soon as we get the rest of the plateau.

Moved to new CP this evening after supper.

Buckner, June 17

Inspected naval base developments on East coast.

No progress by our XXIV Corps and stiffer resistance as result of Japs' 32nd Div remnants reinforcing line there. About 700 yds progress in units of III Phibcorps zone.

Stilwell, June 18

Hot. Eleven [A.M.] saw Doug and went over the dope on new weapons. He agreed on all points. Then there was a lot of talk about commanders and units. He has the dope on them all except Krueger. Refused to take Bradley.

This reference is to Gen. Omar N. Bradley. General Marshall wanted units from the European theater to fight in the invasion of Japan and he wanted Bradley to command an army during this operation. This suggestion was essentially a demotion for Bradley, who was in command of an army group. On April 26, 1945, Gen. of the Army Dwight D. Eisenhower, the theater commander in Europe, sent a cable to Marshall adamantly opposing the idea. Eisenhower wrote, "would make it appear to all soldiers in this theater and to the public that this was rather a minor league affair and would have the further effect of diminishing Bradley's stature in the postwar Army and public opinion." Eisenhower stopped and phoned Bradley after composing the last sentence to check with him about his feelings. Eisenhower reported that Bradley would go wherever his orders dictated. "Nevertheless, I distinctly got the impression that he feels that to go to the Pacific as an army commander would be belittling in the American mind the magnitude of American accomplishments here, and the services of more than 3,000,000 U.S. soldiers. However he did not—repeat not—express an opinion as to his personal desires." A day later, Marshall responded, "In view of your message he will no longer be considered for such an assignment."[32]

Wants NO group commanders. Talked about Sultan as possible chief of staff.[33] Asked me if I would take the job. Told him NO, I fancied myself as a field commander. [Emphasis in original.] Then he said "How about an Army? Would you be willing to step down?"

Told him I would take a division to be with troops. He had asked about Okinawa and I told him. He has not a high opinion of Buckner. Agreed he [is] facetious. Told me he would rather have me as an army commander than anyone he knew, and if GCM was willing, he was.[34] This is contingent on a change in the Tenth Army. He will welcome Buckner's relief and my transfer. Navy refused to give up Tenth Army. If they persist, he will just take the troops and let them keep the army, asking for another, which I am to command. So I tell Marshall that if Buckner is relived, I go to the Tenth Army, and if Navy does not turn it lose, Doug asks for another one for me. (If Navy gives in and Buckner is not relieved, I get nothing.)

* * *

On June 18, Buckner decided to visit the 1st Marine Division. His troops did not always welcome these visits, because they often provoked Japanese fire. He ar-

rived in a jeep flying his three-star flag accompanied by a large gaggle of staff officers. Instead of wearing subdued insignia on these visits, Buckner wore three silver stars displayed prominently on his helmet. These symbols of his rank were highly visible, and a marine officer recalled that the insignia's presence usually provoked a Japanese artillery barrage in an attempt to kill the high-ranking officer wearing it. In most cases, the shelling started just after the general left. Climbing a hill up to a forward observation post, the general expressed concern about the plight of Okinawa's civilians. Marines at the post saw Buckner's helmet with its three shiny stars and asked him to remove it and wear one that was less conspicuous. Buckner said no, telling the marines that he was not afraid of the Japanese and that he had no intention of hiding. Minutes later, a battalion command post on a nearby hill radioed a warning that Buckner's stars were clearly visible to them. The general removed his helmet, placed it on a rock to his left, and put on one that had no rank insignia. But it was too late. A Japanese artillery unit had spotted Buckner, who stood just beyond the crest of the hill with his hands akimbo looking in their direction, and fired a round. The shell exploded on the rock next to the general, tearing a hole in the left side of his chest. Officers standing three feet behind him got up unhurt but saw Buckner lying on the ground, bloody, with mud splattered in his hair. "General Buckner has been hit!" a radio operator yelled into his mike. The marines carried him off the hill on a poncho. Buckner asked if anyone else was hurt and seemed relieved when told that no one else had been harmed. He died a few minutes later in a battalion aid station, where a marine private held his hand and kept repeating, "You are going home, General; you are homeward bound." Silence gripped the small crowd surrounding Buckner, until someone began reciting the Twenty-third Psalm: "Yea, though I walk through the valley of the shadow of death, I will fear no evil: for thou art with me."[35]

Part III

★ ★ ★ ★ ★ ★ ★

STILWELL

June 19

Guam at 7:00. Met by Giles—Rumor that Buckner was killed yesterday.[1] Breakfast at Giles'. To Nimitz office for daily briefing—(Blah, blah). Met Spruance. Nimitz announced death of Buckner. Talked situation over with Giles and sent radio to Doug, telling him where he could get me ("If there is any change in Tenth Army" or if a new one is called for. Is this the "June surprise" I was warned of?)

There are two entries for June 19 because Stilwell crossed the international date line going east and gained a day.

June 19

Richardson passed us during night. On way to PI without doubt. ("I must ask Doug to give me a field command.") I wonder if luck is with me on this? Suppose I had stopped to make speeches, and Richardson had grabbed off an army. Maybe it will all come out OK after all. (But it wouldn't if I had not stirred around and gotten busy.)

Arrived Honolulu at 2:45. Sure enough, Ruffner had radio: "*Do not return to mainland until further orders.*" They have been in a flurry trying to locate me. ???[2] Report that Easley (96th Division) was killed yesterday. Radio from Doug: "Command Tenth Army. Return to Guam at once."

Marshall radioed MacArthur on June 19 and advised him that Nimitz wanted MacArthur to select Buckner's successor. Marshall allowed him to pick from Stilwell; Alexander Patch, Seventh Army commander, Lt. Gen. Lucian Truscott, Fifth Army commander; Gen. George Patton, Third Army commander; Lt. Gen. William Simpson, Ninth Army commander; and Gen. Jacob Devers, the 6th Army Group commander. MacArthur countered that he wanted to give the command to Lt. Gen. Oscar W. Griswold, the XIV Corps commander. If that was not acceptable to Marshall, then his preferences were Stilwell, Patch, and Truscott in that order. On June 20, Marshall informed MacArthur that Stilwell would be Tenth Army's new commander. Although Stilwell received the message informing him of the decision on June 19, it was due to the international date line rather than boldness on MacArthur's part. Since Tenth Army was under the navy's operational control, Stilwell received orders from both MacArthur and Nimitz.[3]

June 20

Went over errand and messages with Donovan and Ty.[4] Took Dorn and Bergin and the C-54 and at 10:15 shoved off for Kwajalein. Ty to go back and move Win and then bring out a plane.[5] Sent for Sgt. Raynaud.[6] Primed

Donovan to get Joe sent out.[7] Hightower wants to come.[8] Sent letter to Win by Donovan. He is to give her the dope.

Drew Pearson has scathing article on Hurley.[9] Jack Service arrested by FBI for espionage.[10] Also the *Amerasia* people who wanted me to write for them. Just as well I didn't.

Twelve hour flight to Kwajalein. Arrived 8:30. Got rid of callers, and had a wack. Turned in at 9:30. Cool Breeze.

Stilwell crossed the international date line going west and lost a day, so there is no June 21 entry.

June 22

Arrived 7:30 at Guam. Rain. Met by McMorris. Breakfast with him. There to Headquarters. Sat there. The bellyache. Then talked to Nimitz and Arnold. Went to Giles' place for lunch. Lowell Thomas there.[11] Left at 1:30. Went to see McMorris. Then talked to Goss and Mandell.[12] Then took a shower. Dinner. Nimitz away at 3rd Mardiv. He came back at 9:30 and gave me my orders. McMorris went to the field and we turned in at 10:00. Left at 12:30 A.M.

On June 21, Gieger announced that U.S. forces had secured control of Okinawa. Generals Ushijima and Cho committed suicide the next morning. A few hours later, a flag-raising ceremony at Tenth Army headquarters marked the capture of the island.[13]

June 23

Sunny. Arrived Okinawa at 7:30. Met by Richardson, Geiger, Hodge, Woods,[14] Post, etc. (Wallace). To CP for breakfast 9:00–11:00—Wallace, Bissett, Nold.[15] Went over construction plane. Usual impasse. 11:00–12: talked to Post. New CP much better than old one. (Crist—military government, in). Tenth Army relieved at not getting an ETO "expert." Operations about over. 5,600 prisoners (!)

P.M.: went to various staff sections (G-2 and G-3). Hot. P.M.: GS meeting. Three casualties to midnight, 22nd.

June 24

Two hundred plus casualties to midnight, 23rd. Hodge and DelValle Called. Long talk with Richardson. He feels dumped on; wanted this command.

P.M.—read the *JUNK*—directives, plans, etc. and almost fell asleep. Very dry. (CORONET-I, VIII, X). [Emphasis in original.][16] Dubbed till supper time. Hubbard in hospital—blown eardrum. Alerts every night. Nothing.

June 25

Kume postponed. High surf. Hot. Eight fifteen [A.M.] left for Iscom. Picked up Wallace and Bissett. To yellow 3 beach. LCM's unloading: up coast to Bolo (VLR field)—September 15 target date. Then up coast and over the Ishigawa isthmus to POW camp. Japs, Okies, and Koreans crowded, all healthy looking and well fed. (Two K rations & 1 C each day!)

Jeep ran on stump, & hit the windshield and cut my forehead. Luckily, glasses did not break. Dorn patched me up. Then out to Chimu field (Marine fighters) ready July 1

Back and out Haten peninsula to unloading point. Back to Awase and out to the dock. Sloppy work. Two long lines of waiting trucks, all empty. Back to Awase airfield. (Target date July 5. They won't make it.) Busier location in rice paddies. Down to lower unloading point, where LST was hit by suicide plane last week. More life there. Called it off and came back for a bath. Very dusty. Wallace not impressive. Bissett improves on acquaintance. Casualties: 23 killed, 118 wounded, 1 missing = 142. Geiger relieved.[17]

June 26

A.M.: 9:00–10:10—Long talk with Adm. Hill. The freight jam must be 1st priority. Radioed for Cheves as terminal commander.[18] Pick to be Iscom, if I get him—very doubtful.[19] Lack of coordination & drive is obvious. I have got to be an SOB or risk disaster.

With Dorn to Naha and called on Geiger. (Graves of Perry's men located.[20]) Rain. Lunch there. Over to XXIV Corps and saw Hodge. They get 5 or 10 Japs every night. Back to CP. Saw Adm. Ring & Feldman.[21] Same old story. Wallace asked for stuff that was already on the way. General dissatisfaction with Wallace. Woods called. Papers from San Francisco with news of appointment. Editorial comments OK.[22]

June 27

At CP in A.M. Filduncan in.[23] Confirms my ideas. Read the files, etc. etc. No lunch. 12:30 to cub strip. Flew to south side. Arnold and Hodge three. To Hill 89 on extreme tip via Hill 95. ("Hi, Uncle Joe!" from various G.I.s). Ninety-five and 89 were tough. Scrambled down to Ushijima's . . . cave. Narrow entrance. Stinking Japs. Back up. All commanders there. Ushijima and adjutant buried on top. Bugler blew *To the Colors,* and flag was raised. Then I made a speech to about 1,000 of 7th Division massed for the ceremony. Back to strip and home.

Today ordered the troops to produce 3 engineering battalions. Five service groups of 1000 each, 3 truck companies and a CB battalion. We have *got* to get tough. [Emphasis in original.] After supper—8:00 P.M. went to Awase, Kuto Saki and Yellow 3 to watch unloading. Back at Midnight.

Story of Jap who tried to surrender, flute player.

Jap lieutenant helping call out Japs. "If the God-damn Japs want to fight, we kill 'em!"

June 28

A.M. at CP. Geiger in griping on the orders. Told him "NO." He took it all right. [Emphasis in original.]

Heinrichs and Duffy, ordnance boys, to say good-bye.[24] After lunch, 1:00, shoved off to Kubo-Sake to see Kirtland.[25] (Kirtland, Mackey, executive,[26] Albright, doctor,[27] flag lieutenant.) Half hour call and back through the dust to CP. Dorn and 2 lieutenants flew by cub to Bolo Point and down to Naha, over to Baten-Ko and up around Awase and home. Number 13 has part of new grade in. Machinato field way back, looks 30–40% along. Awase field will make the date. Great activity on all roads. Naha harbor a mess, and of course, Naha, too.

After supper, recorded a broadcast for Army Hour. Session with Dill.[28]

June 29

Westervelt shot Bergin and me on Wednesday night for typhus and cholera. He had Dr. Phinney up to day to look at my head.[29] Nerve bruised, probably. Neuralgic pains.

Eight thirty to 96th Division CP (1 hour, 10 minutes) via Number through SHURI. A mess. Much like Verdun: *Japs held here nearly 2 months* [emphasis in original]. Road construction going well. Very dusty. On way back, stopped in at Futema air-field. Good start at 77th Division CP. Saw Randle.[30] They'll be out by July 10. Back for lunch.

(Man in 96th mopping up, felt a movement under foot. He was standing on a Jap's chest. They lie down and cover themselves completely except for their noses.)

(One man stumbled into a ditch and fell on top of a Jap. He jumped back and shot the Jap, and then 9 more, all lying covered in the sauce ditch.)

(The cave with 700 in it was sealed yesterday, after 2 doses of gasoline—800 gallons and 900 gallons. Four hundred entrances, 3 levels, access by holes 50 meters deep. Japs refused to come out, except 22, who escaped from their officers.)

(Letter from Mayor of Kerama. "The Americans have treated us very well. Everything is lovely. When may we expect to get the beer?")

(Girl refugee, Okinawan born in Honolulu, caught here visiting family. GI said, "Put a good dress on her and I'd like to take her home." She came right back in English, "Why don't you, then?")

("Eleanor eats powdered eggs.")

P.M.: Feldman in just as I was leaving. He's a wind-bag. Listened to his song and dance and then went to the Kadena, Yontan and Bolo fields. Things are really moving. All kinds of machinery, including "finger cranes," all whooping up and down. The bulldozer operator just goes ahead and does his work. No supervision needed. No dead-beating.

After supper, talked to Nold at airfield and then went out with Post, Dorn, and Bergin to the beaches—white, orange, purple (McDaniels, Rasmussen).[31] Seventy-seventh pulling out; went about on of their LSTs. Back at Midnight.

June 30

Japs over early this A.M. and bombed. Hot Rockey arrived to replace Geiger.[32] Dubbed around CP Had a nap. Sun-bath. Extremely hot and enervating. After supper, out to stumps. (Mail beginning to come) (*Rotten movie.*) [Emphasis in original.] Couldn't find any dumps. West to Awase, Kubosaki and Yellow 3. Dinner hour at latter. (Ninkins)[33] On the job, and knows it. Bueno tonnage for June. Back at 2:00 A.M.

July 1

Up at 7:30. Hot again. Dubbed on papers. P.M.: 1:30, out with Ashton, Quartermaster, Knipper, Engineer, Daniels, Ordnance to go over the dumps.[34] Saw the ration dump, clothing, engineer ordinance, and ammo dumps B and C. DUST [emphasis in original]. Back at 4:15. These staff officers need more of this.

Ex-cook, 7th Division headquarters called. Now Tech. Sgt. in the JASCOs. Saw me on the beach and told his going to be prepared to see me pop up any time right in the middle of there.

Called Wallace in and gave him the dope. He accepts Cheves readily. Today, as I had a blast on Cheves word came he was coming.

July 2

With Westervelt to visit hospital lay-out. To Awase (63 Field) then to Marine Corps Field (#2)—dirtiest I ever saw—bastard organization of Navy personnel, Army nurses, for Marine patients under Army command. Then to 82nd (goes out with 96th Division) and 31st (stays and expands). Back for lunch. Hodge in on PRO matters (Marines hogging the show).

On June 30, General Hodge wrote a four-page memo complaining that the press gave sole credit to the marines for the success on Okinawa. "I read many clippings," he wrote, "giving outstanding exploits of the Marines on Okinawa, often crediting them with moves actually made by my own divisions." The disparity be-

came even worse at the end of the battle: "I have been able to find but little mention of Army troops fighting their hearts out in the last twelve days of the 82-day battle. The big picture and the overall result is that the American public thinks the USMC are the only good troops in the Pacific Area, that they do all the fighting and that no one else can execute amphibious landings."[35]

He stayed for lunch. Out again to Machinato unloading point—good one—and Machinato air-field. Good progress. Down to Naha and looked over the port. Should be good. Back at 5:00. Adm. Cobb here. Queer personality. He stayed for dinner. Got him going on football and that was the key.

Maj. Untermayer in from Guam.[36] He had nothing to offer. Paper work.

July 3

A.M.: Wrote speech and worked on papers

Twelve-thirty: McCaleb of INS in for interview.[37] Hubbard will stay on as ADC

One-thirty: flew to 96th Division strip for decoration of about 60 men. Unusual number from North Dakota. Halloran there. Took off at once for 7th Division strip for similar ceremony there. About 40 men. Band played "Let's GO!"

Back via Yonabam along Route 13. They are getting action on it.

Bath. Early bed.

July 4

A.M.: Dubbed around and worked on papers. Left at 11:30 for broadcast, Col. Carlton, SSO, as guide.[38] So he got lost! We phoned and got to the station OK. CBS and NBC nets in U.S.

Thrown off stride by a photographer making flash picture.

From there to the Okinawan local radio and broadcast same speech to the troops. The lunch with Wallace, Arnold and Jones. Then back to CP and had a bath. Hot as hell. In evening, grand display of pyrotechnics to celebrate the 4th. (Speech apparently went over all right.)

Big day in the evening, when the mail came. Letter from Win! The first.

Out looking over the beaches till 11 P.M.

In his Fourth of July speech, Stilwell told his troops: "I hope and trust that our next Fourth of July will see you all back where you want to be. The harder we pour it on now the sooner we'll all go home. This has been a tough fight; nobody but the men who've fought in it can possibly realize how tough. It's also been a very satisfactory fight, but no one who wasn't in it can possibly feel the same sat-

isfaction as the men who were. That's where the soldier has it all over the rest of the world; he belongs to a select group who have a first-hand knowledge of war. For that reason, I'm not going to wave my arms around and get off a lot of baloney about your heroic deeds, glorious victories and what not. You'd just say 'horsefeathers,' or worse, shut off your radios. All I want to do is to remind you of the satisfaction that you all feel that you've stood up to your work and done in your time what all real Americans have found guts to do in our past wars from the Revolution on." After reminding the combat troops of the contribution service and support personnel made, he added: "The Okinawa campaign has been a big step forward. But if we are going to get the war over as soon as possible we've got to keep going. Extra sweat we put into it now will pay off as we close in on the Jap in his home islands." The New York Times*'s editorial board noted, "This is the sort of language that American soldiers and marines are likely to understand and respect."*[39]

July 5

Started for 27th Division. At 8:45, just before getting to strip, dump "C" began to explode—a big white cloud of smoke with phosphorus streamers on all sides. I went up and watched it, but it kept getting worse so I came back to the CP. Apparently much quieter at 9:45, so tried again. No soap. Much worse again. Back to CP. By 11:30 it was a continuous barrage over 1,000 yds wide and getting deep. Occasional heavy explosions, and then HE, phosphorous, pyrotechnics, colored smoke. So much in clusters and what have you. Origin unknown. Defective ammo stored there. (Jap?) [Stilwell had good reason to suspect enemy stragglers. Sentries killed four Japanese soldiers outside the ammunition dumps the night before as they were trying to throw hand grenades into the compound.[40]] Ordered thorough search in A and B and double guards. This is a bad set back. Notified Nimitz. (One explosion nearly tipped our plane over.)

Racket kept up all P.M. with occasional lulls. Worst concussion about 6:15—by 8:15 it had quitted down. If it just doesn't get over into the other areas! About 10,000 tons have probably gone up.

Mail—all the boys want to come out.

July 6

Eight-thirty off to Nago. Arrived [at] 9:00. Griner met me. To CP, met staff (Ovenshine, chief of staff, Bradford assistant chief of staff, Ferrin, artillery and others.[41] By jeep to 165th (Hart); 105th (Winn) latter very unimpressive.[42] Up to barrier line and Sawa post. Back for lunch, chewed the rag shoved off at 1:50.

Back to CP. Five P.M. press conference—usual blah.

Eight P.M. Kenney, Giles, Bissell, Wallace, Hutchinson in.[43] They talked till 10:45.

July 7

A.M.: Called in the special staff for talks. Judge Advocate (Walsh), Inspector General (Buchanan), Artillery (Edwards), Signal Corps (Taylor), Quartermaster (Ashton), Adjutant General (Garfield).[44] Paper shuffling. One-thirty [P.M.]: Gave Post T/E radio asking for Merrill, Condon, Cannon, Wells, Grindley, Jones.[45] Post took it very nicely and agreed to stay on if Merrill can't come. I'd be well satisfied. He's OK.

Sent back the list of makes with only Post and Hamilton on it. (Buckner had recommended 10 staff officers and 1 combat soldier!)

Left to Naha. Went around with Col. Violante.[46] Saw the engineer—Lt. Col. McMillan.[47]

Looked over the harbor works.

Went on down to 6th Mardiv Shepherd and Clement.[48] Lecture on operations of the 6th. Back at 6:00. Hot day again. No rain. Much dust.

July 8

Many press clippings from Paul. (Kenney's story of Mrs. Bachrach and Jap atrocities in north Manila. Rape and murder every where.) A.M. in CP. 1:50 to see Woods at TAF Headquaters. Traffic Jam. Back at 3:30. Woods sent a case (36 bottles) of coke down by his aide! Young turned up.[49] Letter from Win says he wasn't much help. Win got home on the 3rd. Letter from Al—roof is on the new house.

Air alert, 1/2 hour, then all clear.

July 9

A.M. Letters and papers. Gen. Jones leaving.[50] One of the vagrant and vapid "inspectors." Two P.M. to Ie Shima. Met Thomas and Greely (chief of staff) and went all over the island.[51] Good breaks there, plenty of coral, good water supply, good beach. Cargo daily 2800 tons; will to 5000. At first 2500 was to be the limit. Field construction ahead of plane arrivals. Back at 4:30. ("You will get a bang out of our products." (Bomb dump.) "The Gay 90's" (AAA) "We haven't time to paint fancy signs," etc. etc.) Old Frederick Palmer called.[52] Wanted an interview. No.

Got a radio receiver.

Movie—DOMEI. "Succession of the strong-willed and arrogant Gen. Stilwell to command of the Tenth Army is significant because Stilwell is known as an advocate of the win-the-war-quickly school of thought."

July 10

A slug signing several hundred officer efficiency reports.

Jap ammo went up, killing a captain and 4 men.

Two-thirty, Post shoved off. Bergin and Ruffner in. Nap. (Nineteen cokes for the crew working on the house.)

After supper to ASP 6 and area D (ammo). No guard. Farcical patrols. Sloppy personnel. Told Daniels to do something about it.

July 11

A.M.: Bawled out Wallace and company for ordinance dump deficiencies.

Saw Fitzgerald (PM), Green (G-1), Turner (FO), Pulsifer (Sig), Heilman (PX).[53] Haircut. Matthews of Tucson and Stern, *Philadelphia Record* in to talk.[54] Very friendly. Giles in. Drinks before dinner. Young told me at 6:50 about I and E talk at 7:00. Went down and sounded off. Men seemed to like it. Worked till 11:30 on general officer board.

July 12

All day on general officer list. (Cheves arrived.) (Giles, Bergin, Hodge, Ruffner, I on the board.) Finished at 5:00. Limmie air marshal in—Lloyd.[55] The God-damn Lancaster outfit.

July 13

Oh-oh AM at CP. Paper shuffling. P.M. to Machinato loading site and airfield. To Futenma field via 30 to Awase and south on 13—new location. To Awase field and back.

Cheves says we should make the grade. It looks better. White, Seventh Air Force reported in.[56]

July 14

Seven weeks here. Efficiency reports, etc.

"C" dump is exploding again. Oh, Christ. Wallace is just like . . . Pitts.[57] Chased him out to get some facts, and got after Col. Gibson.[58] Luckily the damn thing blew itself out towards 5:30. At 8:30 inspected "C, D and B" areas also. Awase dock. No action on cause way. Radio that Carl has gone to parachute school![59]

July 15

A.M.: Papers. 2:00 P.M.to 1st Mardiv cemetery for dedication. Back at 3:15. At 4:00 Adm. Price,[60] Cotter, Kirtland in with Bissett. This and that; indication that Navy don't like the Cheves plan.

Gibson reported on dumps. Wallace in with report on July 5 affair at 10:00 A.M. (Needled him last night). Adm. Cobb got nasty.[61] "I have withdrawn the P.T. boats till COMGENTEN can guaranty that they will not be shot at." Ordered 15 get them back on.

—NEWS—Sherry [Maj. Gen. Claire Chennault] reported to have announced his "resignation" as head of Fourteenth Air Force. Hooray if true.

July 16

Hot day. Worked on CORONET geography. Whitehead (Fifth Air Force) reported in.[62] Congressional committee coming—Christ. Richardson pulling more of his administrative crap.[63] (We answered a question from Nimitz direct). Cook (BG) from air depot at Naha in. Nap.[64]

July 17

Hot again. All A.M. on papers. Bradley in to say goodbye. Worked on *Nihon* [Stilwell used the kanji characters for Japan.] G-2 stuff. Doolittle arrived at 5:30 with Smith.[65] Stayed for dinner. (Spaatz to have strategic Air Forces—Eighth and Twentieth.[66] Eighth is old Twentieth and Twentieth is old Twenty First.) Kenney will have Fifth, Seventh, and Thirteenth tactical.) Eighth will drop 120,000 tons a month—double the close on Germany. Two and three-fourths tons over the beach = 1 ton on Japan, instead of 5½ tons into England for 1 ton on Germany. Personnel—100,000 instead of 200,000. Daily requirements here, 10,000 tons. (1,000 B-29s.) Doolittle will be easy to work with.

MEMORANDUM FOR THE CHIEF OF STAFF, U.S. ARMY

The following notes are perhaps obvious and have probably already been considered. They may at least serve as a check list.

1. The terrain in Japan is rugged and lends itself to defense; unless we are prepared for the conditions we are likely to meet not only a determined defense in well dug-in positions in depth, but the fanatical opposition of the entire population, who will resort to any extremity to oppose us.

2. To ensure the heavy fire support needed in the early stages of a large landing in Japan, an increased proportion mobile weapons is indicated. Specifically, 4.2 mortars, pack 75's, recoil-less guns, rockets, and self-propelled artillery.

3. To lessen casualties in reducing pillboxes an increased proportion of tank-dozers and tank flame-throwers is indicated.

4. Immediate attention should be given to the matter of supplying body armor to infantry that has to work against dug-in positions.

5. Close-support aircraft should be used to the limit available and their operations carefully controlled. This field has not been developed as it should be.

6. Since we will command the air and the enemy will move and supply himself mostly at night, we should be prepared to harass him during the hours of darkness. Consideration should be given to a wide use of bomb-carrying liaison planes of this purpose.

7. The latest development in radar and television should be made available for test and use.

8. There is a fertile field for the employment of airborne troops. The Jap is sensitive to attacks on his rear and since we will control the air, the hazards of such attacks from the air will be considerably reduced. If any operations are contemplated in China, where there is a friendly population, where the Jap garrisons are scattered, and where distances are big, this type of operation should receive careful consideration. All airborne divisions should be retained. They are equally good as infantry divisions.

9. The straits of Tsushima should be covered with submarines and aircraft constantly, to cut off any further movement of troops from the mainland, and if subs cannot operate in the Sea of Japan, the shipping routes from Korean east-coast ports should be attacked from the air. The ports of Fusan and Shimonoseki should be wrecked as a high-priority mission.

10. In future operations, some feint or diversionary attack should be added to the main attack in order at least to make the Japs face in two directions.

11. Enough units should be provided to permit of periods of withdrawal for rest and reorganization.

12. Consideration should be given to the use of gas. We are not bound in any way not to use it, and the stigma of using it on the civilian population can be avoided by restricting it to attack on military targets.[67]

July 18

Efficiency reports. Nine [A.M.] to Kadena, Yomitan, and bolo. Back to Yellow 3. CP at 11:30. Sunbath. Twenty-three hundred. . . . Tank Bn. Commanders in on the Back Scratcher matter. Smart boy Dumas approved the scheme. No tank Commanders. Favored it. So I disapproved it.

The "Back Scratcher" was a collection of antipersonnel mines located on the side of tank turrets. The weapon's purpose was to kill or incapacitate Japanese soldiers attempting to dive under tanks with satchel charges strapped to their

bodies. Tank crews were supposed to detonate their Back Scratchers before a suicide bomber got underneath the vehicle. The devices proved ineffective.[68]

Englehart here from Hawaii.

Blakelock back from Guam.[69] Rumors—December 1 release 10 Army. October 1 release 7th and 27th. We can plan in the meantime.

July 19

Dubby day. Woods in, back from Guam and Oahu. Booze from Nimitz—Old Forrester. Wallace in—more Richardson administration. (Saw engineers home.) RCR, Jr. is a prick to put it plainly.[70]

Chennault case to be told to Congress by Patterson![71] "The brass hats are pushing him around."

Five Jap planes downed last night. Alerts every night, but little doing. Wind and rain. Rotten tonnage yesterday—22,000.

July 20

At 10:00 last night Schick brought the JCS separation message. By August 1 we are to be under Doug, who takes over all U.S. Army forces in the Ryukyus, and the defense of the area. Blakelock and Shaw go to Guam as Tenth Army representatives.[72] Ambiguous radio. The whole thing is snarled up. Today, dubbed around with papers. Rain again. Not a ton came ashore yesterday.

Briefed Dumas, Blakelock, Wallace for trip to Guam.

July 21

Old Mama Englehart shoved off. He thinks he's giving orders around here. "Staff officer from COMGENPOA." Hot stuff. Richardson probably told him to throw his weight about.

Kenney and Whitehead in on Army and Navy separation. They will play ball.

Trip to Awase, Kubosaki, Yonabaru, Naha, Naha air depot, Machinto and home for late lunch. Bergin and Dorn along. (Kenney had a copy of JCS radio that classified ours "Naval air installations" only, to Nimitz.)

July 22

Dumas reported. Complete separation of Army and Navy. Tenth Army *sits* till December 1—then turns over to base command. Mama Richardson folding up. No administrative control. No supply after December 1. (Maybe only 2 armies do CORONET. Maybe Tenth is *not* one of them.) Army and Navy separately reports and freight. Doolittle takes the Limmies. Kenney and he run the air. Everything else on me.

Did the west beaches—8:00–10:30. Usual jams of empty trucks. Morris on LST's, etc.[73]

July 23

Eight-thirty, shoved off for Kubosaki. Boat of "Taney" Adm. Cobb's ship, down near Yonabaru. Three picket boats waiting for my "party." Young again. Cobb talked and talked. Back at 11:30. Freight moving now.

P.M.: Borden in on new weapons.[74] Hillyer (Chaplains) going to Oahu. Movie at night.

July 24

Dubby A.M. Papers—1:30 to Yontan to meet the politics. Strike coming in. Air full of planes. The visitors arrived at 2:30. Sent them to Iscom and came back. Dumas back from Guam with agreements. Politicos came in at 5:30. Drinks at 6:30 and dinner. Loud-mouthed Maas (ex-congressman), Marine colonel.[75] A mess. Izac a good sort. Farrington, etc.[76] Not bad on the whole. They had a press conference. I went to bed.

July 25

Breakfast at 6:00 Politicos off at 6:30. Dubby day on papers. Wallace in about military government. GS conference at 4:00 on Army and Navy separation. Bum movie.

July 26

Still rainy. A.M.: office. Radio from Merrill. Arrive about 29th. P.M.: to Bolo, Ishikawa and down Number 1 through the mud to Chima. Then home through a cloud burst. Top down on the jeep. We were soaked. Cobb did not show up . . .

Legion of Merit star for Blake.[77]

July 27

Merrill and Higgins arrived.[78] Long talk on staff and etc. *GCM* has lost confidence in Wedemeyer.[79] Three hundred fifty WACs for CKS.[80] One hundred seventy-five already there. Strat's Headquarters total of 647 officers. One hundred forty-two in A-2 section. Total overhead in China now *6,000* [emphasis in original].

British participation in CORONET. One corps of one Canadian, 1 Australian, and 1 Indian division to be under my command. Good God. This was brought up in war ministry and they *recommended* it [emphasis in original]. They said they knew where they stood with me. Mountbatten has to give up units for this operation! Ain't life funny?[81]

Merrill looks well and agrees on Caucox,[82] Wells and Condon. Says no on Willey.[83]

Ft. Bayard to be opened. Five ships in August. Wedemeyer shot off about what escort rocket ships, etc. were needed. GCM told him to shut up. *Aid to CKS is for the emergency only*, with no strings beyond that. [Emphasis in original.]

Doug coming up.

July 28

Message from PJ about maximum air capabilities of island.[84] Good God, more air. Blakelock and Dumas left this A.M. Cheves in about freight arrangements. Doolittle and Griswold (chief of staff) in to call and have lunch.[85] Radio that Cannon is coming. Further notice on Condon, Wells, and Grindley. One bomb on Yontan last night. Japs have been crying wolf on us for 8 days straight, but they don't come.

July 29

Hot. Alert at 1 A.M. Nothing. A.M.: dubbed around. Visitors—Ordinance and A.A. (Marquat, Handwerk, Holmes, etc.[86]) P.M.: walk with Bergin. Back and forth about rearrangements for Iscom to Ascom. Teddy White here—giving out much dope.[87]

July 30

A.M.: in the office. Woods in—sent a case of coke over. 1:30—meeting of major commands. Quick acceptance of practically everything. Price is OK. Navy generally is OK. Ran it off in about 40 minutes. Army Air Force wants infantry to protect them. Told them NO. Hodge in—told him he would be defense commander.

Bergin and I walked. Got a good sweat up. Bum movie. YOUNG asked if he could go to China! Told him NO. [Emphasis in original.] He has been lousy lately. No good about his work. This confirms my suspicions.

July 31

White left.

Rousseau said, "If there were a people of fools, they would govern themselves as a democracy. So perfect a form of government is not suited for men."

"The best and most natural order is, that the wise should govern the multitude, provided that one is sure that they govern it for the profit of the multitude, and not for their own."[88]

A.M.: paper-shuffling. McNutt coming in. Bergin to field at 11:00. No word. Friendly coming in at Naha.[89] Then, no. Then Gen. McMullen coming.[90] Called Bergin back at 2130—very considerable business. Rain at 3:00. Sun-bath. Dubbed in office. (Thirty-eight thousand tons yesterday).

August 1

Rainy. With Merrill to Kuba to call on Hodge. Then to NOB and saw Price. (He suggested Korea, and we had just been talking about it). Price is simpatico. Jap attack did not come in last night. Leaving tanks on air-fields couple of days more.

P.M.: nap. More rain. Rotten movie. We averaged 30,675 tons a day for July.

August 2

Rain. Worked over Chosen [Korea] possibility. Paper work all A.M. Dubbed in P.M. Nap. *Zero tonnage* [emphasis in original]. Ships left on typhoon alert.

August 3

Dubby day. Went over 96th Division report. Papers. Dumas and Blakelock back. Much pressure. The BLACKLIST scheme is here. (Seoul). Manila is optimistic about it.

Henry and Edwards (War Department, G-1 and G-2) arrived in P.M.[91] They are working on the point system and releases. McNutt arrived at 5:45 with a dozen stooges.[92] Sent him off on a trip by Cub, with 5 of his entourage. Went over BLACKLIST with Merrill. Eighth Army in Taiwan. Sixth Army in center. Tenth Army in Korea. It will be OK if the Kuantung gang don't act up.

August 4

Clearing. Henry and Edwards off. Woods in, to say good-bye to Tenth Army. Sorry to lose him. Merrill and I at 8:30 shoved off for Motobu field. Met DelValle and rode through his muddy area. Started back at 11:30. Campaign hat blew out of plane; feel in water inside reef. Went back. Volunteer search. No luck. Pilot circled. No luck. Offered $25 or 5 bottles of Scotch reward. Came back and sent Young up to look. Cpl. Donahue had the hat. Young brought him down. He took the Scotch. The newsboys took pictures. Everything lovely now.[93] Woods in with Gen. Moore, FMF air chief.[94] Woods to come back to us.

Hodge and Struthers in to get word up on BLACKLIST.[95] Labell and Ritchie, smart boys from CJS (or JCS)—in for no reason whatever.[96] All air squirts. God, they knew *every*thing [emphasis in original]. (The Russians are dumb). (The Japs are dumb). (Japan is wiped out by air bombing). Etc., etc. Very tiresome pricks. Rain again.

August 5

Air raid twice in early A.M. Went over us. Plenty ack ack, but no hits. A.M.: office. Commo. Stone in from Guam.[97] SO for Nimitz. Wurtsmith of Thirteenth Air Force in.[98] Had Pulsifer in on JCC Cover plan for OLYMPIC in. Usual crap. Apparently, Tenth Army is cut out of any part in CORONET (First [Army] and Eighth [Army] to be used). Result of the Doug-Nimitz HATE [emphasis in original]. Nimitz has been trying to have Navy cut in on occupation forces, and wants Tenth Army, with III and XXIV Army Corps. This raises Doug's back, so, fearing it may come off, he plans with other units, leaving us to sit on our hands. Even in BLACKLIST, we get the hot spot to one side, instead of real participation. Maybe the Limmie pressure, plus the Navy will force Doug's hand. All I can do is wait it out.

The planning for the invasion of Japan was clearly in a state of flux. On August 15, Eichelberger wrote his wife: "Joe [Stilwell] has been entirely eliminated as anything but a supply man according to the rumors. Even the corps which may go to Korea will be under GHQ." John Ray Skates, in his study of the preparation for the invasion, notes that MacArthur's planning staff had removed Tenth Army from Coronet and assigned the XXIV Corps and III Marine Amphibious Corps to First Army. Skates further notes that MacArthur had reluctantly accepted British forces for use in the combat operations in Japan that would follow the landings.[99]

P.M.: Nap.

August 6

Air raid at 2:00. Knocked down two. They come in every night now. Yesterday afternoon, 50 Japs attacked Machimato air-field—rifles & grenades. Engineers got 10. Infantry company after the rest of them. (Possibly part of a "knife" project).

A.M.: new Judge Adjutant reported—Col. Haynes.[100] Looks like an improvement on Walsh. Gen. Starr (AAA) in from Manila. (Formerly AGF).[101]

To JIC and got bored stiff by Ely's drool. He's just terrible. Looked over ADC set up. Down Route 5 to new hotel on hill top. Plush lay out in Quonset "huts." Jap waitress. Steaks. Parker house rolls.

P.M.: Gard (96th Division arty) in to say good bye.[102] Walk. Movie. Usual breaks and jams on machine.

August 7

(As soon as Wheeler got control in IB he put in for Legion of Merit for his tramps—Kohloss, Holcombe, Lansing, and company.[103] Wheeler is a two-faced bastard).

Greer BG, BPR in.[104] Yount, air corps training command in.[105] Papers all A.M. Sun bath in P.M. Walk. Heavy rain in early A.M. Styer on way, reported lost.[106] Turned back to Philippine Islands. (Richardson's heavy campaign in Honolulu papers). Mail from Win, Joe, Nance,[107] Paul.

August 8

Indications of repetition of papilonia. That would be just too ducky. Papers all A.M. Schick left on leave. Styer and entourage of eight stooges blew in. They don't seem to know much more than we do. Rumor that Doug is coming. No message. No answer to my radio. Letters from Win and Joe.

A Jap in the CP last night. Much shooting. He got away, wounded. *Air raid*; I slept right through it, AA fire and all. [Emphasis in original.]

Boland got a bad leg at baseball yesterday.[108] The new *atomic bomb* hit Hiroshima and leveled 2½ square miles of it [emphasis in original]. (So they say). Plane 10 miles away got severe concussion. Special meeting of Diet supposed to have been called. Wishful thinking is rampant—(G-2 bust on *OLYMPIC* estimate. Six divisions to 10 divisions; top limit that can be supported. Ha-ha. Fourteen already).

Atomic bomb. "Leveled 7 plus square miles." Blinds within wide radius. Gives x-ray burns (the gamma ray), etc. Weight 9 tons (Kenney). Weight 9,000 tons (Daniels). "Causes cancer," (Daniels) etc. etc. Latrine dope everywhere.

Went to Yontan on hurry up call. Nobody came. At 6:45 came on back. Snafu performance. Nobody knew anything. Styer in at 8 P.M. with Wallace. Told him how our soviet works. He sat till 9:30. Missed the movie. Then went over BLACKLIST with stinking breath Dumas, till 11 P.M. Solution for landing by Dumas rather childish.

August 9

Russia entered the war at midnight [emphasis in original]. (In 1918 August 8 was the Black Day for the German Army, 27 years ago). At 9:30 Nagasaki gets one bomb. Hope it goes off. Much blah and sputter about the atomic bomb. Revolutionary, all right. Human civilization approaching suicide rapidly. I will now acknowledge that the Japs may quit. Russia, plus the bomb, should do the trick.

Papers all A.M. Sun bath in P.M. Adler (*New York Times*), Knight (*Chicago*

Daily News), Cowles (*Minneapolis Star*) in for a drink and dinner.[109] All sound on Russia, compulsory training, the *British Empah* and unified command.(!)

Good move. Second bomb was dropped on Nagasaki at 10:30. No further news of Russia.

August 10

(Looks like a recurrence of the papiloma Doc Gibson burned off in '41.[110] At the worst possible time.) Got Col. Martin over (consultant, medical service) and gave him the dope.[111] He can do it here, if they have the apparatus. Otherwise go the Mariannas. Will let me know.

Russians reported 14 miles inside Manchuria. No report on Nagasaki. Japs say they have a similar bomb, but were too humane to use it!

Four P.M.: Col. Martin in to say they did *not* have all the necessary junk here to handle contingencies and I'd have to got to *Saipan* to get it [emphasis in original]. He'll go ahead and arrange things. Bad news. (Permission to go. Loose talk, etc.)[112] Now of all times. I thought it over and wrote out a letter to Doug. Told Merrill and detailed Eyestone to go.[113]

Good Movie—During it report came in that Japan had surrendered. A lot of loose shooting went on, flares, etc. Like a National Guard outfit. Finally quieted down. Message delivered to me at 10:00 PM giving San Francisco intercept from Domei that Potsdam terms would be accepted, providing prerogatives of Emperor were not compromised. No other dope. *SO IT'S OVER.* I don't feel any particular elation. (Ben's case now OK and is that a relief.)[114] Now for BLACKLIST and Korea. I don't feel any particular elation. Maybe this is bunk. We go on as before, anyway, and if the report *is* bunk, won't have *any psychological setback.* [Emphasis in original.]

August 11

Rain in night. Nothing new on situation. Except 11th Airborne Division coming here to hop to Japan. Adler, Knight, and Cowles in, nosing around. I gave them "Why We Fight" to read, and they grabbed it. They decided to let UP, AP, INS take it, instead of restricting it to their papers. (They all offered me jobs writing! What a laugh.)

Merrill has gotten things well under control. He is good. Air is not sending any bombing missions out. Rumor (radio) peace terms in next 12 hours at Okinawa. (Mush).

Three hundred fifty hospital cases from crazy shooting last night. Dope from Dumas. B-day is day negotiations start in Tokyo(!) V-J day is day hostilities cease. Eleventh Airborne Division jumps off on V-J day.

Arnold and Ty in. All sorts of stuff—booze, food, clothing, books, etc., etc. Letters from Win and Ben. Shoes, accordion, jello, etc., etc. Bing hank.

August 12

Dubby day. Papers. Hodge and Griner in. K. B. Wolfe,[115] Burtandsian (?)[116] and Timberlake for lunch.[117] HOT. Sunbath. Read. (Just dead beat.) Eleventh Airborne Division arriving. No new developments. "Bomb at Nagasaki made the first one obsolete"(!!)

August 13

At 6:00, radio from GHQ. Tenth Army out of BLACKLIST; we give XXIV Army Corps assistance, and they do the job! Tenth Army sits on its ass in Okinawa. I wonder. Is it because we don't belong to the club? Can Doug possibly be unwilling to have me around? Have Krueger, Eichelberger, Hodge, Sutherland done it?[118] What's the use of wasting 15 or 20 years getting ready, if when the time comes, the job is police officer in a back area? I shove off for Manila at 10:00 to try and find out. Maybe they will break up Tenth Army entirely. I may be nearer to Carmel than I think. Taking Col. Martin along to arrange for bladder clipping. May get it done in Manila.

Off at 10:40 with Martin and Carl. Good trip in new B-17. Arr. Manila at 3:30. To administrative apartments, and down to GHQ. Saw Wheeler and Gunner. Doug in at 4:45 and I saw him for half an hour. He had an eyes alone. (*Peanut radioed that he had heard a rumor that Gen. S. would be in command of U.S. troops landed in China coast.*[119] *Truman* answered that Gen. S. would *not* land on China coast).[120] [Emphasis in original.] So they cut my throat once more. Why did they let me come out here if they were not going to back me up? Doug says: It would delay BLACKLIST 4 days to shift me to Japan. So he had to order XXIV Corps to Korea. If things don't break all at once, he will put Tenth Army in Japan. If it breaks *now*, I'm *sunk* [emphasis in original]. He advises do nothing for few days. Wire to Washington to ask if Korea is included in "China coast" would undoubtedly be answered "Yes." So I told him about the bladder and said I would hang around and see what develops. He said the *only* time he and Washington ever agreed was about my appointment [emphasis in original]. His list was

1. JWS
2. Patch
3. Truscott,[121]

and Washington said OK on me. (He had already sent me my orders.) So, here's the end of the line, and I am thrown to the lions again. Rumor: press notice I accepted the "Blue Sky White Sun" from CKS. Told Carl to deny it.[122]

Martin went out to 80th General to make arrangements at 5:30. Back at

7:30. We had dinner top-side. (Chamberlin, Gunner, Russell, Willoughby, etc. etc.[123] All the brass of GHQ there). Out to the Hospital. Saw Col. Holman and Maj. LaDue (San Diego) and went to be in room with L. W. Maddox.[124]

August 15

Apparently the war is over. The Japs accept. Glad to hear that bombing missions went out today.[125]

⋆ ⋆ ⋆

August 16

⋆ ⋆ ⋆

Japs due in here tomorrow A.M. to report to Doug.

Carl and Martin in. I chased them out to go riding. Diller got out my denial of receiving *any* foreign decorations.[126]

⋆ ⋆ ⋆

August 17

⋆ ⋆ ⋆

Nap. Ridgway here.[127] Blamey, a big fat tub.[128] The Russians get Korea north of 38° (north of Seoul). The Japs are being a bit nasty in correspondence. Chamberlin says we may have to jump on them again. I don't believe it. Notification will take minimum of 48 hours to max of 12 days. Birthday was the 15th. Schedules for Sixth and Eighth Army backed up 10–15 days.

August 18

Win's birthday. Boat trip on Sixth Army launch all day. Down the bay to Corregidor, around the island, over to Ft. Drum and Carabao Island and back to the Pasig. Nice quiet day. Lunch on board. Cut out supper and went to bed.

⋆ ⋆ ⋆

August 19

Teddy White in. China a mess. Danger of U.S. getting embroiled. Reds linking up with Russians. . . . New Sixth Army to be flown to Peking, Tien Tsin, Tsing Tao and Shanghai. Reds blocking off RR out Kalgan and Sheih Chia Chiang. We ought to get out—*now* [emphasis in original].

Saw Doug at 11:00. Good talk. Brought up the plebe revolt in '99. He gave me the full story. First Army being sent back to the states. XXIV Corps to Korea—a 4 way command there. Hodge directly under Doug. Tenth Army just a staff. Sit tight on Okinawa. Later a spot will be made for them in Japan. Doug will keep all the dealings in the open with the newsboys. He agrees we should close out in China. He will tell CKS to make all arrangements for Jap surrender in China.[129] (Civil war.)

I am to go to Tokyo for the surrender on the 28th. Arrive there not later than day before. No further orders about this. [Emphasis in original.]

Off at 1:20. Good trip. In at 6:20. Merrill at feed. Chow at new house. Orchestra played. We're nicely fixed now. ***Mail.*** Win having the usual trouble with Al. [Double emphasis in original].

August 20

Rain. 10:30: With Merrill to look over camps of GHQ and Eighth Army, and then down to 11th Airborne. Saw Swing.[130] He is in a jam about plans. FEAF trying to grab the headlines. Back for lunch. Office on papers. Read and bummed. Fine dinner. Good movie.

August 21

Dubby day. Alexander for breakfast. He and Ryan called later. Bradley and Meyers at 2:00. (96th Division and 40th Division). Sun-bath. Read. Capts. Faust and Miller and WO Hughes for dinner.[131] Talbot got pork loin.[132]

August 22

Rain AM office. Nap. 4–6 office again. Movie. Claudia and the Stilwell Road. No new developments. Surrender set for the 31st.

August 23

All A.M. on papers. Nap 3:30. Letter. Then down to Seventh Air Force to call on White. He is fixing up a native house. Then up to Eighth Air Force to call on Doolittle.

★ ★ ★

August 24

Typhoon predicted for this P.M. Papers all A.M. Read and napped and office in P.M. Richardson, Hutchinson, and Davenport for dinner.[133] Pinned Legion of Merit on Woods. Kidded him about "a document bearing on conduct of the Marine Corps." Good egg. Typhoon did not materialize. Opper in.[134] Newsboy from China.

August 25

Yesterday Adm. Andrews in with Price.[135] Andrews is now red and director for Pacific. He puts a Mr. Gibson here under me.[136] Very cooperative. Opper confirms situation hopeless. Hurley impossible.

A.M.: to 27th Division. Saw Griner, who is all set and satisfied. Went over to Chimu Wan and looked over the beaches. Military Government had grabbed part of EM beach. Chief of staff told to kick their teeth in. POW cage. Our pampered pets have everything.

Back at noon. Eichelberger, Byers, and Barrows in.[137] Eichelberger knows about CKS' action.[138]

P.M.: nap. Dorn came around at 6:00 for dinner. Swing could not make it. Dorn fishing for information but did not get it. He makes me a bit tired.

British Empah is in "a serious condition financially" because L-L is cut off! Ain't that just too bad?—and Churchill says we shouldn't tell those Russian bastards about the atomic bomb!

August 26

Further two day delay on occupation, because of typhoon in Tokyo area. The whole move has been bitched up.

A.M.: office. Sunbath instead of lunch. Read in P.M. Office again. Eichelberger, Byers, Barrows for dinner. Orchestra Japs say they have "only enough trucks for themselves"!!

August 27

Doc Ayers from Cheng Chow in.[139] Doolittle in with Adm. Durgin, CVE commander.[140] Orders to take surrender in Ryukyus. (Contrary to orders from Nimitz to take the island). Grindley begged off. O.K. Tansey and Duff in.[141] Move to Japan starts tonight. Mail from Win. Dedicated Soldiers Bowl with a bottle of Scotch. Won by a burly named Marker. (A Lieutenant came up and I declared him ineligible, amid loud cheers).[142] Kay Kyser and his crowd in for coffee and salad.[143] Stayed till midnight. Attractive girls, all kids. Well behaved. Carl put his big foot in it by passing my photos around, including the caricature. I could have killed him.

August 28

Bawled Carl out. Paper work all A.M. Bishop Kennedy in.[144] Seems like a good egg. Doolittle in. Dubbed. Nap. Rain. Office. We *do* take the Ryukyu surrender [emphasis in original]. Sent out notices for Japs to radio us.

Eleventh Airborne Division begin to arrive at Atsugi. Dinner with Eichelberger. A horse's ass named Sverdrup ruined it with his big mouth and conceit. Reserve Major General.[145]

August 29

A.M.: office. Art Steele, Stewart, and White in.[146] No chance to talk. Spaatz appeared with Giles and Doolittle.

P.M.: read and wrote. Sunbath. Doug came in at 3:30 and talked a bit and he shoved [off]. Told him I wanted to take Merrill to Tokyo. OK. Then Richardson appeared. We talked till chow time. After supper, Richardson went to see Eichelberger and his crowd. The Japs are very respectful in their answers to me. Amami and Niyako both checked in. The guy on Amami is rounding up the Navy units there.

The party in Tokyo is not organized and promises to be a riot.

August 30

A.M.: office. Richardson to 27th Division and XXIV Corps. (Hodge and Griner are teacher's pets).

The labor press came in and we had a good talk. There were OK. Sent them on their way happy. Had a sunbath. Griner here calling on Richardson. Five-thirty [P.M.] the appropriations sub-committee for the War Department of the House of Representatives came in—Snyder, Engel, Talbot, Case, Hendricks, Norrell, etc., etc.[147] Gave them a drink and made them a speech. They are *all right*—want to hold what we've taken and stand on our hind legs. [Emphasis in original]. Want me to put in put in permanent construction here. Don't realize my limitations. More crap from RCR about his great command and how the Navy snubbed him, etc., etc.[148] Very, very tiresome.

In contact *with all Jap commanders now* [emphasis in original].

August 31

Reported to Col. Martin on bladder. Papers. Off at 10:15 to Kadena. Left field at 10:50—over water all the way; let in over Oshima, then Numazu, Kamakura, Enoshima to Sagami . . . and up to Atsugi. [Security considerations required this zigzag course when flying into the Tokyo area.] Raining. No distinct views. Usual conditions at the field. Jap driver in ramshackle sedan to Yokohama. Bad road. Dilapidated buildings. Well-fed people. Soldiers saluting. Yokohama pleasant sight. Shanty town in the ruins. Damage mostly by fire. Town dead. Few people. Electric line running. People had left town for fear of raping and what not. Billet at New Grand Hotel on water front. Harbor empty. Contrast. Navy units off Enoshima and Yokohama. RCR at dinner, spouting as usual. The Great I Am. Farrell here;[149] talked about atomic bomb at dinner; that is when not interrupted by RCR, Jr. He went from table to table, being gracious and dispensing information.

September 1

Rain. Wind. Dirty weather. Up at 6:00. Breakfast with Farrell. Dorn came in. "I was in the first plane." "I was the first in Yokohama," etc., etc. He is running the motor pool! Kidded him about working up a HQ Commandant.[150] Wainwright here.[151] Dutch, French, Australians, Limmies (Percival). A mob.

We snubbed the Jap "president of the hotel." Chow is fish cakes, heavy bread, potatoes, grapes, and coffee. Beef last night.

Passed convoy yesterday. It will beat the air move from Oki. Doug here. White, Stewart,[152] Adler, etc. GHQ gang. Eighth Army had to move out. They had marked everything "reserved."

Farrell loaned me Smyth's report on the atomic bomb.[153]

★ ★ ★

Eight-thirty: weather very dirty. Farrell says the atomic scientists are a bunch of temperamental bugs. Screw each other's wives. Squabble. Rush off on tangents. Have to be herded and pushed around to keep their noses on the job. Only war could get them together. He says they are capable of solving *any* problem whatsoever [emphasis in original]. Oppenheimer the keenest brain.[154] Many Jews among them. The Limmie Anderson violated the agreement, and gave Joliott's associates unauthorized information.[155] Joliott wild because French not included. Threatened to tell the Russians. U.S. is stockpiling materials and will strip the Belgian Congo of raw stuff as quickly as possible. We control secrets of manufacture. Bomb arrived by 4 barometric devices and detonated by proximity fuses. Force of explosion is measured by blast instruments on parachutes dropped by accompanying planes. Light of explosions = 1000 suns.

In New Mexico, 5,000 tons of sand blown up and made radioactive—the super-bomb for which this one would act as detonator would produce force of 100,000 tons of TNT. The scientists were ordered to stop work on it. (It might burn up the world's atmosphere.) Sixteen thousand tons of TNT at Hiroshima. Thirty thousand tons at Nagasaki. News spread over Japan in 24 hours. Appalled. (At upper end of atomic scale, energy by splitting. At lower end—investigation fast beginning—energy by combining elements.) Target from making 235. One kilo a day by January 1. Fifteen bombs a month by June, '46. (Heat of summer is given by oxygen changing to helium. Bottom of atomic scale.) First pile experiment at Chicago. December 1942. First chain reaction. First explosion in New Mexico—July 6, 1945. Cook, asleep, blinded at 5 miles. Radioactive particles carried 300 miles.

★ ★ ★

At 1:15, rode through town, up the bluff to race-course and CP, Eleventh Airborne. Back and all through town to Kawasaki. The place is *ruined* [emphasis in original]. Completely gutted. Soul-satisfying sight. Only the stone, brick and concrete buildings remain standing. Safes standing where the stores burned down around them. Shanties dot the rusty landscape. Almost impossible to locate anything. Main routes remain, but business is 100% dead. Naturally the place looked dead when we came in. It is whatakick to stare at the arrogant, ugly brown-faced, buck-toothed, bowlegged bastards, and realize where this puts them. Many newly demobilized solders around. Most police salute. People generally apathetic. We gloated over the destruction and came in at 3:00 feeling fine. Rain continues.

Saw Beebe and Wainwright.[156] Latter was slapped by a private and had to heard goats. Some prisoners beaten on buttocks with a baseball bat.

Muddle by GHQ. Dope issued at 9:00 P.M. Four Air Corps officers out of Bocolod in Jap whore-house. Stole the girls' fancy kimonos. A soldier stole a watch from a Jap on the street. Bertandias seized Sutherland's car. Hell to pay over that. Swing in; plenty of worries. Can't disarm Jap soldiers. The U.S. Army is making a spectacle of itself.

September 2

Further change of plans by GHQ in middle of night. Breakfast at 5:45. Carl got coffee and we ate K-rations. . . . Car with Curley the tough guy as driver. Went to pier and bummed from 6:15 to 7:30. Eleventh Airborne Division band. About 7:00 the Japs came and got on a destroyer. Shigemitsu, Umezu and others.[157] Six thug Japs. MPs also there. Hard, cruel, hateful mugs under excruciating humiliation as we stared at them. Lots of fun. Off at 7:30 on the *Nicholas*. Down to Yokosuka and went along side the *Missouri*. With us were, Spaatz, Kenney, Krueger, Eichelburger, Richarson, Blamey, LeClerc,[158] Helfrich,[159] van Oyen,[160] the Russians, Australians, Canadians, etc. I took a crap and then went on deck. *Missouri* is 45,000 tons on paper, and 60,000 in the water. We went aboard at 8:00 and I led the way to the quarter deck. (Ranking U.S. Army officer.) Perry's U.S. flag had been flown out from Annapolis and was hung on the ship's side. They put us in our places and we waited. Doug and party came aboard at 8:40 and went to Admiral's cabin. At 8:50 the Japs came and formed up. Everybody just stood and stared at them. Terrible experience for those bastards. The downfall of Japan in complete disaster, and they had to stand and take it. Shigemitsu and Umezu in front. Then an officer, a civilian, and an officer and a civilian and American officer. In the third row, 4 officers. They stood stiffly and suffered. How we loved it.[161] Then Doug came back, and at 9:00 made his speech—his hands and legs trembling markedly. Krueger says it is not nervousness, but palsy, but it looked like hell. His voice was firm. The Japs came up and signed. Shigemitsu had a cane and had trouble with a stiff leg. After him Umezu. Doug then signed for the allies calling Wainwright and Percival out to stand behind him.[162] He used about 5 pens and gave one each to Skinny and Percival. Then Nimitz for the U.S. Hsü Yung-Ch'ang for China. Fraser for Great Britain. Derevyanko for Russia. Blamey for Australia. Cosgrove for Canada. LeClerc for France. Helfrich for Holland and Isitt for New Zealand.[163] Cosgrove for Canada, like Merkle for New York, failed to touch 2nd base.[164] He signed in the wrong place . . . Good God. Sutherland's fault, of course, for not watching out. It was terrible. Then Doug announced that the session was over, and the Japs beat it. I had avoided the Chinese, but now went over and spoke to them—Hsü Yung and Chu.[165] They were much relieved and very friendly. Had coffee in the ward room with the kids and signed short-snorters. Got aboard the *Nicholas* and reached the pier at 11:10. Went straight out to Atsugi and found typhoon reported at Okinawa. Had lunch on plane. Got a jeep, and drove down to Fujisawa and on to Kamakura. Saw the daibutsu and drove back to Fujisawa and on to Enoshima. Walked to the island and climbed to top. Then back and along coast to Oiso, which was completely burned out. Finally found road to Atsugi, after asking dumb cop if he spoke Japanese. Back to Atsugi about 5:30. Still grounded. The crew have been "collecting" souvenirs and Jap rations. Canned mikan, etc. (Jap MPs are looting and running out truck loads of rations, furniture, etc.)

Whatley, GHQ HQ commandant arrived last night![166] Hodge was present and ***dumb*** as ever [double emphasis in original]. Air corps gang in the next room had a pow-wow on how the Air Corps won the war. Principal speech by Kenney. He needs killing.

Percival is the weakest sister I have ever seen, even in the British Army. God, help terrible. A furtive, weak-chined ferret looking sort of nut. Long, skinny and stop shouldered. Q: Why did Doug have *him* step up while Doug was signing? [Emphasis in original]. The allied signers were a scratchy looking crowd. Nimitz OK. Hsü OK. Fraser a fat red dumpling. Blamey a tub of guts. Cosgrove an elderly masher or gigolo type. LeClerc rather trim, but his helpers a pair of dirty looking Apaches. Helfrich amateur looking. What a crew of caricatures in the eyes of the Japs. The human race as poorly represented. And the God damn Canadian signed in the wrong place! O, Christ. Met Halsey. Saw Nimitz as I left. Talked with the sobs on the *Nicholas.* Good kids.

Doug, when photogs wanted a repeat on a picture with Spaatz. "You just took one."

"But they would like to have one more with you shaking hands."

"I told you I have already shaked hands with him." Period. No love lost on Spaatz. Giles' 600 B-29s fizzled dismally. Navy planes went over in grand style. B-29s in scattered groups of 6–8–10, all over the lot. Total of not more than 50. Blooey.

Slept on the plane.

★ ★ ★

General dilapidation in Japan. Business zero. Nothing in the stores. Teahouses and restaurants dead. No one in the streets. Buildings, rolling stock, roads, all in very bad repair. Good crops, but that's all. The country is ruined. Thank God. People docile. They want to be friendly. That's the great danger.

September 3

Up at 5:15 and had coffee and nut-cake. Off at 6:00. Fuji stuck up through cloud layer, with a cloud wrapped around its top. At Hamamatsu took off over the sea. About 10:15 over Amami. Okinawa at 11:15. Heavy cross-wind. Cut motors at 11:30 (5 1/2 hours). Jeeps came in 5 minutes. Junk lot of mail. (*This Week* offers $500 for an editorial.) Caught up on papers.

September 4

Schick back in to say good-bye. Ditto Hodge. Col. Wiley (Benning '30–'33) called.[167] Bishop Spellman in for lunch.[168] Typical Boston Irishman. Hot against the *British Empah*. We had a good talk. Sunbath. Wrote an editorial for *This Week*. Reported to Win about Tokyo trip. Japs in from Miyako and Amami. Ten of them. At 7:30 brought them in and lined them up. Ely handed the requirements. Then Merrill told them they could ask questions at 10:00 tomorrow. All very gruff and firm. Gen. Honai wrote to me asking help to prevent Ryukyus from becoming another Alsace-Lorraine.[169] Army docile. Navy truculent. (The old Satsuma stuff.)[170]

September 5

Got the article off to *This Week*.[171] A. Smedley's actor friend in (Manson).[172] Wrote letters. One P.M. to Futema to see the "Yank" planet. Read and dubbed around. Paul and Grindley in.[173]

★ ★ ★

September 6

Condon in late P.M. Japs arrived for surrender. A.M.: papers. Out to *New Jersey* (40,000 tons) to call on Spruance. She was way out. Had a good talk with him; he's a good egg. Looked in at a 16" gun turret, and the crew worked the loading gear. (Twenty seconds to load.) Twenty-seven hundred pound projectile—650 lbs of powder. (*New Jersey, Iowa, Wisconsin,* and *Missouri*. Ahead of them, three more. Ahead of them *North Carolina* and *Washington*.) Back at noon. Nap. Three P.M. Newspaper men—three of them, including Dealey from Dallas.[174] Good eggs. Had a good talk. Five-thirty to dinner with Woods and his staff. Big filet steaks. Ice cream. Crab cocktails. My God. Good letter from Al.

★ ★ ★

September 7

Surrender day in the Ryukyus. Checked up on arrangements. Guards and band in at 11:00. Band played till 11:20. Japs came at 11:20 and stood at attention. At 11:30 I went out to the table. Ruffles and general's march. Sgt.

Oda, Nisei, beside me.[175] "Direct the Jap representative to sign the article of surrender." They did so. Then I signed. "Tell the Jap representatives that I hold them personally responsible for carrying out all instructions." Then, "Have the Jap representatives withdraw." No action; dumb Ely's crowd just stood, with their mouths open. So I yelled "Take 'em out," and go[t] same action. Then I announced the end of the ceremony, and we all adjourned for lunch.

Sixty B-29s and 100 fighters went over M-26s and 155 SP massed on road. Honor guards—Army and Marines. About 40 guests. Big press and photo coverage. Fliers on way to U.S. at 3:30. Guests beat it at 1:00 P.M. O. P. Smith's brother here—he *is* a prick [emphasis in original]. Everybody said it went off well. We threw the hooks into them. Just cold, hard, business.

Two P.M. to U.S. prisoners' camp on Number 1. Twenty-three hundred there. Looked it over and talked to some of them. CAC running it. Back to Number 24 to see set-up for women and children. No one in it. Then to 233rd General Hospital and looked it over. Talked to Executive and neuro psych man. Back at 4:45. Cannon, Condon, Grindley, Jones for dinner. Movie. Bogart and his tart Bacall.[176] She can't act.

September 8

★ ★ ★

Eleven [A.M.] Spruance called, and we had a long talk. I like him; he's a high class guy. Arranged for junior officers to visit the new BBs. Fine day. Sun bath. For dinner. Col. Bethune, Capt. Anderson, Capt. Brenner.[177] Talbot leaving in A.M. Isaacs in.[178] Long talk. On his way to Korea. He is pessimistic; situation in Far East just where it was before. No step forward for native populations. We have survived attack. . . . Russia got all she wanted *for now* [emphasis in original]. Big fact of the future is an expanding Russia. Outlook is "Peace by Expedient" or a series of them. OK. It's still compromise—the Doctrine of the Mean. It may get us by.

September 9

(Hurley considers himself the *counsel for the defense*, and he'll do everything possible for this client! That's the American Ambastardor.) (One word for Hurley—INDIGESTIBLE—spew him out.) [Emphasis in original.]

At the surrender the GIs were yelling, "That's right, Joe—make 'em wait! Keep 'em waitin! Joe!" They would have been pleased to stand there for hours.

A.M.: Papers. Sunbath, under clouds. Spruance in about evacuation of our POWs. Date for lunch Tuesday. Tenth Army—Fifth Air Force (6 to 3) baseball. Excellent game. (The GIs are the Real Guys.)

Six [A.M.]—Eighth A.F. cocktail party by Doolittle. Usual standing around, followed by buffet. Home at 8:15. Doolittle leaving Tuesday for Washington.

September 10

A.M.: office. Talked to Paul about this and that. P.M.: wrote and slept. Davidson (Tenth Air Force) for dinner.[179] Going home to retire. Ulcers in stomach. Nold joined the mess. Saw the "This is the Army" show. Excellent. One hundred sixty in the cast. Had ten of them come up for a drink and bite to eat. Very interesting group of lads, interested in politics and anxious to get going straight. * * * Sgt. Manson corresponds with Agnes Smedly and had some of her letters. Got one from her, telling about J. B. Powell's lies.[180]

Doug has gone crazy [emphasis in original]. Jap officers keep their swords! They have only to say they are personal property, and not issue stuff: Thus he sets up military shrines all over Japan. It gives the game to the Japs. Letter from Win about Ben; he is pretty low over it, but he'll come out of it.

September 11

To bed at 1:00 AM Good thing I had a nap.

A.M.: papers. Weather too bad to make the trip to the *New Jersey* at 10:15. Price phoned it was OK. Fraser there. Took a look around ship with Wooldridge the Capt.,[181] and Spruance. Lunch with Spruance and staff. (He as total of 45 officers.) Fraser here on *Duke of York*.[182] Back to Tenth at 2145. Nap. Read. "Leaflet" tank (searching it) demonstration at 7:30. Young horsing around for special treatment. I am fed up on him. Arnold wants to go home, too.

September 12

A.M.: office. Read. . . . *Doug revokes* orders about swords [emphasis in original]. What happened?

One forty: down to Yonabaru and around Chinen Peninsula to Shichiya, military government village. To see about fishing for the Okinawans. Heavy rain; tail of a typhoon. Back via number 9 and 48 to 44 and up number 5. Ambulance off the road. Back at 6:00. No mail; no business.

September 13

A.M.: papers. Sun bath. P.M.: ball game—XXIV Army Corps and coon team. EYESTONE, McMillan and Hall for dinner. 7:30: Dick Jurgen's show.[183]

THE AXE [emphasis in original]. "Return of Tenth Army to the U.S. 15 October." So Doug's promise means nothing. We just don't belong to the club. Well, the war is over, so what the hell.

September 14

A.M.: papers. Got Nold and looked over ammo storage dumps with Rosenberg.[184] Then to new ammo dock and back (11:30). Sun bath. Read. Five-fifteen to TAF dinner with Woods. Fights afterwards. Mostly niggers.[185] Not so good. Holiday. Rosenberg for lunch.

September 15

A.M.: papers. Read and wrote. Hubbard and Arnold for lunch. Sun bath. Read. Depot, Schubert and Abbink for dinner.[186] To Gracie Fields' show.[187] Had her and husband, Monty Banks, over after the show for a drink and nibble.[188] They stayed till 10:30. Kendrick (Medical), Jefferds (Ordinance), and Stienette (Chaplain) in to meet them.[189]

September 16

Typhoon coming in. Sixty m.p.h. wind forecast. Getting strong at noon. Higgins and Young for lunch. Young says Arnold is low about life.[190] Now I've got to cheer *him* up [emphasis in original]. Heavy rain and wind all P.M. Put the shutters up in the house. Two or three leaks. Movie. By 10:30 wind coming in from west. 180° turn—typhoon passing over.

September 17

By midnight it was heavy and we had a stiff wind all night. All flimsy stuff going down—tents down unless anchored. God-damn swinging base board banged all night long like a pistol. Still blowing at 7:00. Cleaned up room. Dubbed in office. For lunch, Ty and Prof. talked to Carl and got him straightened out. Talked to Paul. Nap. Wind gone by 3 P.M. A lot of damage to docks: little on shore.

September 18

Papers as usual. Krueger and Decker called at 2:45–4:30.[191] Nothing new. Invited to Kyoto. Krueger is looking over the Miyako Hotel.

Fracas at Tokumo. One of our crazy flatheads machine gunned Japs and trucks near the air-field. Not details yet. Garfield's party up there. Jesus, what jackasses. No mercy if we can just get the dope.

Edwards and Ely for dinner. Cannon did not get back in time. Cornell (7th Division) and Berry—RAMPS here.[192] Sent Hubbard to bring them up. Had long talk with them. Same old story about the Limmies. One Limmie had 15 pairs of shoes and wanted $150.00 gold for 2 pairs. Our people detest them for their hoggish, inconsiderate ways. They also hate the God-damn Jap. Cornell picked up in Leyte. Was not at Bataan.

September 19

Sgt. Friendly (*CBI Roundup*) for interview.

During the interview, Stilwell spoke about the importance of Japanese-American veterans, the Nisei: "We can't allow a single injustice to be done these Nisei without defeating the very purposes for which we fought this whole war. We may have to give these Nisei veterans something special to wear in their lapel, but we must never let them down. These Nisei have bought an awful big chunk of America with their own blood. I know that Gen. Mark Clark is very proud of what his Nisei regiment did in Italy, and Gen. Frank Merrill is a constant rooter for those who fought with his Marauders in Northern Burma." Friendly noted that Stilwell banged his desk for emphasis. Stilwell also offered a working definition of the G.I., which is included at the end of this entry.[193]

Hoods in, on decoration for Col. Auton.[194]

P.M.: looked over Navy installations on Katchin Hanto.

Garfield back from Tokumo. (Let the Japs *entertain* him.) He's *out*. [Emphasis in original.] Dumas, Daniels and Westervelt for dinner.

RUMOR. Richardson to take over when MacArthur goes to U.S. for hero worship. My God.

Definition of a G.I.

A G.I. (pronounced "gee-eye") is a special breed of American who inhabited North Africa, Italy, France, Germany, Guadalcanal, Saipan, Okinawa, Luzon, Burma, China, Iceland, India, Korea, Japan, and other places during the war years 1941 through 1945.

Very few of them were to be found within the continental limits of the United States during that time. The term G.I. is usually applied to enlisted men and has a negative effect when applied to officers. The G.I. was superbly equipped, but happiest when in dirty fatigues with a baseball cap.

He cooked meals in his helmet, in which he also shaved and washed. He swore in good style, liked pretty girls, milk, steak, beer, cheesecake, swing music, and was a sucker for a place called the U.S.A.

He hated Japs, Germans, C-rations, draft dodgers, and a thing called 'chicken' (not to be confused with the fowl of the same name).

Race—all races. Just go visit the cemeteries for proof. Names—Murphy, Jones, Galliopolis, Cohen, Dambrowski, Smith—the works. Ways to recognize the G.I.—No matter where you find him he gripes when things are going well; he keeps his mouth shut when the going is tough.

Accomplishments of the G.I.—he beat the hell out of the Japs and Germans.[195]

September 20

Usual morning paper fight. Adm. Barbey in—well informed guy.[196] Sun bath. One-thirty to Yonabaru and Naha with Carl. Dusty on 44. Many wrecks in Baten Ko. Back at 4:30.

Sgt. Manson in to say good-bye and plug me for the AVC. Radio from Nichols (*This Week*) about the message to the G.I.s. He wants more![197] Letters from Win. *BEN* is in the *NAVY*! [Emphasis in original.] He has been broadcasting already. Casey, Beald OK. He likes it. Cannon, Blakelock, Buchanan for dinner.

Sparks up to get photos. Nimitz sent a good picture of the surrender.

September 21

Papers as usual. Visit to 161st Ordinance M.M. plant. Group photo. Woods put on air show for the RAMPS. A good one. Scared the doctors in the 75th Station Hospital.[198] Sunbath. Read and dubbed. Fifteen in for buffet and drinks. Good crowd. They ate up everything. Movie afterward—*Laura*—not bad.[199]

September 22

Papers in A.M. Hair-cut. The "Burma Survivors" had photo taken—Merrill, Jones, Grindley, Bergin, Young, Arnold, JWS. Took Bergin for a walk. Cut lunch. One-fifteen off for Yontan and flew to Tokumo. Watched the landing. Four Lorrals. About 80 planes demonstrated. Our "fleet" was 1 CL, 1 DD, 2 LSTs, and 1 LCT. Very imposing. Circled beach several times and came home. Beautiful colors up there; water and racks. Back at CP at 4:00. Read. Turned in early.

September 23

A.M.: papers. Eleven: walk with Bergin. Air corps birds took over picture on Number 20. Passed us 4 times before they dared to stop. Board on Tokuno shooting bawled out by Smith, Fifth Air Force, who says it's none of my business. His board whitewashed the culprit—a Maj. Vogel. Merrill got it straight with him. He accepts my jurisdiction and apparently will cooperate. Fifth Air Force lost out on wrecking their building. Alson on sending their men home.[200] Navy got their backs up. Call from Adm. Badger and Big Boy Shafroth.[201] On their way home.

Definite orders to pick a list to take with me and break it up on Oct. 15.

Going to Tokyo Wednesday to say good-bye. Joe should be here any time now and go along.

September 24

Eight-thirty to Yontan. Off at 9:00. Miyako at 10:15. Circled till 11:45. Small island, but well dug in. Our "fleet" lying off—mines are thick there. Jeeps ashore. Back at 12:15. Circled till 2:00. Very bad weather. Heavy rains. Late lunch, shuffled papers. Dinner for Price, Larsen,[202] Jones, Woods. Very jolly crowd. Congenial. All enjoyed it.

Three thousand ships here now—biggest shipping concentration in history. Woods gave me clipping with photo of Ben as a sob.[203]

September 25

Rain. Piddled in the office. Tom Wells turned up. Discussed his case. Had him for lunch. Sent him out with Hubbard. Rockey in to call. He goes to Teing Tal and Tientsin with two division. Orders to help CKS disarm Japs and take weapons. Christ again.[204]

Nap. At 5:45 went to Machinato to wedding of Capt. Siegel and St. Boody.[205] Jewish ceremony. Very short and common sense. In the chapel built by GIs. Crowd of quiet GIs watched the show. Back at 7:20. Tom Wells in. Daniels came to say good-bye. Paul, Carl, and Grindley came, and we all talked till 10:00. Good-bye to the last of the old crowd.

Boland turned in my extra junk. All set to take off for Tokyo tomorrow. Joe went to Manila. Tom saw him in Guam and got letters from Ben, Al and Win. We are shipping Tom back to Honolulu. Seventh Division delegation in last night with letter from Arnold about air transport. No can do.

September 26

Up early. Tom for breakfast. Said good-bye. Did the papers. Wrote Ben a note. Got photos of the guard.[206] Passed off at 8:30. In the air at 9:15. Chofu at 2:30. Circled Tokyo and had a good look at a good job. Patchy, but big patches.

Fine weather coming in past Shizuoka and Numazu, Odawara, Lake Hakone, Oiso, etc. Beautiful country. Too bad the people are bastards. Met by Maj. Anderston—in to Imperial Hotel past palace grounds.[207] (Guarded by U.S. soldiers!!) Anderston says electric power plants are untouched. RRs not hurt, except rolling stock. Seventy-five percent of Tokyo population is gone. Casualties not known. Doug operates from 5 P.M. to 8 or 9:00. (Hard day).

At 5:00 saw Doug (Daichi Ginko Building). OK on Merrill and Bergin. Okinawa for Kyoto and Seoul. Radio GCM for Peking.[208] (Fellers got the message off).[209]

Ryukyu surrender. Press notices. Navy insistence that it was Nimitz's job. Directive to Doug. He objected and said it was an independent surrender to me. Neither his nor Nimitz's business. Apparently Navy was insistent. Doug was "re-directed" to do it with me as stooge for Nimitz. He simply ignored the order. Nimitz radioed asking him what he was doing to implement the directive. Doug answered "nothing" and got away with it.

Touchy about being sniped at. Spoke of Summerall's speech "I can take Cote de Châtillin, if you will keep my rear from being sniped at." As a result Pershing gave Dickman the Army of Occupation, instead of Summerall.[210]

This comment is a reference to the battle the 42nd Infantry Division and its commander, Douglas MacArthur, waged from October 14–16, 1918, to take the Cote de Châtillin during the Meuse-Argonne Offensive. MacArthur promised Maj. Gen. Charles P. Summerall, the V Corps commander, that his division would take the hill or he would die trying. When initial efforts to take Châtillin failed, Summerall put considerable pressure on MacArthur. Summerall, however, allowed MacArthur to retain command of his division—unlike most other unit commanders, who he removed when they failed to reach their objectives. When the 42nd Inafntry Division took the hill, Summerall nominated MacArthur for the Medal of Honor and promotion to major general, both of which were denied. Although Maj. Gen. Joseph T. Dickman, the I Corps commander, took command of the Third Army during the American occupation of the Rhineland after the war, Summerall eclipsed him by becoming the army chief of staff and achieving four-star rank.[211]

Eisenhower. "He will compromise and yield to protect his prestige. He will not fight for principles." "It may well be a sad day for the Army when Ike goes in as chief of staff." "The fact that he has political aspirations may keep him from being made chief of staff."

Doug sore about Drew Pearson stuff. Insisting that War Department B.P.R. should issue counter statements. (They were telling him to avoid being the cause of such statements.)

Gen. Wang, fat slob, greeted me at dinner.[212] Russians, Limmies and Chinese here of course.

September 27

Up at 5:30. Off at 8:00 to Yokohama. Saw Nogi's home, where he harakiri'd.[213] Then down to 47 Ronins' shrine. No admittance to military personnel! On to Eighth Army HQ at Yokohama. Continuous destruction all the way. Eichelberger being presented with a sword by a Jap admiral! And accepting it. He's just a blah hand shaker. Spruance came in. Refused invite to go on trip with Eichelberger. (He was taking Mrs. Doug to Miyashita today.) Back to 47 Ronins and got in with a pass.

The shrine Stilwell is referring to is a monument to an incident that occurred at the beginning of the eighteenth century. In 1701, a fight broke out in Edo Castle between Asano Naganori and Kira Yoshinaka, two feudal lords. Asano drew his sword despite the shogun's prohibition against such actions inside the castle. As a penalty for this violation of decorum, the shogun ordered Asano to commit suicide in the traditional manner of the samurai, which he did. Many in the Asano household believed that this decree was unjust since the attitudes of the day held that each party in a dispute was equally at fault, and Kira had a reputation for corruption. A year later the Asano household's samurais struck, even though they had promised the shogun they would obey the law prohibiting vendettas. On the night of December 14–15, 1702, forty-seven ronins—samurai without masters or lords—formerly of the Asano house attacked and killed Kira and later placed his head on their lord's grave. They then reported their actions to the authorities and were promptly arrested. Uncertain if the ronin were loyal retainers fulfilling their duty of loyalty or conspirators, the shogun compromised. He ordered their deaths, but allowed them to commit suicide in honorable fashion, which they did on the day of the verdict.[214]

Then to the field at Chofu and shoved off at 12:00. Lunch on board. Up to Utsunomiya and Nikko. Circled, saw the temples, red bridge and Lake Chuzenji. Then up to Sendai and Matsushima. Landed at field beyond mountain and meet Swing and Pierson and Griswold.[215] Dorn at Yamagata. Took Swing and flew to Tendo. Very thick weather. Dorn not there. Went to hotel billet and waited till 3:35. Then beat it. As we left the ground, Dorn arrived. Too late. Took Swing to Matsushima and at once took off for Tokyo, at 4:45. Reached Chofu just after dark. Rain Hell of a time getting down. Reached hotel at 7:15. Met Atcheson,[216] Service, Isaacs. Dinner together. Very boring evening with Atcheson, who sat on his ass till 11:30. I could have killed the booby.

Isaacs on Korea. Russians are rough. Divided control—how do anything? Hodge over his depth. Food will be a problem.

Helmick for Hurley in China?[217] Atcheson to Siam. Ignored by GHQ. Hirohito went to see Doug today.[218]

September 28

Diller announces return to U.S. of Stilwell and Merrill—(They are making sure.)[219] Rain. (GI lesson in manners on a street car. Yanked Jap man up and seated the women.) ("It is not necessarily degrading to be polite to women in foreign countries"—Instructions to Jap diplomatic corps.) (Reminded CLEAR of his call at Carmel, when he told me how nice the Japs were!)

Got money changed. Cleared off at noon. Left for field at 12:45—left about 1:30 via Fuji south side. Fine look at Gotemba line, Hakone Lake, shore line. Over the Akaishi mountains—rugged and steep—5,000–7,000 feet. No roads. Down on Nagoya—a wreck. Really terrific. On over a low range to Biwa and down to Kyoto. Skirted the hill twice. Looked at the field. Wet and soft. National Guard went on to OSAKA. [Emphasis in original.] Again terrific—burned out like Nagoya. More impressive than Tokyo. Found a field east of Osaka and sat down. Harper coming in with 98th Division.[220] Bummed a car and came to Kyoto in 1 1/2 hours after diddling around in Osaka looking for the way. Kyoto untouched. Japs watching the troops come in. To Miyako and found rooms ready. Krueger had just arrived. Had supper with him and Decker. Merrill and I have a suite. Very elegant.

Corps: I, Kosaka; Swift. X, Kure; Sibert. III Amphibious, Sasebo; Schmidt.[221] Krueger doesn't know he is to go to U.S. December 1. Escape to bed at 9:00 P.M.

September 29

Eight-thirty: out to look for Shinmonzen. Back and forth, right on it. Finally ran it down. NOTHING [emphasis in original]. Everything closed down tight. . . . Walked to Chion In. Big bell still there. Then over to Kiyomizu. Unchanged. But no activity. No bustle. No business. Got tea. Visitors said to old lady, "They are quieter than was to be expected." The authorities here were looking for reprisals in a big way and could not understand our forbearance. "Aren't you going to punish us?" Walked back to hotel for lunch. At 1:30 took jeep and rode to Otsu and on up to Karasaki (the old pine tree). Looked over an air-field and got souvenirs. Back to town and down to Higashi Honganji (hair ropes). Then out to Kinkakuji, southwest of town. Beautiful grounds. Back to town looking for Nijo Shiro, but missed it. Walked hotel grounds. Bath. (Krueger has not yet heard about December 1.) The EM came up this A.M. and are having a grand time. Billeted in hotel.

September 30

A.M.: walked to HEIAN temple (big cemetery). Stopped at zoo, which is all run down. (Monkeys in a pit.) Then walked out to Ginkakuji. (Just like Kinkakuji.) Beautiful grounds. Back to hotel. (The hillside over there is full of temples.) Got jeeps (11:10) and went to NIJO castle. All the carvings down, and building all boarded up. Walked around the citadel. Hotel at noon—(about 3 hours hiking).

P.M.: out to Arashi Yama and on to Moss Temple (sai-ho-ji). Another good one near by. Beautiful walk through moss temple. Surprisingly far out. How did we do it in 1911?[222] Back via Kitano temple—very interesting. Usual BAZOO at dinner. God, he's dumb. [Emphasis in original.]

October 1

"Most clean and sonorous shop." (Barber) "This porisher has flavorous elegance and odiferous brilliance." No answer to radio yet. Took a walk to pigeon temple and otter at entrance to Maruyama Park. (Eight Moons Temple.)

To Shinmonzen. Shops opening. Got a Kokusai copy. Hubbard bought obi, lacquer, etc. Back to hotel. P.M., sat. Sent Hubbard to Kyoto to get message, if any. Merrill and I rode to Arashi yama and walked up river. Pretty inn on bank. (Good CP) Back at 5:00—hot bath. Hubbard got off from Taisho at 4:10. "No one can be a pitcher until he has been a catcher. . . ." aphorism of Andrew Johnson.[223]

October 2

Goodbye to Dorn, Paul and Decker. (Bache at breakfast.[224] Q: What has GCM[225] done for the ARMY? A: Nothing. It is still dis-united—the National Guard is still in the saddle. We are still operating on the 1916 Defense Act.) Fine weather.

Sat around all day waiting for Hubbard. Plane finally came over at 3:00 P.M. Merrill and I took a walk. Hubbard in at 4:30. Went in at Asugi; late into Tokyo. Decided to cut out Korea and go to Okinawa direct in morning, G-Mo having refused permission for *Beijing* [Stilwell wrote Beijing in kanji characters].[226] (September 26 to October 2 to get an answer!)

October 3

Up at 5:30. Off at 6:30. Accident in Osaka. Jap bicyclist. Stopped in old citadel. Taisho field take off at 8:30. Over Osaka, Kobe, Okayama, Kure, Hiroshima, Miyajima, Shinseki, Moji, Kokusa, Yawata, Sasebo, Nagasaki, Kagoshima. Desolation. All stacks standing. Queer. Hint on future design. Remnants of Jap fleet. At Kure 25 SS, 25 DD, 1 CL, etc. At Sasebo, 4 or 5 DD, 2 CL, few SS. Wooden freighters being built off Miyajima. Floods had covered hotel grounds there with sand. SS aground. Dirty weather. Rain from Kure on.

Hokusai views all the way.[227] He had the right colors.

Seven hour flight. In at Okinawa at 2:45. Yontan closed. Landed at Awase. Ten minutes later, all fields closed. Everything OK here. The Vogel case is closed. He crashed in a P-38 *with a nurse*—both killed [emphasis in original]. Heavy rain. Cleaned up papers and turned in early.

October 4

Papers all day. GCM's and decorations. (Nap.)

★ ★ ★

October 5

Papers all A.M. Sunbath—good weather. P.M.: read and wrote. (First Annual Amami Regatta.)

October 6

Tried to hop off for Miyako. Plane not ready. Our Air Force an indifferent, sloppy, dirty, inefficient lot. Will get a plane from the Marines. Sunbath. Quiet day.

October 7

Off from Awase at 7:50 in Marine plane. Clean and ready to go. Pilot Sweetser.[228] Miyako at 9:00. To docks with Col. Levin.[229] Off for Ishigaki at 10:00. Arrived 10:30. Met Cannon. Visited docks. Cannon hustling to beat typhoon. Getting out tonight. Lunch at field. Left at 12:30. Awase at 2:00. (Japs at Ishigaki eighty percent sick with Malaria.) Dead-beated the rest of the day. Typhoon coming.

October 8

A hell of a night with the rats. Trap outside[;] they were inside, gnawing out. Brought trap in and they jumped over it and kept on gnawing out. Twelve to 1:00 went after them with a stick, then gave up and read till 3 A.M. They gnawed until dawn.

Papers and letters. Nap. Walk in rain with Bergin. Cocktail party for 35. Good party. This HQ never got together. Letter from Joe. He is down.

October 9

"Louise" [typhoon that hit Okinawa that day with incredible force] getting worse. Rain and wind. At 2:30 it got bad and at 4:30 we moved out, down to the office. Wind 80 knots. Roof paper blowing off. Everything getting soaked. Tentage going down all around. At 6:00 even worse. A struggle to get to the mess hall. Typhoon moving north at 20 knots. Worst blow I've seen. Hard to stand up. Dates all called off.

October 10

Inspected damage to Naha and back. Bad. Up north in P.M. Bad. Party at 5:30. Nurses, Red, and staff. About 70. Big whoops.

October 11

Piddled in office in A.M. Early lunch at 12:15. Shoved off to Kunishi ridge. Arrived 1:35—at 2:00, ceremony to unveil Buckner marker. Short and snappy. Back again at 3:50. beautiful day—sunny with strong breeze. Expected Joe, but no soap.

October 12

Fruitless flight to Nunnami Daito, with Woods. Did not land. No personnel visible. Looked over derelicts (over 90) on east shore and islands. Price is against a big base here. Sun bath. Doddered around. Radioed Joe.

October 13

A.M.: papers. Leavey in (AFWESPAC).[230] Two P.M. funeral of Col. Dickey—Marines.[231] (Heart failure.) Joe here. Talked all P.M. and evening. Preliminary packing.

October 14

Last day at Okinawa. Joe and I talked and at 9:00 I made a speech to the staff. Decorated Hubbard, Edwards, and Bentley. After sun-bath, heard Army-Michigan game.[232] Two P.M.: staff cocktail orgy. Took Joe for a ride. Condon in for dinner. Lawson, Leavey, and Jones in to say good-bye. Joe and I talked till late.

Stilwell's Farewell Message to the Tenth Army

Now that you are on the way back to the farm, the shop, the desk, or the mine, or soon will be, listen to a few words from an old brass hat who has watched the generations pass by. You are not required to listen any more; nobody can call you to attention; you are free from red tape, discipline, censorship, and restrictions; the wraps are off you at last. But give me a chance to speak to you briefly with the wraps off me, too. Even brass hats are tied up in red tape, and sometimes they don't like it any better than you do.

My great regret is that I can't expect to go along with your generation much longer. I have seen how you respond in a crisis and it is okay. I have heard you cuss and gripe, and that's normal and proper. You can take it on the nose and you can dish it out, with interest. You have made the grade, as soldiers, sailors, and Marines, and you can have my shirt any time you need it.

When you get home, they will make a fuss over you. They will be shouting, "Welcome home, heroes," "The thanks of America," etc. How you will squirm and wish you could get down to Clancy's with the boys! All you can do is sweat it out, make your speech, and be thankful that it doesn't last very long.

The home folks think a lot of you and they will only be trying to show their appreciation. You want your own people and your own community to feel that you made good, anyway. They never doubted that you would; it was only you who had any qualms about it. And here is where you cash in; you have been through the mill, you have stood the gaff, and you have the satisfaction of accomplishment that nothing can buy. That is the real reward of your service. From now on you can live with yourself, without regrets.

But unless I read you wrong, you will not think your work as Americans is all done because the war is over. In the face of aggression, we got together and submerged all our little differences. In the big issues, everybody came through. You did not hesitate to go forward and pull a buddy out of machine-gun fire at the risk of your own neck. And it didn't count that you were maybe a college graduate and he never got beyond the eighth grade, because you know he'd have done as much for you. You wouldn't know, except incidentally, who were Protestants, Catholics, or Jews in your company, who were union men and who non-union. It wouldn't have made any difference anyway.

The war has proved the essential cohesion of America. If the Germans and the Japs had looked us over carefully, and had had the brains to evaluate what they saw, they would never have been crazy enough to try to pull us down. If we can lick a problem such as this war has been, are we going to let the comparatively minor problems of peace bother us? Why if we put the effort on solving our domestic problems that we have put on licking the Germans and the Japs, we could make over the United States of America the way we'd like to have it.

It is too much to expect that we should continue the same pace when the urge is gone, but 11,000,000 ex-servicemen can have a lot to say about what we will do. I am sure of one thing—you like the way America is headed, or you wouldn't have put up such a fight for it.

Maybe in the near future your machine gunner will make a million dollars and you will run a filling station. What the hell! It may be that you will make the million and the gunner will run the filling station. That's America—everybody on his feet, and nobody on his knees.

One more thing before I stop talking. You have left your outfit and exchanged the bugle for the alarm clock, but you will never be alone again. There are 11,000,000 men now who have had similar experiences. You have, all of you, seen a lot of the world and can better appreciate what we've got in the United States of America. Because I have faith in the outlook and ideals of your generation, I should like to live long enough to see what you do with your opportunities. But though it is a fine day in the morning for you, it is getting late in the afternoon for me.

Good luck, soldier. I am proud to have known you.[233]

Epilogue

Taps

So, what are we to make of these two generals, their legacies, and their impact on military operations in the last days of World War II? Part of that answer can be found in looking at reactions to their deaths. Buckner was buried the day after he died. A muddy army ambulance brought a simple coffin to the cemetery and the pallbearers, six enlisted men who had served under the general as clerks and orderlies, carried the body to the grave. A crowd of officers and men stood outside the cemetery's white picket fence. A color guard and Col. Roy Hillyer, a Protestant chaplain in the Tenth Army, stood among the white crosses as Buckner was laid to rest in the barren, yellow ground. A reporter for the *New York Journal-American* observed that the "funeral was stirring in its simplicity."[1]

The reaction to his death in the United States showed that the newspaper controversy the week before had done little to discredit Buckner, the highest-ranking officer to die in combat during the war. His death was front-page news across the country. The accounts that followed were effusive with praise. A *New York Times* reporter on the island called Buckner the "defender of Alaska, liberator of the Aleutians," and "conqueror of Okinawa." The article concluded with quotes from King, Nimitz, Secretary of War Henry Stimson, and Navy Secretary James Forrestal praising Buckner's ability and leadership. No marines were quoted, although Forrestal observed that he was "held in high regard in the Navy and Marine Corps." The *New York Herald Tribune* ran an extremely flattering obituary that included a section on the Okinawa campaign.[2] Editorial writers commenting on his passing fell into one of two groups. A number of journalists praised him as a tough, demanding warrior, but one who was considerate of his men's needs and interests. Robert B. Atwood, the publisher and editor of the *Anchorage Times,* wrote: "General Buckner was tops in everything that he did and represented." Atwood also noted: "His fighting was consistent with his living and with his thinking—hard, sincere, and thorough." Back in Kentucky, the Louisville *Courier-Journal,* the modern incarnation of the paper his father had once edited, noted: "General Buckner was a professional soldier" and that "he died as such a man would choose to die, in action with his men." The *Cleveland Plain Dealer* praised him simply as a "soldier's general," while the *Los Angeles Times* called him "a soldier's ideal of a fighting leader."[3] Other journalists chose to defend him against Bigart and Lawrence. The *Honolulu Star-Bulletin* and Portland *Oregonian* argued that recent events, including Nimitz's defense and the impending defeat of the Japanese, had repudiated any criticism of the general. Admiral William V. Pratt, *Newsweek*'s military affairs columnist, made similar comments. He rhetorically asked if Lawrence even had the expertise to comment on amphibious landings: "Does the source of the criticism, coming from an excellent reporter but one who, nevertheless, is not thoroughly versed in the art of war, insure its complete reliability?" The *Washington Evening Star,* which ran Lawrence's column in the District of Columbia, retreated from his criticisms of Buckner: "If there had been a less costly method of reaching the same objective, it is inconceivable that it would not have been chosen. For decisions on strategy are seldom those of one man, but of many men."[4]

Others outside of journalism also commented on the general's passing. On the floor of the U.S. Senate, Albert "Happy" Chandler and Alban Barkley, both from Buckner's native state of Kentucky, praised the fallen general. "It was the will to win that characterized Simon Bolivar Buckner as he met his death on Okinawa," Chandler stated. "A man who attacked life aggressively, he never asked the men under his command to do a job he would not do himself." Barkley, reflecting on his long admiration for the general's father and his association with the younger Buckner when the general lived in Washington, added, "By his gentlemanly qualities and his personality, his sincerity and his devotion, he endeared himself to all people who came in contact with him."[5]

In the years that followed, Buckner was remembered in ways large and small. On July 4, 1945, Nakagusuku Bay was renamed Buckner Bay, and three days later the army posthumously decorated him the Distinguished Service Cross. The navy followed in October, giving him the Distinguished Service Medal. That same year, the army renamed the Tactical Training and Firing Center, used for cadet summer training at West Point, Camp Buckner. Three and a half years after his death, he was reburied at the foot of his father's grave in Frankfort, Kentucky's capital. All of the state's public offices were closed for an hour in his honor, flags few at half-staff, and a minute of silence was observed at 2 P.M. More than eighteen hundred people attended, including Kentucky governor Earle C. Clements and the current army chief of staff, Gen. Omar Bradley. A number of old friends, high-ranking officers, and members of the Tenth Army staff served as honorary pallbearers. Several marine generals were also present. At the request of his widow, the services were the same as those accorded to returning enlisted men. Buckner was posthumously promoted to the rank of general in 1954.[6]

Since that time, there have been many studies of the Okinawa campaign.

Buckner appears as a character of importance in each of them, regardless of a work's focus. However, he has never been a dominating figure in the drama. No previous author has had access to his diaries or letters and, since he did not live to write memoirs or give interviews, his perspective and voice have been uncharacteristically mute.[7]

Stilwell lived a bit longer than Buckner and his return to the United States was front-page news, at least in the San Francisco Bay area.[8] He was assigned to duty as president of the War Equipment Board and in January, 1946, became commander of the Sixth Army, headquartered at the Presidio of San Francisco—a short drive from the house he owned in Carmel, California. The main mission of this peacetime command was the deactivation of service and support units in the western United States. In July, Stilwell was the War Equipment Board's observer at the testing of two atomic bombs at Bikini Island. When he returned home, his wife thought he looked ill. Stilwell was hospitalized in late September and on October 3 doctors operated and discovered that he had a highly developed case of cancer in his stomach that was spreading into his liver. On Friday, October 11, Secretary of War Robert Patterson presented the Combat Infantryman's Badge to Stilwell in recognition of his combat service in an infantry unit. He died in his sleep shortly after noon the next day.[9]

Since he was the first of the major theater commanders to die and did so only a year after the end of the war, his fate was major news. Announcement of his passing spread quickly, interrupting play of the Army-Michigan football game. Newspapers in western time zones announced his death on the front pages of their afternoon and evening editions. In several publications, banner headlines appeared above the masthead.[10] Stilwell's death dominated the front pages of Sunday editions all across the rest of the country. Most of the articles focused on his service in China. In London, a *Times* reporter called him "one of the greatest authorities on Chinese life and culture in the United States." His stay on Okinawa was usually mentioned only in passing, although the *Chicago Daily Tribune* mentioned the lost hat episode and the *Fort Worth Star-Telegram* quoted his Fourth of July speech.[11]

Since Sunday editions were often prepared several days in advance of their publication, editorial tributes took another day or two to appear. These essays focused almost entirely on his acid personality and blunt honesty. The *Herald Statesman,* published in Yonkers, New York, where Stilwell grew up, noted that these traits made Stilwell great copy and explained his popularity among journalists. These personality characteristics, however, had little to do with his significance in World War II, which was his mission in China. Most editorial writers avoided in-depth discussions of his actions on the Asian continent or his feud with Chiang Kai-shek and subsequent removal from command. There were some exceptions, however. The *Baltimore Sun* and *Washington Post* respectfully noted that Stilwell lacked the temperament and personality for diplomatic duty. Jack Bell, a columnist for the *Miami Herald,* and the *Boston Globe*'s editorial board were almost alone in their defense of Stilwell's actions in China.[12]

Funeral services, in keeping with Stilwell's nature, were simple. After his death, flags at the Presidio were immediately lowered to half-staff, and an artillery salute was fired every half hour in his honor. At 5 P.M., the Presidio's military band marched onto the parade ground and played ruffles and flourishes as the flag was raised and then lowered. A seventeen-gun salute followed, while Maj. Gen. George P. Hays, Sixth Army deputy commander, Brig. Gen. Frank Merrill, Sixth Army chief of staff, and Col. George Slaney, headquarters commandant, faced the flag and saluted. Mrs. Stilwell and her family watched from a car parked on the side of the field. Four days later, on October 16, flags were flown at half-staff and businesses closed from 2 to 2:15 P.M. in Stilwell's hometown of Carmel as the city held a small memorial service in his honor. Colonel Roy Hillyer, the chaplain who had supervised Buckner's funeral on Okinawa, addressed the crowd. In accordance with Stilwell's wishes, his body was cremated and his ashes were spread over the Pacific that afternoon.[13]

Stilwell remained controversial after his death. Theodore White, a reporter in China during the period of Stilwell's command, arranged with the general's family to edit and publish his diary and letters from that period. Published in 1948 as *The Stilwell Papers,* the book was a publishing sensation. The edited material contained Stilwell's blunt and frank assessments of a bad situation in the sharp, uncompromising language that was so typical of him. Portions of the text first appeared in the *Ladies' Home Journal,* then the *Infantry Journal,* and for three weeks as a series in the *San Francisco Chronicle.*[14] The book, which offered the first public explanation for the general's removal, appeared just as Chinese Communist forces were making strong gains against the Nationalists. This timing intensified the attention the book received. Stilwell's account featured devastating portraits of Chiang Kai-shek, Franklin D. Roosevelt, and Claire Chennault. The *New Yorker* called it "a posthumous blast at the Generalissimo."[15] Chiang appears to be both corrupt and incompetent in its pages, while Stilwell's words make Roosevelt out to be an irresponsible lightweight, and Chennault an unprincipled man totally committed to his ideology of airpower. Since Stilwell took on such highly placed targets, the book was the subject of much editorial commentary. Most of the interest was in the deceased president. "The Roosevelt myth can't survive many more such revelations as this one," a *Chicago Daily Tribune* editorial declared.[16]

The volume was the subject of cover articles in the *New York Times Book Review,* the *New York Herald Tribune Weekly Book Review,* and the *Saturday Re-*

view of Literature.[17] Publications large and small ran their own original reviews.[18] The bulk of the comments focused on the general's candid, blunt language. A number of reviewers also noted that Stilwell had an almost impossible assignment. In large part, however, the reviewers were neutral on the issue of the general's feud with Chiang. China was a volatile issue, and those who found fault with the Chinese leader were often labeled as communist sympathizers. Chiang had some strong American defenders. Chennault wrote a series of articles that appeared in Scripps-Howard newspapers that put most of the blame for the things that went wrong in China on Stilwell. Far more influential was Henry Luce, chairman of Time-Life, Incorporated. A *Time* magazine article called Stilwell "insecure and suspicious" and also stated that he "fell for the 'liberal' line that the Chinese Communists were really agrarian reformers." Harold Isaacs, a reporter who had known Stilwell, was closer to the mark in his review for the *New York Herald Tribune Weekly Book Review.* He explained that the general's interest in deploying the communists had clear limits: "Stilwell actually never deviated from the narrow bounds of strictly American national and military interests."[19]

The subject of Stilwell and China proved it could still garner attention twenty-three years later when Barbara Tuchman published *Stilwell and the American Experience in China, 1911–1945,* a life-and-times biography of the general. The nature of the response was different, however. In the wake of America's painful experience in Vietnam, most reviewers were more than willing to concede the wisdom of Stilwell's recommendation that the United States withdraw from the Asian continent and did not hesitate to express their outrage at how he had been ignored and maligned.[20]

Looking at the reaction to the deaths of these two men only answers part of the question of what we are to make of these two generals and their impact on military operations in the last days of World War II. The diaries themselves are important windows into combat operations in the waning days of the war. First, let us focus on Buckner. He was a competent and professional officer. It is true that he lacked combat experience and he did, as a result, make several bad decisions. It would be a mistake to call his errors minor, if for no other reason than the fact that they resulted in his own death. That point having been made, it is important to note that much of the criticism directed at Buckner is similar to the commentary aimed at Field Marshal Sir Douglas Haig, commander of the British Expeditionary Force in the First World War.

Buckner most likely would not have enjoyed the comparison as Haig had already developed a bad reputation by the start of the Second World War. Nevertheless, more recent British military historians have come to revise their views. Haig is still a controversial figure and is hardly free from blame for battles like the Somme and Passchendaele, but several historians argue that the field marshal kept up with innovations in both tactics and technology, especially the use of new weapon systems like the tank and airplane. In writing about Haig's generalship on the western front, British military historian Gary Sheffield argues, "The employment of attritional warfare *per se* is not necessarily a sign of strategic bankruptcy or stupidity on the part of commanders; indeed, in battles fought between evenly matched foes attrition is virtually inevitable."[21] With only slight modification this statement could describe the campaign in the Ryukyus. It is not that Buckner failed to achieve his objective, but rather that the price was more costly than observers thought it should have been. This faultfinding must take into account the caliber of the opponent he faced. The Japanese Thirty-second Army on Okinawa was well prepared. In fact, it was the best-equipped unit the U.S. armed services faced in the Pacific theater. General Ushijima's main objective was to inflict as many casualties on the invading Americans as possible. He made no serious effort to deny the invaders control of the island. Such an objective was beyond the capacity of his men. As a result, American victory on Okinawa was assured—if the attackers were willing to pay the butcher's bill.

Many historians, however, have attributed responsibility for the costly operation not to the tenacious and brave defenders, but rather to Buckner's poor command ability. Williamson Murray and Allan R. Millett liken the campaign to those waged in the First World War and charge, "What made the carnage at Okinawa so different from Iwo Jima, and so much worse, is that Simon Bolivar Buckner's flawed generalship contributed to the slaughter." His rejection of the second landing was a sign of his inexperience in combat. "Sadly for his troops, Buckner did not have the experience to make such a critical decision." Murray and Millett note that the marines in the III Amphibious Corps had more expertise than the Tenth Army's commanding general. "Compared with his subordinates, Buckner was hardly fit to command a corps, let alone a field army." These two historians are not alone in their views. William L. O'Neill also compares Okinawa to World War I and states flatly, "Buckner ought to have been relieved."[22]

These criticisms do not stand up well to close scrutiny, however. Although Murray and Millett contend that Buckner was unqualified to command a field army, they say nothing about Generals Kreuger, Simpson, Hodges, Clark, and/or Devers. These five had no real prior combat experience, yet they each were given army commands—and Devers graduated to command of an army group. The two historians also tend to show a lack of familiarity with naval matters and do not really think much about maritime logistical issues.

Given the strength of the defenders, no action or inaction on Buckner's part could have significantly reduced the carnage on the island. Nor would any other commander have won a significantly cheaper victory; they would have faced the same problems that confronted Buckner. The United States faced massive logistical problems far beyond Buckner's immediate control and those shortcomings limited his options in several ways. The issue about landing on Okinawa's southern tip should not be would it have worked—although it probably would have helped bring the battle to an end sooner. The real question should be: Was such an operation within Tenth Army's capacity at a time when logistical units were straining to supply current operations? As the official Marine Corps historians note in the their study of the campaign, the massive size of the Okinawa operation, "coupled with the long distances over which supplies had to travel, created logistical problems of an immense nature beyond all that which had transpired in earlier operations." Operation Iceberg consumed twice the amount of matériel required in the Marianas and three times the amount needed on Iwo Jima. "Quick and easy solutions were seldom if ever within grasp, for amphibious logistics has always been an immense and complex factor."[23] Quartermaster issues might not be all that colorful or exciting, but that in no way changes their fundamental importance in combat operations. Buckner fought not as he would have liked, but as he was able.

The Joint Chiefs of Staff believed this point and exonerated Buckner to none other than the president of the United States, Harry S. Truman. Troubled by the high cost of the operation in the Ryukyus, Truman called the chiefs to the White House on June 18 for a special meeting about the proposed invasion of Kyushu, the southernmost Japanese home island. Secretary of War Henry Stimson and General Marshall both shared Truman's concern that the attack on Japan would be a larger, more gruesome version of the debacle on Okinawa.[24] Fleet Admiral Ernest King, chief of naval operations, made an important point that both reassured Truman and validated Buckner's decision about a second landing. Kyushu was much wider than Okinawa, which meant there would be more room for maneuver. There had been only one way to go on Okinawa, making frontal assaults on well-fortified positions almost the only alternative. Buckner had conducted the only campaign possible.[25]

Stilwell would have disagreed with this assessment of Buckner. His diary certainly offers support to some of Buckner's critics, but the importance of his journal lies in its description of events in the summer of 1945. No one knew that the war would end as quickly as it did. For a short time, Stilwell had the field command that he had always wanted. He was preparing to lead the Tenth Army into combat. As a result, his diary is a unique record of command.

As a historical document, Stilwell's jottings suggest that the end of the war in the Pacific was far more complex, dangerous, and uncertain than many have allowed. Trying to solve logistical problems dominated much of Stilwell's time. The problems that the United States faced in the Pacific had, if anything, become worse than they had been during the Okinawa campaign. Staff planners estimated that operations against Japan would have required 53.88 million measurement tons of supply. The capacity of ports on the U.S. West Coast was 44 million measurement tons. Using Gulf and East Coast ports would make up this shortfall, but the real problem was that total military cargo capacity in the coming year, including that needed to supply the army of occupation in Europe, was 25 million dead-weight tons per quarter. The War Shipping Administration had a capacity of 32 million per quarter, which would have meant civilian requirements for all other purposes would have had to get by with 7 million dead-weight tons—much less than civilian society was using in the middle of 1945.[26] Efforts to develop reception capacity on Okinawa, which would have helped to reduce this bottleneck, were developing in a less than satisfactory manner according to Stilwell's notes. Operations Olympic and Coronet were at the edge of U.S. logistical capacity.

Just as significant, Stilwell's diary indicates that command arrangements in the Pacific were far from settled. What role, if any, Tenth Army would have played in either operation was still an open question. The feud between the army and navy in the Pacific had yet to be resolved when the war ended. As a result, the planners in MacArthur's headquarters removed Tenth Army from the plans for Coronet. In private, Nimitz and King were both dubious about the prospects for that operation's success.[27] There was, of course, no need to find a solution to this problem after Japan's surrender, but with the basic issues still unresolved, MacArthur would have faced enormous difficulties initiating Olympic and then Coronet on schedule.[28]

Appendix A

Glossary of Terms

AA	Antiaircraft
AAA	Antiaircraft Artillery
ADC	Aide de camp
AF	Air Force
AAF	Army Air Forces
AFWESPAC	U.S. Army Forces, Western Pacific
AGF	Army Ground Forces
AP	Associated Press
Arty	Artillery
Ascom	Army Service Command
ASP	Ammunition Supply Point
AVC	American Veterans Committee
BB	Battleship
BG	Brigadier General
Blacklist	MacArthur's plan for the occupation of Japan and Korea
Bldg	Building
BPR	Bureau of Public Relations
Bn	battalion
CAP	Combat Air Patrol
CB	Construction Battalion
CBS	Columbia Broadcasting System
C&GS	Command and General Staff School
Chap.	Chaplain
CINCPOA	Commander in Chief, Pacific Ocean Areas (Nimitz and his command)
CJS	Combined Joint Staff
CL	Light Cruiser
CO	Commanding Officer
Co	Company
Coronet	Code name for the invasion of the Tokyo plain, planned for March 1, 1946. Coronet was a

	component operation of Operation Downfall, which was the plan for the final defeat of Japan.
COMGENPOA	Commanding General, U.S. Army Forces, Pacific Ocean Areas (Richardson and his command)
COMGENTEN	Commanding General, Tenth Army
CP	Command Post
CVE	Escort Carrier
DD	Destroyer
DSM	Distinguished Service Medal
Div	Division
EM	Executive Manager
ETO	European Theater of Operations
FA	Field Artillery
FMF	Fleet Marine Force
ft.	Feet
G1[1]	Personnel officer/office for a division or larger sized unit
G2	Intelligence officer/office for a division or larger sized unit
G3	Operations and training officer/office for a division or larger sized unit
G4	Logistics officer/office for a division or larger sized unit
G5	Civil affairs officer/office for a division or larger sized unit
GHQ	General Headquarters
GI	Government Issue
GS	General Staff
HE	High Explosive
HMS	His Majesty's Ship
HQ	Headquarters
IB	India-Burma
Iceberg	Code name for the invasion of Okinawa
in.	Inch
Inf	Infantry
Iscom	Island Command
JASCO	Joint Assault Signal Companies
JCC	Joint Chiefs Communication
JCS	Joint Chiefs of Staff
JIC	Joint Intelligence Center
INS	International News Service
lb.	Pound

LCT	Landing Craft, Tank
LL	Lend-Lease
LST	Landing Ship, Tank
LVT	Landing Vehicle, Tracked
mm	Millimeter
MP	Military Police
Mardiv	Marine Division
mi	Miles
NBC	National Broadcasting Corporation
NCOs	Noncommissioned Officers
NOB	Naval Operating Base
NW	Northwest
NY	New York
Olympic	Code name for the invasion of Kyushu, the southernmost Japanese home island, scheduled for November 1, 1945. Olympic was a component operation of Operation Downfall, which was the plan for the final defeat of Japan.
OP	Observation Post
Phibcorps	Marine Amphibious Corps
PI	Philippine Islands
POW	Prisoner of War
PM	Provost Marshal
PRO	Public Relations Office or Officer
PT	Patrol Torpedo Boat
PX	Post Exchange
RAMP	Recovered Allied Military Personnel
RCT	Regimental Combat Team
Recon	Reconnaissance
Regt	Regiment
Regtl	Regimental
RR	Railroads
SF	San Francisco
SO	Signal Officer
SS	Submarine
SSO	Services of Supply Office/Officer
SWPA	Southwest Pacific Area (MacArthur and his command)
TAF	Tactical Air Force
T/E	Table of Equipment
TF	Task Force

TNT	Trinitrotoluene (an explosive)
UDT	Underwater Demolition Team
UPI	United Press International
USS	United States Ship
USMC	United States Marine Corps
V-E Day	Victory in Europe Day; end of the war in Europe
V-J Day	Victory over Japan Day; end of the war in the Pacific
VLR	Very Long Range
WAC	Women's Auxiliary Corps
Weasel	Tracked amphibious vehicle
WD	War Department
yds	Yards

Appendix B

Persons Mentioned in the Diaries

More than four hundred individuals, ranging in rank from corporal to the president of the United States, are mentioned in these two diaries. In many cases, Buckner and Stilwell mentioned people without giving their full name. Neither man had reason to do so, since he was writing for himself, not others. Given the large number of individuals who appear within these pages, the editor made no effort to provide biographical information, such as dates of birth and death, education, or previous positions held. The editor fully identified slightly more than 80 percent of the people mentioned.

This glossary lists all those who are identified in the diaries and includes their full name, rank or title, and the position they held *at the time.* All individuals are footnoted and identified the first time they are mentioned in the text. In several instances it was difficult, if not impossible, to fully identify individuals the two generals mentioned. In more than a few cases, Buckner and Stilwell did not know an individual, particularly when they were meeting junior officers. When such occurred, the two generals would simply note that they had met a Captain Miller or a Lieutenant Jones. Trying to identify these individuals more fully hardly seems worth the time and energy that such a task would require.

Name	*Position*
1st Lt. John Abbink	Tenth Army operations staff officer
Brig. Gen. Julius O. Adler	Vice president and treasurer, *New York Times*
Comdr. Carl "Squeaky" Anderson	Alaskan cannery owner and U.S. Navy officer
Sir John Anderson	Director of British atomic bomb research
Maj. Gen. Archibald V. Arnold	Commanding general, 7th Infantry Division
Maj. Carl Arnold	Stilwell's aide de camp
Col. Donald Ashton	Tenth Army quartermaster officer
George Atcheson	General MacArthur's political adviser in Japan

Lauren Bacall	American film actress
Rear Adm. Oscar C. Badger	Commanding officer, Task Force 31
Monty Banks	Italian-born American film and stage actor and director
Vice Adm. Daniel E. Barbey	Commanding officer, VII Amphibious Force
Col. Frederick Barrows	Editor, *Military Review*
Brig. Gen. Lewis C. Beebe	U.S. Army Forces, Philippine Islands, chief of staff; became a prisoner of war in 1942
Col. William C. Bentley, Jr.	Buckner's and Stilwell's pilot
Brig. Gen. William Bergin	Tenth Army chief of staff
Brig. Gen. Kearie L. Berry	Commanding general, 1st Regular Division, Philippine Army; became a prisoner of war in 1942
Maj. Gen. Victor Bertrandias	Commanding general, Okinawa Air Depot
Col. Philip H. Bethune	Tenth Army intelligence staff officer
Homer Bigart	*New York Herald Tribune* correspondent
Maj. Gen. Clayton L. Bissell	U.S. Army Air Forces assistant chief of staff for intelligence
Commodore Andrew G. Bissett	Commander, Island Command Construction Troops
Lt. Col. Delbert Bjork	Commanding officer, 184th Infantry Regiment, 7th Infantry Division
Brig. Gen. David H. Blakelock	Tenth Army assistant chief of staff for logistics
Gen. Sir Thomas Blamey	Australian representative at Japan's surrender
Vice Adm. William H. Blandy	Commanding officer, Amphibious Support Force (Task Force 52)
Humphrey Bogart	American film actor
Col. Robert H. Booth	7th Infantry Division chief of staff
Brig. Gen. William A. Borden	Director, New Development Division, War Department General Staff
Brig. Gen. William B. Bradford	Assistant commanding general, 27th Infantry Division
Maj. Gen. James L. Bradley	Commanding general, 96th Infantry Division

Capt. Allyn Brenner	Tenth Army intelligence staff officer
Maj. Gen. Andrew D. Bruce	Commanding general, 77th Infantry Division
Col. Milo Buchanan	Tenth Army inspector general
Adele Buckner	Buckner's wife
Brig. Gen. Clovis Byers	Eighth Army chief of staff
Rear Adm. Richard E. Byrd	Noted explorer
Brig. Gen. Robert Cannon	Tenth Army civil affairs officer
Lt. Col. John Carlton	Tenth Army Services of Supply officer
Clifford P. Case	New Jersey member, U.S. House of Representatives
Maj. Gen. Hugh Casey	Chief engineer officer, U.S. Army Forces, Pacific
Maj. Gen. Stephen Chamberlin	Chief, Operations Section, U.S. Army Forces, Pacific
Maj. Gen. Claire Chennault	Commanding general, Fourteenth Air Force
Maj. Gen. Gilbert X. Cheves	Tenth Army island commander
Chiang Kai-shek	President, Republic of China
Lt. Gen. Chu Shih-ming	Chinese representative, Allied Council for Japan
Winston Churchill	British prime minister
Brig. Gen. William T. Clement	Assistant commanding general, 6th Marine Division
Rear Adm. Calvin H. Cobb	Commanding officer, Naval Forces Ryukyus
Brig. Gen. Orval Cook	Commanding general, 7th Air Service Area Command
Vice Adm. Charles M. Cooke, Jr.	U.S. Fleet assistant chief of staff for plans
Col. Theodore M. Cornell	Commanding officer, Leyte Provincial Regiment; became a prisoner of war in 1942
Col. L. Moore Cosgrove	Canadian representative at Japan's surrender
Rear Adm. Carl H. Cotter	Director, Pacific Division, Bureau of Yards and Docks, U.S. Navy
Lt. Col. William S. Cowart	Buckner's aide de camp
	John Cowles, Sr. Publisher, *Minneapolis Star*
Brig. Gen. William E. Crist	Tenth Army deputy commander for military government

Col. Robert W. Daniels	Tenth Army ordnance officer
Maj. John M. Davenport	Tenth Army Judge Advocate General Section staff officer
Maj. Gen. Howard C. Davidson	Commanding general, Tenth Air Force
Rear Adm. Arthur C. Davis	Fifth Fleet chief of staff
Ted Dealey	President, *Dallas Morning News*
Brig. Gen. George Decker	Sixth Army chief of staff
Maj. Gen. Pedro A. Del Valle	Commanding general, 1st Marine Division
Capt. John B. Depot	Tenth Army Adjutant General Section staff officer
Lt. Gen. Kuzma Derevyanko	Soviet representative at Japan's surrender
Lt. Gen. John DeWitt	Commanding general, Western Defense Command
Rear Adm. Morton L. Deyo	Replaced Oldendorf as commanding officer, Gunfire and Covering Force (Task Force 54)
Maj. Gen. Joseph T. Dickman	Commanding general, I Corps, World War I, and Third Army during the postwar occupation of the Rhineland
Col. Ward E. Dickey	Commanding officer, Marine Aircraft Group 33
Col. Macey L. Dill	Commanding officer, 382nd Infantry Regiment, 96th Infantry Division
Brig. Gen. LeGrande "Pick" Diller	General MacArthur's public information officer
Cpl. Edward P. Donahue	Soldier who recovered Stilwell's hat
Maj. Gen. Leo Donovan	U.S. Army Ground Forces operations officer
Maj. Gen. William "Wild Bill" Donovan	Director, Office of Strategic Services
Lt. Gen. James H. Doolittle	Commanding general, Eighth Air Force
Brig. Gen. Frank Dorn	Tenth Army staff officer after Stilwell took command
Brig. Gen. Robinson E. Duff	Commanding general, Service Command C
Brig. Gen. Walter A. Dumas	Tenth Army assistant chief of staff for operations
Rear Adm. Calvin Durgin	Commanding officer, Task Group 77.4

Brig. Gen. Claudius M. Easley	Assistant commanding general, 96th Infantry Division
Nancy Easterbrook	Stilwell's daughter
Col. Edmund Edwards	Tenth Army artillery officer
Maj. Gen. Idwal Edwards	Chief, Military Intelligence Division, U.S. War Department
Lt. Gen. Robert L. Eichelberger	Commanding general, Eighth Army
Gen. of the Army Dwight D. Eisenhower	Supreme commander, Allied Expeditionary Forces, European theater of operations
Col. Louis B. Ely	Tenth Army intelligence officer
Clair Engel	California member, U.S. House of Representatives
Brig. Gen. Francis A. Englehart	Chief ordnance officer, U.S. Army Forces, Pacific Ocean Areas
Maj. Gen. Graves B. Erskine	Commanding general, 3rd Marine Division
Maj. Raymond T. Eyestone	Tenth Army Chief of Staff Section staff officer
Brig. Gen. Thomas F. Farrell	Deputy commander, Manhattan Engineer District
Joseph R. Farrington	Hawaii delegate, U.S. House of Representatives
Brig. Gen. Herman Feldman	Executive assistant to the assistant chief of staff for logistics, U.S. Pacific Fleet and Pacific Ocean Areas
Brig. Gen. Bonner Fellers	General MacArthur's military secretary
Brig. Gen. Charles S. Ferrin	Artillery commander, 27th Infantry Division
Brig. Gen. Kendall Fielder	U.S. Army Forces, Pacific Ocean Areas, assistant chief of staff for intelligence
Gracie Fields	English comedienne, singer, and film actress
Col. John "Mickey" Finn	Commanding officer, 32nd Infantry Regiment, 7th Infantry Division
Col. Maurice Fitzgerald	Tenth Army provost marshal
Adm. Sir Bruce Fraser	Commander in chief, British Pacific Fleet; United Kingdom representative at Japan's surrender
M.Sgt. Fred "The Man" Friendly	*CBI Roundup* correspondent
Brig. Gen. Robert G. Gard	Artillery commander, 96th Infantry Division

Col. James Garfield	Tenth Army adjutant general
Brig. Gen. Cump Garvin	XXIV Corps chief of staff
Maj. Gen. Roy S. Geiger	Commanding general, III Amphibious Corps
Col. Elmer J. Gibson	Tenth Army ordnance staff officer
Lt. Gen. Barney Giles	Commanding general, Central Pacific Air Forces
Brig. Gen. Wentworth Goss	U.S. Pacific Fleet and Pacific Ocean Areas assistant plans officer
Lt. Col. Leonard J. Greely	Island Command, Ie Shima, chief of staff
Col. Kirby Green	Tenth Army assistant chief of staff for intelligence
Col. Roy A. Green	Commanding officer, 184th Infantry Regiment, 7th Infantry Division
Brig. Gen. Frank Greer	Bureau of Public Relations, U.S. War Department
Maj. John Grindley	Tenth Army Chief of Staff Section staff officer
Maj. Gen. George W. Griner, Jr.	Commanding general, 27th Infantry Division
Brig. Gen. Francis H. Griswold	Eighth Air Force chief of staff
Lt. Gen. Oscar W. Griswold	Commanding general, XIV Corps
Brig. Gen. Matthew Gunner	U.S. Army Forces, Pacific, deputy chief of staff
Rear Adm. J. L. Hall	Commanding officer, Southern Attack Force (Task Force 55)
Col. Michael E. Halloran	Commanding officer, 381st Infantry Regiment, 96th Infantry Division
Fleet Adm. William F. "Bull" Halsey	Replaced Spruance as commanding officer, Central Pacific Task Forces (designated Third Fleet when at sea under Halsey's command)
Col. Stephen S. Hamilton	Commanding officer, 307th Infantry Regiment, 77th Infantry Division
Howard Handelman	International News Service correspondent
Brig. Gen. Morris C. Handwerk	Commanding general, 53rd Antiaircraft Brigade, Tenth Army
Maj. Gen. Arthur Harper	Commanding general, 98th Infantry Division
Lt. Col. Joseph T. Hart	Commanding officer, 165th Infantry Regiment, 27th Infantry Division
Col. Ashton Haynes	Tenth Army Judge Advocate General Section staff officer

Maj. Gen. F. A. Heileman	Director of supplies, U.S. Army Ground Forces
Lt. Col. John L. Heilman	Tenth Army post exchange officer
Adm. C. E. L. Helfrich	Netherlands representative at Japan's surrender
Joe Hendricks	Florida member, U.S. House of Representatives
Maj. Gen. Stephen G. Henry	Chief, Personnel Division, U.S. War Department
Capt. Elbert V. Higgins	Tenth Army Chief of Staff Section staff officer
Col. Roy Hillyer	Tenth Army Baptist chaplain
H.I.M. Hirohito	Emperor of Japan
Adolf Hitler	Führer, Reich Chancellor, and President of Germany
Maj. Gen. John R. Hodge	Commanding general, XXIV Corps
Gen. Courtney Hodges	Commanding general, First Army
Hokusai Katsushika	Eighteenth- and nineteenth-century Japanese artist
Brig. Gen. Henry B. Holmes, Jr.	U.S. Army Forces, Middle Pacific, artillery officer
Gen. Hsü Yung-Ch'ang	Republic of China representative at Japan's surrender
Maj. Frank Hubbard	Buckner's and then Stilwell's aide de camp
Maj. Gen. LeRoy Hunt	Commanding general, I Corps
Maj. Gen. Patrick Hurley	U.S. ambassador to China
Maj. Gen. Donald R. Hutchinson	Commanding general, 308th Bomb Wing
Bob Huttle	Chief, Anchorage Police Department
Lt. Gen. Noel Irwin	Former British commander in India
Harold Isaacs	*Newsweek* correspondent
Lt. Gen. Cho Isamu	Japanese Thirty-second Army chief of staff
Air Vice Marshal Leonard M. Isitt	New Zealand representative at Japan's surrender
Ed Izac	California member, U.S. House of Representatives
Lt. Col. Joseph C. Jefferds	Tenth Army ordnance officer
Andrew Johnson	Seventeenth president of the United States
Dr. Frederic Joliott	French physicist and Nobel laureate
Maj. Gen. Junius Jones	Air inspector, Headquarters, U.S. Army Air Forces
Brig. Gen. Louis R. Jones	Assistant commanding general, 1st Marine Division

Dick Jurgen	Composer and bandleader of the Dick Jurgen Orchestra
Vice Adm. James L. Kaufman	Commanding officer, Philippine Sea Frontier Naval Bases
Lt. Col. James H. Keller	Executive officer, 32nd Infantry Regiment, 7th Infantry Division
Col. Gerard W. Kelly	Commanding officer, 165th Infantry Regiment, 27th Infantry Division
Lt. Col. Douglas Kendrick, Jr.	Tenth Army surgeon
Bishop Harry S. Kennedy	Catholic religious leader
Gen. George C. Kenney	Commanding general, Far East Air Forces
Rear Adm. Ingolf N. Kiland	Commanding officer, Western Island Attack Group
Fleet Adm. Ernest J. King	Chief of naval operations and commander in chief, U.S. Fleet
Adm. Thomas C. Kinkaid	Commanding officer, Seventh Fleet
John S. Knight	Publisher, *Chicago Daily News*
Col. Joseph L. Knipper	Tenth Army engineer officer
Col. Fabius H. Kohloss	Lt. Gen. Raymond A. Wheeler's chief of staff
Lt. Gen. Walter Krueger	Commanding general, Sixth Army
Kay Kyser	Bandleader and radio personality who often played himself in wartime films
David Lawrence	Syndicated newspaper columnist
Brig. Gen. Laurence A. Lawsen	Tenth Army deputy island commander
Maj. Gen. Edmond H. Leavey	Deputy commander and chief of staff, U.S. Army Forces, Western Pacific
Gen. Jacques LeClerc	French representative at Japan's surrender
Air Vice Marshal Sir Hugh Lloyd	Senior Royal Air Force officer in the Pacific theater
Col. Melvin Maas	U.S. Marine Corps Reserve; former member, U.S. House of Representatives
Capt. Donald M. Mackey	Adm. Fred D. Kirtland's executive officer
Brig. Gen. Louis W. Maddox	U.S. Army Forces, Pacific, fiscal director
Brig. Gen. Harold C. Mandell	Assistant to the chief, Plans Section, U.S. Pacific Fleet and Pacific Ocean Areas

Sgt. Alan Manson	Actor and member of the *This is the Army* troupe that entertained troops on Okinawa
Maj. Gen. William F. Marquat	U.S. Army Forces, Pacific, chief antiaircraft officer, and commanding general, 14th Antiaircraft Command
Gen. of the Army George C. Marshall	U.S. Army chief of staff
Col. Joseph I. Martin	Tenth Army surgeon
William Matthews	Editor and publisher, *Arizona Daily Star*
Col. Edwin T. May	Commanding officer, 383rd Infantry Regiment, 96th Infantry Division
Gen. of the Army Douglas MacArthur	Commander in chief, Southwest Pacific Area and later commander in chief, U.S. Army Forces, Pacific
Kenneth McCaleb	International News Service correspondent
Vice Adm. Charles H. McMorris	U.S. Pacific Fleet and Pacific Ocean Areas chief of staff
Maj. Gen. Clements McMullen	Commanding general, Far East Army Service Command
Paul V. McNutt	Chairman, War Manpower Commission
Maj. Gen. Frank Merrill	Tenth Army chief of staff
Sgt. Sid Meyers	Staff writer, 96th Infantry Division newsletter
Vice Adm. Marc Mitschner	Commanding officer, Fast Carrier Force (Task Force 58)
Maj. Gen. James T. Moore	Commander, aircraft, Fleet Marine Force, Pacific
Adm. The Lord Louis Mountbatten	Commander in Chief, Southeast Asia Theater Command
Maj. Gen. F. P. Mulcahy	Commanding general, Tactical Air Force, Tenth Army
Benito Mussolini	Former Italian premier
William T. Nichols	Managing editor, *This Week*
Fleet Adm. Chester W. Nimitz	Commander in chief, U.S. Pacific Fleet and Pacific Ocean Areas
Brig. Gen. George J. Nold	Tenth Army engineer officer
W. F. Norrell	Arkansas member, U.S. House of Representatives
Sgt. Robert Oda	Interpreter at the surrender of Japanese forces in the Ryukyus
Vice Adm. Jesse B. Oldendorf	Commanding officer, Gunfire and Covering Force (Task Force 54)

Dr. J. Robert Oppenheimer	Director, Los Alamos Laboratory
Frederick "Fritz" Opper	Editor, *Evening Post and Mercury* (Shanghai)
Col. Richard Ovenshine	27th Infantry Division chief of staff
Lt. Gen. L. H. van Oyen	Netherlands delegation member at Japan's surrender
Col. Francis Pachler	Commanding officer, 17th Infantry Regiment, 7th Infantry Division
Frederick Palmer	Journalist, author, and historian
Lt. Gen. Alexander "Sandy" Patch	Commanding general, Seventh Army
Robert Patterson	Undersecretary of war
Gen. George S. Patton, Jr.	Commanding general, Third Army
Drew Pearson	Syndicated newspaper columnist
Lt. Gen. Arthur Percival	British general who surrendered Singapore to the Japanese in 1942
Commodore Matthew Perry	Nineteenth-century American naval officer responsible for establishing diplomatic relations with Japan
Gen. of the Armies John J. "Black Jack" Pershing	Commander of the American Expeditionary Force during World War I
Brig. Gen. Albert Pierson	Assistant commanding general, 11th Airborne Division
J. B. Powell	Editor and publisher, *China Weekly Review*
Brig. Gen. Elwyn D. Post	Tenth Army chief of staff
Rear Adm. John D. Price	Commanding officer, Advanced Naval Operating Base, Ryukyus
Don Prior	Combined American Radio Networks correspondent
Col. Arthur Pulsifer	Tenth Army communications officer
Brig. Gen. Edwin H. Randle	Assistant commanding general, 77th Infantry Division
Sgt. Jules Raynaud	Stilwell's cook
Brig. Gen. Joseph L. Ready	Assistant commanding general, 7th Infantry Division
Rear Adm. L. F. Reifsnider	Commanding officer, Northern Attack Force (Task Force 53)

Lt. Gen. Robert C. Richardson, Jr.	Commanding general, U.S. Army Forces, Pacific Ocean Areas
Maj. Gen. Matthew B. Ridgway	Commanding general, XVIII Airborne Corps
Brig. Gen. William Ritchie	Chief, Southwest Pacific Operations Division, U.S. War Department
Maj. Gen. Keller E. Rockey	Commanding general, III Amphibious Corps
Lt. Col. Henry A. Rogan	Commanding officer, 31st Field Hospital
Franklin D. Roosevelt	Thirty-second president of the United States
Jean Jacques Rousseau	Eighteenth-century French philosopher
Maj. Gen. Clark L. Ruffner	U.S. Army Forces, Pacific Ocean Areas, chief of staff
Brig. Gen. Carl A. Russell	Chief planning officer, Operations Section, U.S. Army Forces, Pacific
Brig. Gen. Lawrence E. Schick	Tenth Army deputy chief of staff
Maj. Gen. Harry Schmidt	Commanding general, V Amphibious Corps
1st Lt. Glendon A. Schubert, Jr.	Tenth Army Signal Corps Section staff officer
Jack Service	Foreign Service officer and political adviser, U.S. Army mission to Chinese Communist Forces
Col. Virgil Shaw	Tenth Army assistant chief of staff for operations
Maj. Gen. Lemuel Shepherd, Jr.	Commanding general, 6th Marine Division
Rear Adm. Forrest P. Sherman	U.S. Pacific Fleet and Pacific Ocean Areas deputy chief of staff and chief, War Plans Division
Robert E. Sherrod	Time-Life correspondent
Shigemitsu Mamoru	Japanese foreign minister
Maj. Gen. Franklin C. Sibert	Commanding general, X Corps
Agnes Smedley	Freelance American journalist in China
Lt. Gen. Holland M. "Howlin' Mad" Smith	Commanding general, Fleet Marine Forces, Pacific
Brig. Gen. Joseph Smith	Deputy commander, Eighth Air Force
Brig. Gen. Oliver P. Smith	Tenth Army marine deputy chief of staff
Maj. Gen. Ralph Smith	Commanding general, 27th Infantry Division
Dr. Henry D. Smyth	Princeton University physicist

J. Buell Snyder	Pennsylvania member, U.S. House of Representatives
Lt. Gen. Carl "Tooey" Spaatz	Commanding general, U.S. Army Strategic Air Forces, Pacific
Archbishop Francis Spellman	Archbishop of New York and military vicar of the United States
Adm. Raymond A. Spruance	Commanding officer, Central Pacific Task Forces (designated Fifth Fleet when operating at sea under Spruance's command)
Marshal Joseph Stalin	Soviet premier
Brig. Gen. Rupert E. Starr	U.S. Army Forces, Pacific, antiaircraft artillery officer
Col. Albert K. Stebbins	Commanding officer, 105th Infantry Regiment, 27th Infantry Division
Archibald T. Steele	*Chicago Daily News* correspondent
David Stern III	Publisher, *Philadelphia Record*
Brig. Gen. George C. Stewart	U.S. Army Forces, Western Pacific, chief transportation officer
James Stewart	Columbia Broadcasting System correspondent
Capt. Charles R. Stienette, Jr.	Tenth Army Episcopalian chaplain
Benjamin Stilwell	Stilwell's son
Lt. Col. Joseph W. Stilwell, Jr.	Stilwell's son
Winifred Stilwell	Stilwell's wife
Commodore Earl Stone	U.S. Pacific Fleet and Pacific Ocean Areas assistant chief of staff for communications
Lt. Gen. Wilhelm D. Styer	Army Service Forces chief of staff
Lt. Gen. Daniel Sultan	Commander in chief, Burma-India Theater Command
Maj. Gen. Charles P. Summerall	Commanding general, V Corps, World War I
Lt. Gen. Richard K. Sutherland	U.S. Army Forces, Pacific, chief of staff
Maj. Gen. Leif "Jack" Sverdrup	Commanding general, Engineering Construction Command, U.S. Army Forces, Western Pacific
Maj. Gen. Innis Swift	Commanding general, I Corps
Maj. Gen. Joseph Swing	Commanding general, 11th Airborne Division
Joseph E. Talbot	Connecticut member, U.S. House of Representatives

Col. Benjamin Talley	Commanding officer, 1st Engineer Special Brigade, Tenth Army
Brig. Gen. Patrick H. Tansey	Army Service Command C chief engineer
Capt. Edwin A. Taylor	Navy officer assigned as Tenth Army signal officer
Brig. Gen. Charles F. Thomas	Commanding general, Island Command, Ie Shima
Lowell Thomas	Syndicated newspaper columnist
Vice Adm. John H. Towers	Deputy commander in chief, U.S. Pacific Fleet and Pacific Ocean Areas
Harry S. Truman	Thirty-third president of the United States
Maj. Gen. Karl Trunesdell	Commandant, Command and General Staff school
Col. Hiram B. Turner	Tenth Army finance officer
Vice Adm. Richmond Kelly Turner	Commanding officer, Joint Expeditionary Force (Task Force 51)
Lt. Gen. Lucian K. Truscott, Jr.	Commanding general, Fifth Army
Gen. Umezu Yoshijiro	Imperial General Staff representative at Japan's surrender
Lt. Gen. Ushijima Mitsuru	Commanding general, Japanese Thirty-second Army on Okinawa
Gen. Alexander A. Vandergrift	Commandant, U.S. Marine Corps
Lt. Gen. Jonathan "Skinny" Wainwright	General who surrendered U.S. Army Forces, Philippine Islands, to the Japanese in 1942
Maj. Gen. Fred Wallace	Commanding general, Island Command, Tenth Army
Col. Edward J. Walsh	Tenth Army judge advocate general
Maj. Gen. Wang Chih	Republic of China delegation member at Japan's surrender
Lt. Gen. Albert C. Wedemeyer	Commander in chief, China Theater Command
Col. F. B. Westervelt	Tenth Army surgeon
Lt. Gen. Raymond A. Wheeler	Deputy commander, Southeast Asia Theater Command
Maj. Gen. Charles White	Assistant commanding general, 7th Infantry Division, under Stilwell, and then his successor in 1941–42
Theodore White	Time-Life correspondent
Brig. Gen. Thomas D. White	Commanding general, Seventh Air Force

Lt. Gen. Enis Whitehead	Commanding general, Fifth Air Force
Col. Noble J. Wiley	Instructor during the 1930s at the Infantry School, Fort Benning, Georgia
Vice Adm. Theodore S. Wilkinson	Commanding officer, III Amphibious Force
Maj. Gen. Charles Willoughby	U.S. Army Forces, Pacific, assistant chief of staff for intelligence
Col. Walter S. Winn	Commanding officer, 105th Infantry Regiment, 27th Infantry Division
Maj. Gen. Kenneth B. Wolfe	Commanding general, XX Bomber Command
Capt. Edmund T. Wooldridge	Commanding officer, USS *New Jersey*
Maj. Gen. Louis E. Woods	Commanding general, 4th Marine Aircraft Wing
Rear Adm. Jerauld Wright	Commanding officer, Task Group 51.2
Maj. Gen. Paul B. Wurtsmith	Commanding general, Thirteenth Air Force
Maj. Richard Young	Stilwell's aide de camp

Notes

Preface

1. A. P. Jenkins, ed., "The Battle Diary of Lt. Gen. Simon Bolivar Buckner, 1945," *Scripsimus* 6 (Oct., 1997): 69–122; idem., "Lt. Gen. Simon Bolivar Buckner: Private Letters Relating to the Battle of Okinawa," *Ryudai Review of Euro-American Studies* 42 (Dec., 1997): 63–113.

Introduction

1. Among the many are: Benis M. Frank and Henry I. Shaw, *Victory and Occupation;* James H. and William M. Belote, *Typhoon of Steel: The Battle for Okinawa;* Gerald Astor, *Operation Iceberg: The Invasion and Conquest of Okinawa in World War II;* Roy Appleman, James M. Burns, Russell A. Gugeler, and John Stevens, *Okinawa: The Last Battle;* Samuel Eliot Morrison, *Victory in the Pacific, 1945;* George Feifer, *Tennozan: The Battle of Okinawa and the Atomic Bomb.*

2. Jenkins, ed., "Battle Diary," 69–122; idem., ed., "Lt. Gen. Simon Bolivar Buckner," 63–113.

3. Adrian R. Lewis, *Omaha Beach: A Flawed Victory,* 33, 57–58.

4. Joseph H. Alexander, *The Final Campaign: Marines in the Victory on Okinawa,* 21.

5. Robert W. Coakley and Richard M. Leighton, *Global Logistics and Strategy, 1943–1945,* 539–604; Frank and Shaw, *Victory and Occupation,* 72.

6. For an example of this argument, see the statement of Theodore White, who edited Stilwell's papers for publication (*Ladies' Home Journal,* Apr., 1948, 3).

7. *New York Herald Tribune,* May 2, 1945.

8. Frank and Shaw, *Victory and Occupation,* 725–26; Jeter A. Isely and Philip A. Crowl, *The U.S. Marines and Amphibious War: Its Theory, and Its Practices in the Pacific* (Princeton, 1951), 576–577; Appleman et al., *Okinawa,* 256–57.

9. Lt. Gen. Merwin Silverthorn, oral history, U.S. Marine Corps Historical Center, Washington Navy Yard, Washington, D.C., 339 (hereafter USMCHC).

10. Roger Willock, *Unaccustomed to Fear: A Biography of the Late General Roy S. Geiger, U.S.M.C.,* 285.

11. Lewis, *Omaha Beach,* 61.

12. Oliver P. Smith, "The Tenth Army and Okinawa," unpublished manuscript, n.d., folder 8, box 22, Oliver P. Smith Papers, Marine Corps University, Quantico, Va., 46.

13. Maj. Gen. Wilburt S. Brown Oral History, 198–99, 214–15; Gen. Vernon Megee, oral history, USMCHC, 64–66.

14. Allan R. Millett, *Semper Fidelis: The History of the United States Marine Corps,* 406–409, 426.

15. Alexander, *Final Campaign,* 21.

16. Millett, *Semper Fidelis,* 431.

17. Smith, "Tenth Army and Okinawa," 25; Lt. Gen. Robert L. Eichelberger to his wife, Feb. 16, 1945, in Jay Luvaas, ed., *Dear Miss Em: General Eichelberger's War in the Pacific, 1942–1945,* 217.

18. Smith, "Tenth Army and Okinawa," 7.

19. Triparte Military Meeting, July 24, 1945, *Foreign Relations of the United States: The Conference of Berlin, 1945,* 2:349.

20. Lloyd J. Graybar, "The Buckners of Kentucky," *Filson Club History Quarterly* 58, no. 2 (Apr., 1984): 202–14.

21. *New York Herald Tribune,* May 2, 1945.

22. Graybar, "Buckners of Kentucky," 212; Douglas Kinnard, *The Certain Trumpet: Maxwell Taylor and the American Experience in Vietnam,* 6–7.

23. Graybar, "Buckners of Kentucky," 202–14; Ronald H. Spector, *Eagle Against the Sun: The American War with Japan,* 178–82; Feifer, *Tennozan,* 237; Belote and Belote, *Typhoon of Steel,* 24.

24. Barbara W. Tuchman, *Stilwell and the American Experience in China, 1911–1945,* 9–20.

25. Ibid, 23–112.

26. Ed Cray, *General of the Army George C. Marshall: Soldier and Statesman* (New York, 1990), 282–83.

27. Tuchman, *Stilwell,* 275–81.

28. Ibid., 651–52.

Part I: Buckner

1. Adm. Chester W. Nimitz, commander in chief, U.S. Pacific Fleet and Pacific Ocean Areas; Adm. Raymond A. Spruance, commanding officer, Central Pacific Task Forces; Vice Adm. Richmond Kelly Turner, commanding officer, Joint Expeditionary Force (Task Force 51).

2. The "southern project" was an invasion of Taiwan, which Buckner opposed. He thought the supply requirements would be far too costly for the United States. Admiral Chester W. Nimitz, commander in chief, Pacific Fleet and Pacific Ocean Areas, accepted that logistical factors worked against trying to initiate this operation and he in turn convinced Adm. Ernest King, chief of naval operations, to abandon the proposal. (Grace Peron Hayes, *The History of the Joint Chiefs of Staff in World War II: The War Against Japan,* 617, 623).

3. Lt. Gen. Robert C. Richardson Jr., commanding general, U.S. Army Forces, Pacific Ocean Areas.

4. Rear Adm. Forrest P. Sherman, deputy chief of staff and head of the War Plans Division, U.S. Pacific Fleet and Pacific Ocean Areas.

5. Gen. of the Army George C. Marshall, U.S. Army chief of staff.

6. During the battle on Saipan, Lt. Gen. Holland M. Smith, a marine and commander of the V Amphibious Corps, relieved Maj. Gen. Ralph Smith as commanding general of the 27th Infantry Division, a substandard National Guard unit. The 27th Infantry Division occupied the middle of the American line and made the least amount of progress, creating a U-shaped salient that jeopardized the marine units on either side. This incident resulted in an interservice dispute because the two generals were from different services. Buckner was in charge of an army commission that investigated the relief of Ralph Smith (Spector, *Eagle Against the Sun,* 314–16; Harry A. Gailey, *'Howlin' Mad' vs. the Army: Conflict in Command, Saipan 1944*).

7. Adm. Ernest J. King, chief of naval operations.

8. Buckner obviously wrote this entry before learning that Admiral King had approved

the invasion of Okinawa during a conference with Admiral Nimitz in San Francisco from September 29–October 1, 1944 (Frank and Shaw, *Victory and Occupation,* 12–13).

9. Lt. Col. William S. Cowart, Buckner's aide de camp.

10. Brig. Gen. Elwyn D. Post, Tenth Army chief of staff.

11. Maj. Gen. Fred Wallace, commanding general, Island Command, Tenth Army.

12. Brig. Gen. Edgar Colladay.

13. Maj. Gen. Karl Trunesdell, commandant, Command and General Staff School.

14. Gen. Douglas MacArthur, commander in chief, Southwest Pacific Area Forces.

15. Brig. Gen. Morris C. Handwerk, commanding general, 53rd Antiaircraft Brigade, Tenth Army.

16. Brig. Gen. Cump Garvin, XXIV Corps chief of staff.

17. Maj. Gen. John R. Hodge, commanding general, XXIV Corps.

18. General of the Army Douglas MacArthur was commander in chief, Southwest Pacific Area (SWPA), a theater command separate from Nimitz's. The two commanders were rivals for supplies, equipment, and men. Buckner and the Tenth Army were in Nimitz's command.

19. Brig. Gen. Herman Feldman, executive assistant to the executive assistant to the assistant chief of staff, logistics, U.S. Pacific Fleet and Pacific Ocean Areas; and Brig. Gen. Francis A. Englehart, chief ordnance officer, U.S. Army Forces, Pacific Ocean Areas.

20. Maj. Gen. Roy S. Geiger, commanding general, III Amphibious Corps.

21. Lt. Gen. Albert C. Wedemeyer, commander in chief, China Theater Command; Vice Adm. Charles M. Cooke Jr., Admiral King's chief of staff; and Maj. Gen. William "Wild Bill" Donovan, director, Office of Strategic Services (OSS). Created during the war, the OSS recruited and trained spies and conducted espionage and covert operations.

22. Pres. Franklin D. Roosevelt; Soviet premier Marshal Joseph Stalin; and British prime minister Winston Churchill.

23. Brig. Gen. Kendall Fielder, assistant chief of staff, intelligence, U.S. Army Forces, Pacific Ocean Areas.

24. Vice Adm. John H. Towers, deputy commander in chief, U.S. Pacific Fleet and Pacific Ocean Areas. Emphasis in original.

25. Rear Adm. Arthur C. Davis, Fifth Fleet chief of staff; Vice Adm. Charles H. McMorris, U.S. Pacific Fleet and Pacific Ocean Areas chief of staff.

26. This abundance also made its way down to the troops in frontline fighting units. "We ate three good meals a day," one lieutenant from the 96th Infantry Division remarked. "We even had ice cream!" (Astor, *Operation Iceberg,* 129.)

27. Maj. Gen. Harry Schmidt, commanding general, V Amphibious Corps.

28. Maj. Gen. Graves B. Erskine, commanding general, 3rd Marine Division.

29. This is the text of a letter to Buckner's wife, Adele.

30. *Japan and the Japanese,* originally published as the April, 1944, issue of *Fortune* magazine; Fairfield Osborn, *The Pacific World: Its Vast Distances, Its Lands and the Life upon Them, and its Peoples.*

31. Adm. Thomas C. Kinkaid, commanding officer, Seventh Fleet.

32. Col. Benjamin Talley, commanding officer, 1st Engineer Special Brigade, Tenth Army.

33. Vice Adm. James L. Kaufman, commanding officer, Philippine Sea Frontier Naval Bases.

34. Maj. Gen. F. P. Mulcahy, commanding general, Tactical Air Force, Tenth Army.

35. Brig. Gen. Walter A. Dumas, Tenth Army assistant chief of staff for operations.

36. Maj. Gen. Andrew D. Bruce, commanding general, 77th Infantry Division; Rear Adm. Ingolf N. Kiland, commanding officer, Western Island Attack Group.

37. Douglas Southall Freeman, *Lee's Lieutenants: A Study in Command,* vol. 2, *Cedar Mountain to Chancellorsville.*

38. Rear Adm. J. L. Hall, commanding officer, Southern Attack Force (Task Force 55). Admiral Hall was the commander of Amphibious Force "O" at Omaha Beach on D-Day in Europe (Lewis, *Omaha Beach,* 228).

39. Maj. Gen. Archibald V. Arnold, commanding general, 7th Infantry Division; and Maj. Gen. James L. Bradley, commanding general, 96th Infantry Division.

40. Don Prior, Combined American Radio Networks correspondent.

41. Lt. Gen. Robert L. Eichelberger, commanding general, Eighth Army.

42. Lt. Gen. Noel Irwin. Buckner incorrectly identified the former British commander in India as a major general.

43. Brig. Gen. Clovis Byers, Eighth Army chief of staff.

44. Vice Adm. Marc Mitscher, commanding officer, Fast Carrier Force (Task Force 58).

45. On March 18, planes from the Fast Carrier Force (Task Force 58) struck airfields on Kyushu, one of the main Japanese islands. During counterstrikes, kamikaze planes hit the carrier *Wasp.* Another plane struck the *Franklin.* A ball of fire instantly replaced the carrier on the horizon. Afterward, observers said its flight deck resembled a "half-eaten Shredded Wheat biscuit." The ship became the mostly heavily damaged carrier to survive a kamikaze attack. See Samuel Eliot Morison, *Victory in the Pacific, 1945,* vol. 14, History of the United States Naval Operations in World War II, 94–98.

46. Buckner was incorrect. The casualties that the Army of Northern Virginia suffered at Gettysburg were slightly higher than those of the Marine V Amphibious Corps at Iwo Jima (Jenkins, ed., "Lt. Gen. Simon Bolivar Buckner," 74).

47. Douglas Southall Freeman, *Lee's Lieutenants: A Study in Command,* vol. 3, *Gettysburg to Appomattox.*

48. Col. Louis B. Ely, Tenth Army intelligence officer.

49. Vice Adm. William H. Blandy, commanding officer, Amphibious Support Force (Task Force 52).

50. Hiromichi Yahara, *The Battle for Okinawa,* trans. Roger Pineau and Masatoshi Uehara, 23.

51. Thomas B. Buell, *The Quiet Warrior: A Biography of Admiral Raymond A. Spruance,* 358.

52. Diary entry, Apr. 24, 1945, Col. Stevens/Sgt. Burns Okinawa Diary, folder 110–0.6, box 2942, Tenth Army Files, World War II Unit Operations Reports, Record Group 407, National Archives, College Park, Maryland.

53. Rear Adm. L. F. Reifsnider, commanding officer, Northern Attack Force (Task Force 53).

54. International News Service correspondent Howard Handelman.

55. According to Tenth Army's original plans, the second phase of combat operations included the capture of Ie Shima and northern Okinawa. The third phase was the seizure of additional minor islands and their development as air bases for use in the invasion of metropolitan Japan (Appleman et al., *Okinawa,* 17).

56. *Time-Life* correspondent Robert E. Sherrod.

57. On March 31, a kamikaze plane struck the USS *Indianapolis,* killing nine and wounding another twenty on board. A careless repair crew did more damage to the shaft, forcing the ship to leave the Okinawa area for extensive repairs (Morison, *Victory in the Pacific,* 138).

58. On April 6, the Japanese launched the first attack wave of Operation Ten-Go, the plan for Japan's aerial defense. The American armada suffered considerable damage that day. Seventeen ships were hit, six of which were sunk or scuttled (ibid., 181–98, 390).

59. The damage was worse than Buckner knew. Seventeen ships were hit. The two carrying ammunition were *Logan Victory* and *Hobbs Victory* (ibid., 196, 390).

60. MacArthur was given command of the force set to invade Japan. His SWPA command became the U.S. Army Forces, Pacific, which gave him authority over all army units in the Pacific (Paul P. Rogers, *The Bitter Years: MacArthur and Sutherland,* 276).

61. Morison, *Victory in the Pacific,* 199–209; Arthur J. Marder, Mark Jacobsen, and John Horsfield, *Old Friends, New Enemies: The Royal Navy and the Imperial Japanese Navy,* vol. 2, *The Pacific War, 1942–1945,* 432–38.

62. The Japanese scuttled the destroyers *Isokaze, Asashimo,* and *Kasumi* (Morison, *Victory in the Pacific,* 208).

63. Maj. Gen. Pedro A. Del Valle, commanding general, 1st Marine Division.

64. Maj. Gen. George W. Griner Jr., commanding general, 27th Infantry Division.

65. Frank and Shaw, *Victory and Occupation,* 45, 48, 51; Thomas M. Huber, *Japan's Battle for Okinawa, April–June, 1945,* Leavenworth Paper no. 18, 1–3, 6–8, 60, 63; Appleman et al., *Okinawa,* 101–30.

66. A week and a half into the campaign, Tenth Army was consuming artillery shells at a much faster pace than anticipated. Other factors such as the weather, shortages in merchant shipping, the limited capacity of the beaches to handle supply traffic, and a lack of experienced logistical personnel made it difficult for supply efforts to keep pace with the advance. Logistics, as a result, was a constraining force on offensive operations. The problem would only get worse (Frank and Shaw, *Victory and Occupation,* 71–72, 192, 240–41).

67. Col. Macey L. Dill, commanding officer, 382nd Infantry Regiment, 96th Infantry Division.

68. Maj. Frank Hubbard, Buckner's aide de camp.

69. The USS *Hopping* was struck by coastal battery fire on April 9 and suffered two killed and eighteen wounded (Morison, *Victory in the Pacific,* 391).

70. General Bruce proposed that Buckner use the 77th Infantry Division to launch an amphibious landing on the island's southern shore and have it march north, attacking the enemy positions from the rear. Buckner rejected this idea, concerned that it would complicate logistical efforts. This decision became controversial even before the battle ended.

71. Rear Adm. Calvin H. Cobb, commanding officer, Naval Forces Ryukyus.

72. The number of battleships Buckner cites here is incorrect. Only one battleship, the *Tennessee,* was hit. However, the figure he gives for destroyers on radar picket duty is correct. A kamikaze and a *baka* bomb struck the USS *Mannert L. Abele,* which sank in just five minutes. (Morison, *Victory in the Pacific,* 223–24, 391).

73. President Franklin D. Roosevelt died on April 12 in Georgia, which was April 13 in Okinawa. Buckner's statement was short: "We deeply mourn the loss of our Commander in Chief, who, like a good soldier, did his duty to the last and inspired us all to do ours. A nation at war must face many tragedies, but in our present grief let us renew our efforts to carry on toward the victory so brilliantly planned and gloriously initiated by our departed leader" (quoted in *New York Times,* Apr. 14, 1945).

74. The Motubu Peninsula was the only portion of northern Okinawa the Japanese defended strongly. There was a reason for this effort. Artillery positioned on the heights of the peninsula fired down onto Ie Shima, a small island just off the Okinawa coast. These guns denied the Americans operational use of the airfields they held on that island (Frank and Shaw, *Victory and Occupation,* 142).

75. Brig. Gen. William E. Crist, Tenth Army deputy commander for military government.

76. Unable to identify Dillon fully.

77. Brig. Gen. Claudius M. Easley, assistant commanding general, 96th Infantry Division

78. The USS *Sigsbee* suffered twenty-two killed and seventy-four wounded (Morison, *Victory in the Pacific,* 391).

79. Maj. Gen. Lemuel Shepherd Jr., commanding general, 6th Marine Division.

80. The ship Buckner is referring to is probably the USS *Bowers.* It was the only ship to lose its captain during the kamikaze attacks on April 16. The casualties were slightly worse

than Buckner recorded: forty-eight killed and fifty-six severely wounded (Morison, *Victory in the Pacific,* 238).

81. Unable to identify Fraser fully.

82. Appleman et al., *Okinawa,* 184–94.

83. The Japanese turned back the attack on April 19. There was no breakthrough at any location on the front. American units failed to gain any ground beyond the point where they encountered Japanese positions (ibid., 207).

84. Col. Albert K. Stebbins, commanding officer, 105th Infantry Regiment, 27th Infantry Division.

85. Col. Gerard W. Kelley, commanding officer, 165th Infantry Regiment, 27th Infantry Division.

86. When Tenth Army encountered strong points that it was unable to take, it would encircle the positions and allow reserve troops to reduce them. Buckner called this process "pinching out" the strong points (XXIV Corps Journal, May 10, 1945, entry, in Col. Stevens/ Sgt. Burns Okinawa Diary).

87. Col. Michael E. Halloran, commanding officer, 381st Infantry Regiment, 96th Infantry Division.

88. The battle for Ie Shima is best remembered for the death of Ernie Pyle, the popular syndicated newspaper columnist. See Appleman et al., *Okinawa,* 163.

89. Brig. Gen. William B. Bradford, assistant commanding general, 27th Infantry Division. Hodge assigned Bradford to lead a special task force to eliminate a pocket of Japanese troops in the town of Kakuzu, which was located behind the American lines and just west of their center. Bradford's task force attacked Kakuzu on April 24, only to discover that it was vacant. See *Appleman et al., Okinawa,* 244–47.

90. Gen. Alexander A. Vandergrift, commandant, United States Marine Corps.

91. Buckner had made similar comments about race before. He resisted the introduction of black troops in Alaska on the grounds that "Alaska is already plagued with problems of Indians who are half Swede, half Chinese, or half something else. Certainly the Army has a responsibility in not further complicating the population characteristics of the Territory by leaving a trail of new racial mixtures" (quoted in *Anchorage Times,* June 19, 1945).

92. Appleman et al., *Okinawa,* 248, 265.

93. Buckner reportedly dismissed Nimitz's complaints about progress by claiming ground combat was none of the navy's business. The admiral is alleged to have replied, "Yes, but ground though it may be, I'm losing a ship and a half a day. So if this line isn't moving within five days, we'll get someone here to move it so we can all get out from under these stupid air attacks" (E. B. Potter, *Nimitz,* 375).

94. Townsend Hoopes and Douglas Brinkley, *Driven Patriot: The Life and Times of James Forrestal,* 192–93.

95. A shortage of service troops was a major factor in Nimitz's decision to call off this effort. Tenth Army needed more support personnel than planners had anticipated. Many logistical units were helping engineers build durable roads on Okinawa and Buckner was facing the effects of U.S. logistical shortcomings (Frank and Shaw, *Victory and Occupation,* 241; Coakley and Leighton, *Global Logistics and Strategy,* 573).

96. Fleet Adm. William F. "Bull" Halsey, Spruance's successor as commander of the Central Pacific Task Forces.

97. On April 27, Buckner announced his decision to attach the 1st Marine Division to the XXIV Corps to replace the battered 96th Infantry Division (Frank and Shaw, *Victory and Occupation,* 197).

98. Gen. Courtney Hodges, commanding general, First Army; Gen. George S. Patton Jr., commanding general, Third Army.

99. This comment is in reference to the press coverage of two incidents in which Patton slapped soldiers showing no sign of physical wounds that he encountered in U.S. military hospitals on Sicily. These incidents resulted in his removal from command of the Seventh Army (see Carlo D'Este, *Patton: A Genius for War,* 521–63).

100. The supply ship full of ammunition that sank was the *Canada Victory.* The *Hutchins* and *Rathburne* suffered no casualties when hit by a kamikaze. On April 28, the *Pinkney* and the hospital ship *Comfort* were struck, suffering heavy casualties (Morison, *Victory in the Pacific,* 391).

101. Vice Adm. Jesse B. Oldendorf, commanding officer, Gunfire and Covering Force (Task Force 54); and Rear Adm. Morton L. Deyo, who replaced Oldendorf.

102. On April 29–30, the 77th Infantry Division replaced the 96th Infantry Division in the fight to take the Maeda escarpment, also known as Hacksaw Ridge (Appleman et al., *Okinawa,* 279).

103. Lt. Col. Henry A. Rogan, commanding officer, 31st Field Hospital.

104. Adolf Hitler, führer of Germany after combining the offices of Reich Chancellor and president; and former Italian premier Benito Mussolini.

105. Appleman et al., *Okinawa,* 282–89.

106. Brig. Gen. Charles E. Thomas, commanding general, Island Command, Ie Shima.

107. Unable to identify Dougherty fully.

108. Appleman et al., *Okinawa,* 289–302; Belote and Belote, *Typhoon of Steel,* 218–26, 230–34; *New York Times,* May 11, 1945.

109. Unable to identify Roney fully.

110. John Hersey's *A Bell for Adano* was a bestseller in 1945. An optimistic and ideological novel about the American occupation of Adano, a small town in Italy, the book won the Pulitzer Prize and was turned into a movie of the same name starring William Bendix, Richard Conte, John Hodiak, Gene Tierney, and Henry Morgan in 1945.

111. Vice Adm. Theodore S. Wilkinson, commanding officer, III Amphibious Force.

112. Buckner joked that "it might be lots more fun killing them rapidly, but if you want to prolong the enjoyment you take a little longer." He turned serious and said it would be "suicidal" to employ American power in direct, open assaults (*New York Times,* May 11, 1945).

113. Appleman et al., *Okinawa,* 311–59.

114. Lt. Gen. Walter Krueger, commanding general, Sixth Army.

115. At a meeting of his staff, Buckner said that the failure to take more ground was a lack of coordination among the various units in the two corps, allowing the Japanese artillery to shift where and when needed (diary entry, May 12, 1945, Col. Stevens/Sgt. Burns Okinawa Diary).

116. With a base about 50 yards from Okinawa's eastern shore of and a peak that rises 476 feet above the coastal plain and dominates the surrounding terrain, Conical Hill was the anchor of the Japanese line in the east (Appleman et al., *Okinawa,* 351).

117. Col. Edwin T. May, commanding officer, 383rd Infantry Regiment, 96th Infantry Division.

118. Eichelberger to his wife, Mar. 4, 1945, in Luvaas, ed., *Dear Miss Em,* 230; diary entry, Mar. 31, 1945, in Weldon Rhoads, *Flying MacArthur to Victory,* 372.

119. According to newspaper accounts, Buckner stated: "It has been admitted by Japanese leaders that our possession of Okinawa spells defeat for Japan. Every effort of Japan to bring aid to its doomed and dwindling garrison in the south has met with disastrous failure" (quoted in *New York Times,* May 21, 1945).

120. Maj. Gen. Hugh Casey, chief engineer officer, U.S. Army Forces, Pacific. Casey was

a member of MacArthur's personal clique and, since this message is similar to others the theater commander made in the past, it was probably relayed correctly.

121. Hiromichi Yahara, *Battle for Okinawa,* 81–83.

122. Rear Adm. Jerauld Wright, commanding officer, Task Group 51.2; Rear Adm. Richard L. Connolly.

123. Commodore Carl "Squeaky" Anderson, Alaskan cannery owner and U.S. Navy officer.

124. Elements of the 6th Marine Division occupied Naha, making it at that time the largest city ever taken by the Marine Corps (Frank and Shaw, *Victory and Occupation,* 276).

125. The report was in error. There were no kamikazes attacks on May 26 (Morison, *Victory in the Pacific,* 392).

126. Lt. Gen. John DeWitt, commanding general, Western Defense Command. Scipio Africanus, also known as Publius Cornelius Scipio or Scipio Africanus Major, was a Roman general who defeated Hannibal at the battle of Zama in 202 B.C.

127. The USS *Braine* and *Anthony* were hit by kamikazes while at Radar Picket 5 off the eastern coast. On fire, the *Anthony* went dead in the water and was towed out of the area (Morison, *Victory in the Pacific,* 260).

128. A battalion of the 1st Marine Division captured Shuri Castle, until that time the headquarters of the Japanese Thirty-second Army. The marines took the castle with the authorization of their division commander, Maj. Gen. Pedro A. Del Valle, even though the objective was in the 77th Infantry Division's operations zone. Del Valle informed Maj. Gen. Andrew D. Bruce, the 77th Division's commander, of his decision only minutes before the marines took the castle. Bruce, who had a prearranged artillery and air strike scheduled to hit the castle, had his staff work frantically to call off the barrage in time (Frank and Shaw, *Victory and Occupation,* 286; Appleman et al., *Okinawa,* 396–97).

129. On May 27, Buckner issued an order to his corps commanders: "Indications point to possible enemy retirement to new defensive positions with possible counteroffensive against our forces threatening his flank. Initiate without delay strong and unrelenting pressure to ascertain probable intentions and keep him off balance. Enemy must not repeat not be permitted to establish himself securely on new position with only nominal interference" (quoted in Frank and Shaw, *Victory and Occupation,* 278).

130. Buckner held to this optimistic view for several more days. The Japanese had withdrawn their forces in time to form a new defensive line on the Yaeju-Dake–Yuza-Dake escarpment, a giant coral wall on the southern tip of the island (Appleman et al., *Okinawa,* 422–25).

131. Karl C. Dod, *The Corps of Engineers: The War Against Japan,* 648–49, 658–59; Frank and Shaw, *Victory and Occupation,* 241.

132. Tenth Army was unable to get sufficient supplies to the frontline troops via the initial landing beaches. Shore party operations expanded to include new beach areas, but the American assault on Japanese defensive positions required more supplies than could be handled (Frank and Shaw, *Victory and Occupation,* 241).

133. The Iheya Islands are located north of the Motubu Peninsula and northeast of Ie Shima. The Americans wanted to take the islands to establish a radar station, which would replace some of the ships on picket duty (ibid., 348).

Part II: Buckner and Stilwell

1. Tuchman, *Stilwell,* 651–62.

2. Brig. Gen. Oliver P. Smith, Tenth Army marine deputy chief of staff.

3. Maj. Gen. F. A. Heileman, director of supplies, U.S. Army Ground Forces; Brig. Gen.

Frank Dorn (Buckner incorrectly identified Dorn as a major general); and Brig. Gen. William Bergin, deputy chief of staff, U.S. Army Ground Forces. Bergin later transferred to Tenth Army and served as Stilwell's chief of staff.

4. At the end of June, construction and engineer units were maintaining 340 miles of roads on the island. The more important roads were expanded to carry two lanes of traffic (Dod, *Corps of Engineers,* 659).

5. After receiving only thirty-six hours advance notice, elements of the 6th Marine Division made an amphibious landing in the early morning hours. The units crossed the open sea in front of the Naha harbor mouth and landed on the Oroku Peninsula on the south side of the harbor across from Naha (Frank and Shaw, *Victory and Occupation,* 299, 304–307).

6. Unable to identify Captain Miller fully.

7. Col. Robert H. Booth, 7th Infantry Division chief of staff; Brig. Gen. Joseph L. Ready, assistant commanding general, 7th Infantry Division.

8. Lt. Col. James H. Keller, executive officer, 32nd Infantry Regiment, 7th Infantry Division.

9. Col. John "Mickey" Finn, commanding officer, 32nd Infantry Regiment, 7th Infantry Division.

10. Col. Roy A. Green, commanding officer, 184th Infantry Regiment, 7th Infantry Division; Lt. Col. Delbert Bjork, commanding officer, 184th Infantry Regiment, 7th Infantry Division.

11. Col. Francis Pachler, commanding officer, 17th Infantry Regiment, 7th Infantry Division.

12. Rear Adm. Carl H. Cotter, director, Pacific Division, Bureau of Yards and Docks, U.S. Navy.

13. Unable to identify De Conter fully.

14. Col. William C. Bentley Jr., Stilwell's pilot.

15. Brig. Gen. Louis R. Jones, assistant commanding general, 1st Marine Division.

16. The marines took the island of Ono Yama in the middle of Naha Harbor to use as a supply depot. They had to wait to build the bridge until they neutralized the heavy machine guns the Japanese on the Oroku Peninsula were using to puncture and sink the pontoons on the bridge (Frank and Shaw, *Victory and Occupation,* 307).

17. Sgt. Sid Meyers, staff writer, 96th Infantry Division newsletter.

18. Maj. Gen. Charles White, assistant division commander, 7th Infantry Division, when Stilwell was the commanding officer, and his successor from 1941 to 1942.

19. Stilwell was quoted in the 96th Infantry Division's newsletter as saying: "The 96th Division has done a magnificent job. . . . They are a damn good slugging outfit and have a damn good commanding general." He also commented on the battle conditions: "Mud is bad anyplace, but where caterpillars and bulldozers sink and spin their tracts, it's damn bad" ("The Deadeye Dispatch," June 8, 1945, folder: Clippings 1945, box 37, Joseph W. Stilwell Papers, Hoover Institute, Stanford University, Stanford, Calif. [hereafter Stilwell Papers]).

20. Col. Stephen S. Hamilton, commanding officer, 307th Infantry Regiment, 77th Infantry Division.

21. Maj. Gen. Leo Donovan, U.S. Army Ground Forces operations officer.

22. *New York Herald Tribune,* June 12, 1946; *New York Times,* June 12, 1946; *New York Sun,* June 12, 1946.

23. Maj. Gen. LeRoy Hunt, commanding general, I Corps.

24. The naval detachment on Okinawa was not under General Ushijima's command. Rear Admiral Minoru Ota, the naval base commander, refused Ushijima's requests to join forces. He insisted on making a last stand on the Oroku Peninsula (Hiromichi Yahara, *Battle*

for Okinawa, 125–26; Frank and Shaw, *Victory and Occupation,* 321–23). This episode is an example of divided command, although the translators and editors of Col. Hiromichi Yahara's memoirs call it an example of consensus management breaking down.

25. Appleman et al., *Okinawa,* 463; *New York Journal-American,* June 12, 1945; Hiromichi Yahara, *Battle for Okinawa,* 136.

26. Col. Roy Hillyer, Tenth Army Baptist chaplain.

27. Rear Adm. Richard E. Byrd, noted explorer.

28. Brig. Gen. Lawrence E. Shick, Tenth Army deputy chief of staff.

29. *New York Herald Tribune,* May 29, 1945. Lawrence's syndicated column can be found in either the *New York Sun,* May 30, 1945; June 4, 1945, or the *Washington Evening Star,* May 30, 1945; June 4, 1945; *Washington Sunday Star,* June 17, 1945. Lawrence continued to demand an investigation long after the end of the war (*Washington Evening Star,* Jan. 10, 1946).

30. Rear Admiral Minoru Ota committed suicide when the marines overran his position (Hiromichi, *Battle for Okinawa,* 125–26; Frank and Shaw, *Victory and Occupation,* 321–23).

31. *New York Herald Tribune,* June 18, 1945. For the lack of coverage in other major publications see the following publications for June 18, 1945: *Washington Evening Star, New York Times, Washington Post, Chicago Daily Tribune,* and the *Los Angeles Times.* For Nimitz's comments, see *New York Times,* June 17, 1945; *Washington Post,* June 4, 1945; Richard Kluger, *The Paper: The Life and Death of the New York Herald Tribune,* 373; *New York Herald Tribune,* June 17 and 18, 1945; Clifton La Bree, *The Gentle Warrior: Oliver Price Smith, USMC,* 89.

32. Eisenhower to Marshall, cable, Apr. 26, 1945; Marshall to Eisenhower, cable, Apr. 27, 1945; Eisenhower to Marshall, Apr. 27, 1945, in Alfred D. Chandler, ed., *The Papers of Dwight D. Eisenhower,* vol. 4, *The War Years,* 2647–48, 2651–52; Omar N. Bradley and Clay Blair, *A General's Life,* 435.

33. Lt. Gen. Daniel Sultan, commander in chief, Burma-India Theater Command

34. The GCM reference is to General Marshall.

35. Buckner's aide, who was also wounded by the artillery round, offered a different version. He told reporters that Buckner never regained consciousness (*New York Journal-American,* June 19, 1945). Several other sources make it clear that Hubbard suffered some light wounds. These, along with Buckner's death, traumatized him, making it difficult to accept his account. See Astor, *Operation Iceberg,* 407; Brig. Gen. Fred Beans, oral history, USMCHC, 90, 93; and J. Fred Haley, "The Death of Gen. Simon Bolivar Buckner," *Marine Corps Gazette,* Nov., 1982, 100–105.

Part III: Stilwell

1. Lt. Gen. Barney Giles, commanding general, Central Pacific Air Forces.

2. Maj. Gen. Clark L. Ruffner, chief of staff, U.S. Army Forces, Pacific Ocean Areas. Emphasis and question marks in original.

3. D. Clayton James, *The Years of MacArthur,* vol. 2, *1941–1945,* 735–36; MacArthur to Stilwell, June 20, 1945, and Nimitz to Stilwell, June 22, 1945, folder A-27 1945, box 28a, Stilwell Papers.

4. Maj. Gen. Leo Donovan, the Army Ground Forces operations officer; unable to identify Ty fully.

5. Winifred Stilwell, Stilwell's wife.

6. Sgt. Jules Raynaud, Stilwell's cook.

7. Lt. Col. Joseph W. Stilwell Jr., Stilwell's son.

8. Unable to identify Hightower fully.

9. Drew Pearson, syndicated newspaper columnist; Maj. Gen. Patrick Hurley, U.S. ambassador to China

10. Jack Service, Foreign Service officer and political adviser of the U.S. Army mission to Chinese Communist Forces.

11. Lowell Thomas, syndicated newspaper columnist.

12. Brig. Gen. Wentworth Goss, assistant plans officer, U.S. Pacific Fleet and Pacific Ocean Areas; Brig. Gen. Harold C. Mandell, assistant to the chief, Plans Section, U.S. Pacific Fleet and Pacific Ocean Areas.

13. Appleman et al., *Okinawa,* 470–71.

14. Maj. Gen. Louis E. Woods, commanding general, 4th Marine Aircraft Wing.

15. Maj. Gen. Fred Wallace, commanding general, Island Command, Tenth Army; Commodore Andrew G. Bissett, commander, Island Command Construction Troops; Brig. Gen. George J. Nold, Tenth Army engineer officer.

16. Operation Coronet was the code name for the plan to invade the Tokyo plain in March, 1946. The planned invasion force consisted of the First, Eighth, and Tenth Armies (John Ray Skates, *The Invasion of Japan: Alternative to the Bomb,* 199–203).

17. Geiger was promoted to lieutenant general and assigned to command the Fleet Marine Forces, Pacific (Frank and Shaw, *Victory and Occupation,* 365 n).

18. Maj. Gen. Gilbert X. Cheves, island commander, Tenth Army.

19. Maj. Gen. Lewis Pick, engineer responsible for the construction of the Stilwell Road.

20. Commodore Matthew Perry, nineteenth-century American naval officer responsible for establishing diplomatic relations with Japan.

21. Rear Adm. Morton L. Ring; Brig. Gen. Herman Feldman.

22. Clippings in the Stilwell Papers include news items from the *New York Journal-American,* June 24, 1945; *Detroit News,* June 21, 1945; *Monterey Peninsula Herald,* 21, 1945; *Washington Times-Herald,* June 21–22, 1945; *Ohio State Journal,* June 23, 1945; *PM,* June 22, 1945. See also *New York Times* and *New York Herald Tribune* editorials of June 22, 1945.

23. Unable to identify Filduncan fully.

24. Unable to identify Heinrichs and Duffy fully.

25. Rear Adm. Fred D. Kirtland.

26. Capt. Donald M. Mackey, Kirtland's executive officer.

27. Capt. Paul M. Albright, navy doctor.

28. Col. Macey Dill, 382nd Infantry Regiment commander.

29. Col. (Dr.) F. B. Westervelt, Tenth Army surgeon; unable to identify Dr. Phinney fully.

30. Brig. Gen. Edwin H. Randle, assistant commanding general, 77th Infantry Division.

31. Unable to identify McDaniels and Rasmussen fully.

32. Maj. Gen. Keller E. Rockey, commanding general, III Amphibious Corps.

33. Unable to identify Ninkins fully.

34. Col. Donald Ashton, Tenth Army quartermaster; Col. Joseph L. Knipper, Tenth Army engineer; and Col. Robert W. Daniels, Tenth Army ordnance officer.

35. Hodge to Stilwell, June 30, 1945, folder A-27 1945, box 28a, Stilwell Papers. Emphasis in original.

36. Unable to identify Major Untermayer fully.

37. Kenneth McCaleb, International News Service correspondent.

38. Lt. Col. John Carlton, Tenth Army Services of Supply officer.

39. *San Francisco News,* July 5, 1945; *New York Times,* July 5, 1945.

40. "Military Government Detachment C-1 Okinawa History of Operations," folder: Island Command Okinawa Background Material and interviews, 1945, box 5–1, Ryukyu Papers, Military History Institute, Carlisle Barracks, Pa.

41. Col. Richard Ovenshine, 27th Infantry Division chief of staff; Brig. Gen. William B. Bradford, the 27th's assistant division commander, whom Stilwell incorrectly identifies here as an assistant chief of staff; and Brig. Gen. Charles S. Ferrin, the division's artillery commander.

42. Lt. Col. Joseph T. Hart, commanding officer, 165th Infantry Regiment, 27th Infantry Division; Col. Walter S. Winn, commanding officer, 105th Infantry Regiment, 27th Infantry Division.

43. Gen. George C. Kenney, commander, Far East Air Forces; Lt. Gen. Barney Giles, commander, Central Pacific Air Forces; Maj. Gen. Clayton L. Bissell, assistant chief of staff, intelligence, U.S. Army Air Forces; Maj. Gen. Fred Wallace, commander, Island Command, Tenth Army; and Maj. Gen. Donald R. Hutchinson, commander, 308th Bomb Wing.

44. Col. Edward J. Walsh, Col. Milo Buchanan, Col. Edmund Edwards, Capt. Edwin A. Taylor (a navy officer), Col. Donald Ashton, and Col. James Garfield.

45. Maj. Gen. Frank Merrill; Col. John P. Condon, U.S. Marine Corps; Maj. Thomas Wells; Maj. John Grindley; and Col. Paul Jones—all staff officers who had served with Stilwell in China.

46. Lt. Col. Andre L. Violante.

47. Unable to identify McMillan fully.

48. Maj. Gen. Lemuel Shepherd Jr., commanding general; Brig. Gen. William T. Clement, assistant commanding general.

49. Maj. Richard Young, Stilwell's aide de camp.

50. Maj. Gen. Junius Jones, air inspector, Headquarters, U.S. Army Air Forces.

51. Brig. Gen. Charles E. Thomas, commanding general, and Lt. Col. Leonard J. Greely, chief of staff, Island Command, Ie Shima.

52. Frederick Palmer, journalist, author, and historian.

53. Met with more members of the Tenth Army staff: Col. Maurice Fitzgerald, provost marshal; Col. Kirby Green, assistant chief of staff, intelligence; Col. Hiram B. Turner, finance officer; Col. Arthur Pulsifer, communications officer; and Lt. Col. John L. Heilman, post exchange officer.

54. William Matthews, editor and publisher of the *Arizona Daily Star,* and David Stern III, publisher of the *Philadelphia Record.*

55. Air Vice Marshal Sir Hugh Lloyd, senior Royal Air Force officer in the Pacific theater.

56. Brig. Gen. Thomas D. White, commanding general, Seventh Air Force.

57. Unable to identify Pitts fully.

58. Col. Elmer J. Gibson, Tenth Army ordnance officer.

59. Maj. Carl Arnold, Stilwell's aide de camp.

60. Rear Adm. John D. Price, commanding officer, Advanced Naval Operating Base, Ryukyus.

61. Rear Adm. Calvin H. Cobb, commander of naval forces in the Ryukyus.

62. Lt. Gen. Enis Whitehead, commanding general, Fifth Air Force.

63. Lt. Gen. Robert C. Richardson Jr., commanding general, U.S. Army Forces, Pacific Ocean Areas.

64. Brig. Gen. Orval Cook, commanding general, 7th Air Service Area Command.

65. Lt. Gen. James H. Doolittle, commanding general, and Brig. Gen. Joseph Smith, deputy commanding general, Eighth Air Force.

66. Lt. Gen. Carl "Tooey" Spaatz, commanding general, U.S. Army Strategic Air Forces, Pacific.

67. Stilwell to Marshall, n.d., folder: 1945 A-27, box 28A, Stilwell Papers.

68. Lida Mayo, *The Ordnance Department: On Beachhead and Battlefront,* 463.

69. Brig. Gen. David H. Blakelock, assistant chief of staff, Logistics, Tenth Army.

70. Lt. Gen. Robert C. Richardson, Jr., commanding general, U.S. Army Forces, Pacific Ocean Areas.

71. Undersecretary of War Robert Patterson.

72. Col. Virgil Shaw, assistant chief of staff, operations, Tenth Army.

73. Unable to identify Morris fully. Emphasis in original.

74. Brig. Gen. William A. Borden, director, New Development Division, War Department General Staff. Borden was on Okinawa to inform unit commanders about new self-propelled artillery. Stilwell told Borden he wanted those weapons as well as more Sherman tanks (Mayo, *Ordnance Department,* 473).

75. Col. Melvin Maas, U.S. Marine Corps Reserve, and former member, U.S. House of Representatives.

76. Ed Izac, California member, and Joseph R. Farrington, Hawaii delegate, U.S. House of Representatives.

77. Unable to identify Blake fully.

78. Maj. Gen. Frank Merrill became Tenth Army chief of staff. Capt. Elbert V. Higgins was a staff officer in the Chief of Staff Section.

79. GCM is George C. Marshall.

80. CKS is Chiang Kai-shek.

81. Adm. The Lord Louis Mountbatten, commander in chief, Southeast Asia Theater Command. Stilwell had been Mountbatten's deputy even though Stilwell was commander of forces in the China-Burma-India theater. Relations between the two quickly became strained and never improved (Tuchman, *Stilwell,* 550, 557–59, 570, 573, 578, 605).

82. Unable to identify Caucox fully.

83. Brig. Gen. John P. Willey.

84. PJ is Col. Paul Jones.

85. Brig. Gen. Francis H. Griswold, Eighth Air Force chief of staff.

86. Maj. Gen. William F. Marquat, chief antiaircraft officer, commander in chief, U.S. Army Forces, Pacific, and commanding general, 14th Antiaircraft Command; Brig. Gen. Morris C. Handwerk, commanding general, 53rd Antiaircraft Brigade, Tenth Army; and Brig. Gen. Henry B. Holmes Jr., artillery officer, U.S. Army Forces, Middle Pacific.

87. Theodore White, *Time-Life* correspondent.

88. Emphasis in original. These two quotes are from separate sections of eighteenth-century French philosopher Jean Jacques Rousseau's *On the Social Contract.* Stilwell was most likely quoting these passages from memory, but his version is close in language to the most recent English-language translation and accurately represents Rousseau's views toward democracy. The most recent translation of the first passage is: "If there were a people of Gods, it would govern itself democratically. Such a perfect government is not suited to men." The second passage is: "In short, it is the best and most natural order for the wisest to govern the multitude, as long as it is certain that they govern for its benefit and not their own" (Roger D. Masters and Christopher Kelly, eds., *The Collected Writings of Rousseau,* vol. 4, trans. Judith R. Bush, Roger D. Masters, and Christopher Kelly, 174–75).

89. M.Sgt. Fred "The Man" Friendly, *CBI Roundup* correspondent.

90. Maj. Gen. Clements McMullen, commanding general, Far East Army Service Command.

91. Maj. Gen. Stephen G. Henry, chief of the War Department Personnel Division; Maj. Gen. Idwal Edwards, chief of the War Department Military Intelligence Division.

92. Paul V. McNutt, chairman of the War Manpower Commission.

93. During a trip by plane Stilwell lost his campaign hat, which he had owned for twenty

years. According to press accounts, Cpl. Edward P. Donahue of Cleveland, Ohio, waded two hundred yards into the ocean to retrieve the hat and accepted the cash. See *New York Times,* Aug. 5, 1945; *New York Herald Tribune,* Aug. 5, 1945; *Washington Times Herald,* Aug. 5, 1945; *Chicago Daily Tribune,* Aug. 5, 1945; *Chicago Daily News,* Aug. 5, 1945; *Philadelphia Inquirer,* Aug. 5, 1945; *New York Journal-American,* Aug. 5, 1945; *Chicago Herald American,* Aug. 5, 1945; *New York Mirror,* Aug. 5, 1945.

94. Maj. Gen. James T. Moore, commander, aircraft, Fleet Marine Force, Pacific.

95. Unable to identify Struthers fully.

96. Unable to identify Labell fully; Brig. Gen. William Ritchie, chief, Southwest Pacific Operations Division, U.S. War Department.

97. Commodore Earl Stone, assistant chief of staff, communications, U.S. Pacific Fleet and Pacific Ocean Areas.

98. Maj. Gen. Paul B. Wurtsmith, commanding general, Thirteenth Air Force.

99. Eichelberger to his wife, Aug. 15, 1945, in Luvaas, ed., *Dear Miss Em,* 300; Skates, *Invasion of Japan,* 202–203, 227–32.

100. Col. Ashton Haynes, Tenth Army judge advocate general.

101. Brig. Gen. Rupert E. Starr, antiaircraft artillery officer, U.S. Army Forces, Pacific.

102. Brig. Gen. Robert G. Gard, artillery commander, 96th Infantry Division.

103. Lt. Gen. Raymond A. Wheeler, Stilwell's successor as deputy commander, Southeast Asia Theater Command; Col. Fabius H. Kohloss, Wheeler's chief of staff; and Brig. Gen. William H. Holcombe. Unable to identify Lansing fully.

104. Brig. Gen. Frank Greer, War Department Bureau of Public Relations.

105. Brig. Gen. Paul F. Yount.

106. Lt. Gen. Wilhelm D. Styer, Army Service Forces chief of staff.

107. Nancy Easterbrook, Stilwell's daughter.

108. Unable to identify Boland fully.

109. Brig. Gen. Julius O. Adler, vice president and treasurer of the *New York Times;* John S. Knight, publisher of the *Chicago Daily News;* and John Cowles Sr., publisher of the *Minneapolis Star.*

110. Unable to identify Doc Gibson fully.

111. Col. Joseph I. Martin, Tenth Army surgeon.

112. Stilwell's concern about rumors was well founded. When he eventually went into the hospital, his disappearance from public sight became the subject of much speculation (Eichelberger to wife, Aug. 15, 1945, in Luvaas, ed., *Dear Miss Em,* 300).

113. Maj. Raymond T. Eyestone, staff officer, Chief of Staff Section, Tenth Army.

114. Benjamin Stilwell, Stilwell's son.

115. Maj. Gen. Kenneth B. Wolfe, commanding general, XX Bomber Command.

116. Question mark in original text. Stilwell was unsure of the spelling for Maj. Gen. Victor Bertrandias, commanding general, Okinawa Air Depot.

117. It is difficult to identify Timberlake from the information available. There were many officers in the U.S. Army named Timberlake, including three brigadier generals.

118. Lt. Gen. Richard K. Sutherland, U.S. Army Forces, Pacific, chief of staff.

119. "Peanut" is his nickname for Chiang Kai-shek, president of the Republic of China.

120. Harry S. Truman, president of the United States.

121. Stilwell; Lt. Gen. Alexander "Sandy" Patch, Seventh Army commander; Lt. Gen. Lucian K. Truscott, Fifth Army commander. See the editor's comments in the June 19 entry to understand better the course of events leading to Stilwell's selection.

122. CKS is Chiang Kai-shek; Carl is Maj. Carl Arnold, Stilwell's aide de camp. Stilwell refused the award while still in China, but a spokesman for the Chinese cabinet claimed he

accepted the award after his return to the United States (Tuchman, *Stilwell,* 644; *New York Times,* Aug. 9, 1945).

123. Maj. Gen. Stephen Chamberlin, operations chief; Brig. Gen. Matthew Gunner, deputy chief of staff; Brig. Gen. Carl A. Russell, chief planning officer; and Maj. Gen. Charles Willoughby, assistant chief of staff, intelligence, U.S. Army Forces, Pacific.

124. Col. Oliver I. Holeman, Maj. Paul E. LaDue, and Brig. Gen. Louis W. Maddox, fiscal director, U.S. Army Forces, Pacific.

125. Gen. of the Army Henry H. Arnold, commander of the Army Air Forces, wanted to send one last combat flight exceeding more than a thousand planes over Tokyo. On the night of August 14–15, a total of 1,014 aircraft flew one last mission (Wesley Frank Craven and James Lea Cate, ed., *The Army Air Forces in World War II,* vol. 5, *The Pacific: Matterhorn to Nagasaki, June 1944 to August 1945,* 732–33).

126. Emphasis in original. An announcement to that effect was released to the press. See *New York Times,* Aug. 17, 1945.

127. Maj. Gen. Matthew B. Ridgway, commanding general, XVIII Airborne Corps.

128. Gen. Sir Thomas Blamey, Australian representative at Japan's surrender.

129. CKS is Chiang Kai-shek.

130. Maj. Gen. Joseph Swing, commanding general, 11th Airborne Division.

131. Unable to identify Captains Faust and Miller fully; CWO John Hughes.

132. Commodore Frank Talbot, naval officer attached to Tenth Army.

133. Maj. John M. Davenport, staff officer, Judge Advocate General Section, Tenth Army.

134. Frederick "Fritz" Opper, editor of the Shanghai *Evening Post and Mercury.*

135. Adm. Adolphus Andrews.

136. Unable to identify Mr. Gibson fully.

137. Col. Frederick Barrows, editor of *Military Review.*

138. CKS is Chiang Kai-shek. In a letter to his wife, Eichelberger wrote: "After we got settled I went down to see Joe Stilwell, who is sorry as the dickens because he is not going to be allowed to go to China, although one of his corps will go but not under his command. He says he doesn't blame Chiang Kai-shek so much for objecting to his coming but he blames our authorities of allowing Chiang to keep him out of Manchuria and Korea when China has no control over those countries" (Eichelberger to wife, Aug. 25, 1945, in Luvaas, ed., *Dear Miss Em,* 305–306).

139. Unable to identify Doc Ayers fully.

140. Rear Adm. Calvin Durgin, commanding officer, Task Group 77.4.

141. Brig. Gen. Patrick H. Tansey, chief engineer, Army Service Command C; Brig. Gen. Robinson E. Duff, commanding general, Service Command C.

142. This event occurred at the beginning of a *This is the Army* soldier show and, according to a reporter for the *Newark Evening News* then stationed on the island as a sergeant, Stilwell "completely won [the] huge audience." He quoted Stilwell as saying: "You guys came to see a movie and not to hear me talk. Okay. I won't waste your time with a lot of baloney. Instead I'll raffle off a bottle of Scotch." The crowd cheered and became even more enthusiastic when he declared the first winner, the lieutenant, ineligible. There was much resentment in the ranks at the time about supply policies that sent liquor to officers' messes while enlisted men were lucky to get a can of beer (*Newark Evening News,* Oct. 15, 1946).

143. Kay Kyser, bandleader and radio personality who often played himself in wartime films.

144. Bishop Harry S. Kennedy, Catholic religious leader.

145. Maj. Gen. Leif "Jack" Sverdrup, commanding general, Engineering Construction Command, U.S. Army Forces, Western Pacific. Sverdrup's main duty at this time was over-

seeing the transfer of engineering command headquarters from Manila to Tokyo (Gregory M. Franzwa and William J. Ely, *Leif Sverdrup: Engineering Soldier at His Best,* 239–40).

146. *Chicago Daily News* correspondent Archibald T. Steele, Columbia Broadcasting System correspondent James Stewart, and Time-Life correspondent Theodore White.

147. J. Buell Snyder, Pennsylvania; Clair Engel, California; Joseph E. Talbot, Connecticut; Clifford P. Case, New Jersey; Joe Hendricks, Florida; and W. F. Norrell, Arkansas, members, U.S. House of Representatives.

148. RCR referred to here and in subsequent entries is Lt. Gen. Robert C. Richardson Jr., commanding general, U.S. Army Forces, Pacific Ocean Areas.

149. Brig. Gen. Thomas F. Farrell, deputy commander, Manhattan Engineer District.

150. Dorn had become the artillery commander for the 11th Airborne Division. On August 30, about thirty soldiers from that division, accompanied by many reporters, were the first Americans to arrive in Japan (Robert W. Desmond, *Tides of War: World News Reporting, 1940–1945,* 443).

151. Lt. Gen. Jonathan "Skinny" Wainwright, the general who surrendered U.S. Army forces in the Philippines to the Japanese in 1942.

152. Brig. Gen. George C. Stewart, chief transportation officer, U.S. Army Forces, Western Pacific.

153. On August 12, the War Department released an official study on the development of the atomic bomb. Henry D. Smyth, a Princeton University physicist wrote *General Account of the Development of Methods of Using Atomic Energy for Military Purposes, 1940–1945,* which quickly became known as the "Smyth Report." Princeton University Press published the study a month later as *Atomic Energy for Military Purposes* (Richard Rhodes, *Dark Sun: The Making of the Hydrogen Bomb,* 182, 215).

154. Dr. J. Robert Oppenheimer, director, Los Alamos Laboratory.

155. Sir John Anderson, director of British atomic bomb research; Dr. Frederic Joliott, French physicist and Nobel laureate.

156. Brig. Gen. Lewis C. Bebe, U.S. Army Forces, Philippine Islands, chief of staff.

157. Shigemitsu Mamoru, Japanese foreign minister; Gen. Umezu Yoshijiro, Japanese Imperial General Staff representative.

158. Gen. Jacques LeClerc, French representative.

159. Adm. C. E. L. Helfrich, Netherlands representative.

160. Lt. Gen. L. H. van Oyen, member of the Netherlands delegation.

161. Theodore White, a *Time* magazine correspondent, wrote: "Complete silence greeted them as they ascended the deck. The American generals watched them come to attention in their designated places with varying degrees of emotion. Stilwell bristled like a dog at the sight of the enemy" (*Time,* Sept. 30, 1945, 30).

162. Lt. Gen. Arthur Percival, the British general who surrendered Singapore to the Japanese in 1942.

163. Present in addition to those officers identified in earlier entries were Gen. Hsü Yung-Ch'ang, the Republic of China representative; Adm. Sir Bruce A. Fraser, the United Kingdom representative; Lt. Gen. Kuzma Derevyanko, the Soviet representative; Col. L. Moore Cosgrove, the Canadian representative; and Air Vice Marshal Leonard M. Isitt, the New Zealand representative.

164. Stilwell's comment is a reference to a controversial play in a baseball game between the New York Giants and Chicago Cubs on September 23, 1908. Fred Merkle was on first base when his teammate Al Bridwell hit a single that advanced the runner on third to home plate for the winning run. Merkle jogged to second and then stopped short as the crowd surged onto the field. The umpires, ruling that Merkle never tagged the base and thus was

out, declared the game a tie instead of a New York victory. The two teams replayed the game at season's end when both tied for the National League pennant. The Cubs won the rematch (Noel Hynd, *The Giants of the Polo Grounds: The Glorious Times of Baseball's New York Giants,* 147–51). This incident reminded others of Merkle. See the coverage of the surrender episode in the *New York Times,* Sept. 3, 1945.

165. Lt. Gen. Chu Shih-ming, Chinese representative, Allied Council for Japan.

166. Unable to identify Whatley fully.

167. Col. Noble J. Wiley, instructor in the 1930s at the Infantry School at Fort Benning.

168. Archbishop Francis Spellman, archbishop of New York and military vicar of the United States.

169. Unable to find a copy of this letter in the Stilwell Papers.

170. In 1868, *samurais* from the *daimyos* of Satsuma and Choshu overthrew the rule of the Tokugawa *shoguns,* establishing the system of cabinet government in Japan. Since that time, the Sat-Cho clique had dominated the leadership position in the government, army, and navy.

171. Stilwell made the following notation on a letter from William I. Nichols, editor of the magazine: "I sent him a blurb, that will probably end up in the wastebasket." The article was published in the October 28 issue of *This Week.* Stilwell also used this piece as a farewell message to Tenth Army. It is included at the end of this diary (Nichols to Stilwell, Aug. 21, 1945, folder: B-15, 1945, box 33, Stilwell Papers).

172. Agnes Smedley, freelance American journalist in China; Sgt. Alan Manson, actor and cast member of the *This is the Army* soldier show that entertained troops on Okinawa.

173. Col. Paul Jones and Maj. John Grindley.

174. Frank Ahlgren of the *Memphis Commercial Appeal* and Bob Walton of the *South Bend Tribune* were the other two journalists with Ted Dealey, president of the *Dallas Morning News* (Dealey to Stilwell, Nov. 13, 1945, folder: B-17 1945, box 34, Stilwell Papers).

175. Sgt. Robert Oda, interpreter.

176. Famed Hollywood duo Humphrey Bogart and Lauren Bacall. The film Stilwell watched was *To Have and Have Not,* a 1944 Warner Brothers release directed by Howard Hawks.

177. Col. Philip H. Bethune, a Tenth Army intelligence staff officer; Capt. George Anderson, a Tenth Army artillery staff officer; and Capt. Allyn Brenner, a Tenth Army intelligence staff officer.

178. *Newsweek* correspondent Harold Isaacs.

179. Maj. Gen. Howard C. Davidson, commanding general, Tenth Air Force.

180. J. B. Powell, editor and publisher of the *China Weekly Review.*

181. Capt. Edmund T. Wooldridge, commanding officer, USS *New Jersey.*

182. Adm. Sir Bruce Fraser, commander in chief of the British Pacific Fleet. The battleship HMS *Duke of York* was his flagship.

183. Dick Jurgen, composer and bandleader of the Dick Jurgen Orchestra.

184. Unable to identify this individual.

185. African-American soldiers served in segregated units led mostly by white officers during World War II. The U.S. military did not completely integrate until shortly after the Korean War.

186. Capt. John B. Depot, a Tenth Army adjutant general staff officer; 1st Lt. Glendon A. Schubert Jr., a Tenth Army Signal Corps staff officer; and 1st Lt. John Abbink, a Tenth Army operations staff officer.

187. Gracie Fields, English comedienne, singer, and film actress.

188. Monty Banks, Italian-born American film and stage actor and director.

189. Lt. Col. Douglas Kendrick, Jr., a Tenth Army surgeon; Lt. Col. Joseph C. Jefferds, a

Tenth Army ordnance officer; and Capt. Charles R. Stienette Jr., a Tenth Army Episcopal chaplain.

190. Maj. Carl Arnold, Stilwell's aide de camp.

191. Brig. Gen. George Decker, Sixth Army chief of staff.

192. Col. Theodore M. Cornell, commander of the Leyte Provincial Regiment, and Brig. Gen. Kearie L. Berry, commanding general of the Philippine army's 1st Regular Division. Both became prisoners of war in 1942.

193. Quoted in *CBI Roundup,* Oct. 11, 1945.

194. Col. Jesse Auton.

195. *CBI Roundup,* Oct. 11, 1945.

196. Vice Adm. Daniel E. Barbey, commanding officer, VII Amphibious Force.

197. In a follow up letter, Nichols wrote: "You are a natural writer, and don't let anyone tell you otherwise." He also repeated his request for more submissions: "Please take seriously my request for more material" (Nichols to Stilwell, Sept. 17, 1945, folder: B-15, 1945, box 33, Stilwell Papers).

198. The marines made several low passes during the flyovers. One inexperienced pilot hit the top of the flagpole that dominated the parade ground in front of Tenth Army headquarters, bending the top third of the structure at a roughly thirty-degree angle. Stilwell later sent the fliers a note saying there would be no charge for the damages (Maj. Gen. John P. Condon, oral history, USMCHC, 74–75).

199. The film Stilwell watched was a 1944 film-noir mystery released by 20th Century Fox and directed by Otto Preminger. The leads in the picture were Gene Tierney and Dana Andrews.

200. Unable to identify Alson fully.

201. Rear Adm. Oscar C. Badger, commanding officer, Task Force 31; Rear Adm. John F. Shafroth.

202. Brig. Gen. Laurence A. Lawsen, deputy island commander, Tenth Army.

203. Benjamin Stilwell's enlistment in the U.S. Navy drew varying degrees of media attention. See, e.g., *New York Times,* Sept. 15, 1945.

204. CKS is Chiang Kai-shek. The III Marine Amphibious Corps went to North China to take the surrender of the Japanese armies in China, repatriate them to Japan, and hold territory until Chinese Nationalist forces could arrive. The marines were in China for a year and a half (Frank and Shaw, *Victory and Occupation,* 529–628).

205. No further identification of Siegel (groom) and St. Boody (bride) is possible. Stilwell gave away the bride. On the back of a photo of the event, he estimated the crowd was 500 strong. "Orderly and silent—just interested to watch the goings on" (notation on back of unmarked photo, Photo Collection, folder V, Stilwell Papers).

206. A small squad of soldiers protected Stilwell from Japanese stragglers.

207. Unable to identify Maj. Anderston fully.

208. GCM is Gen. of the Army George C. Marshall, U.S. Army chief of staff.

209. Brig. Gen. Bonner Fellers, MacArthur's military secretary.

210. Gen. of the Armies John J. "Black Jack" Pershing, commander of the American Expeditionary Force in World War I.

211. D. Clayton James, *The Years of MacArthur,* vol. 1, *1880–1941,* 217–23.

212. Maj. Gen. Wang Chih, member of the Republic of China's delegation at Japan's surrender.

213. General Count Nogi Maresuke was the Japanese commander at the siege of Port Arthur and the battle of Mukden. Despite lackluster results, he retained his command be-

cause of Emperor Meiji's intervention. He committed suicide after the emperor died in 1912 (Hiroaki Sato, *Legends of the Samurai,* 341).

214. Conrad Totman, *Early Modern Japan,* 222.

215. Brig. Gen. Albert Pierson, assistant commanding general, 11th Airborne Division.

216. George Atcheson, MacArthur's political adviser in Japan.

217. Milton J. Helmick, member of the President's Board of Visa Appeals in the State Department and former judge in the U.S. Court in China.

218. His Imperial Majesty Hirohito, emperor of Japan.

219. Brig. Gen. LeGrande "Pick" Diller, MacArthur's public information officer.

220. Maj. Gen. Arthur Harper, commanding general, 98th Infantry Division.

221. Maj. Gen. Innis Swift, commanding general, I Corps; Maj. Gen. Franklin C. Sibert, commanding general, X Corps; Maj. Gen. Harry Schmidt, commanding general, III Amphibious Corps.

222. Stilwell and his wife traveled across Japan between September and November, 1911 as tourists (Tuchman, *Stilwell,* 28).

223. Andrew Johnson, president of the United States from 1865–69.

224. Unable to identify Bache fully.

225. GCM is George C. Marshall.

226. Stilwell used the kanji characters for this Chinese city. G-Mo is a reference to Chiang Kai-shek.

227. Hokusai Katsushika, an acclaimed eighteenth- and nineteenth-century Japanese artist, is best known for his woodblocks and leadership in the *ukiyo-e* school of art. What made his work distinctive was his emphasis on color and shading in pastoral landscapes. His work had an influence on impressionist artists such as Claude Monet, and Henri Toulouse-Lautrec.

228. Unable to identify Sweetser fully.

229. Unable to identify Col. Levin fully.

230. Maj. Gen. Edmond H. Leavey, deputy commander and chief of staff, U.S. Army Forces, Western Pacific.

231. Col. Ward E. Dickey, commanding officer, Marine Aircraft Group 33.

232. Army won this football game, 28–7 (*Los Angeles Times,* Oct. 15, 1945).

233. This address was also published as "Good Luck, Soldier" in *This Week,* Oct. 28, 1945, 2.

Epilogue: Taps

1. Haley, "Death of Gen. Simon Bolivar Buckner," 100–105; photographs of funeral, CPA-45–23108 and CPA-45–23113, folder U, Photograph Collection, Stilwell Papers; *New York Journal-American,* June 9, 1945.

2. *Baltimore Evening Sun,* June 19, 1945; *Baltimore Sun,* June 19, 1945; *Honolulu Star-Bulletin,* June 19, 1945; *Oregonian* (Portland), June 19, 1945; *Los Angeles Times,* June 19, 1945; *New York Times,* June 19, 1945; *Washington Post,* June 19, 1945; *Seattle Post-Intelligencer,* June 19, 1945; *Cleveland Plain Dealer,* June 19, 1945; *Boston Daily Globe,* June 19, 1945; *New York Herald Tribune,* June 19, 1945; *Louisville Times,* June 19, 1945; *Courier-Journal* (Louisville), June 19, 1945.

3. *Anchorage Times,* June 19, 1945; *Courier-Journal* (Louisville), June 20, 1945; *Los Angeles Times,* June 20, 1945; *Cleveland Plain Dealer,* June 20, 1945. Other papers containing tributes to Buckner include the *Boston Daily Globe,* evening ed., June 19, 1945; *Honolulu Star-Bulletin,* June 20, 1945; *Baltimore Evening Sun,* June 19, 1945; *Washington Post,* June 21, 1945; and *Louisville Times,* June 19, 1945.

4. *Oregonian* (Portland), June 20, 1945; *Honolulu Star-Bulletin,* June 20, 1945; *Washington Evening Star,* June 20, 1945; *Newsweek,* July 2, 1945, 36.

5. Remarks in the Senate, June 19, 1945, *Congressional Record,* vol. 91, pt. 5, 6264–65.

6. *New York Times,* July 4, 7, and Oct. 24, 1945; Feb. 9, 1949; July 20, 1954; *Louisville Times,* Feb. 9, 1949; *Courier-Journal* (Louisville), Feb. 10, 1949.

7. A listing of only the major works on this campaign proves this point: Frank and Shaw, *Victory and Occupation;* Belote and Belote, *Typhoon of Steel;* Astor, *Operation Iceberg;* Appleman et al., *Okinawa;* and Feifer, *Tennozan.*

8. *Monterey Peninsula Herald,* Oct. 18, 1945.

9. Rhodes, *Dark Sun,* 261–62; Tuchman, *Stilwell,* 674–75; Maj. Gen. George P. Hays, unpublished manuscript, George P. Hays Papers, privately held by the Hays Family, Gilroy, Calif., 70–71.

10. *San Francisco Call-Bulletin,* Oct. 12, 1946; *San Francisco News,* Oct. 12, 1946; *Berkeley Gazette,* Oct. 12, 1946; *Honolulu Star-Bulletin,* Oct. 12, 1946; *San Mateo Times,* Oct. 12, 1946; *Monterey Peninsula Herald,* Oct. 12, 1946.

11. *Times* (London), Oct. 14, 1946; *St. Louis Post Dispatch,* Oct. 13, 1946; *Fort Ord Panorama,* Oct. 18, 1946; *Newark Sunday Call,* Oct. 13, 1946; *New York Sunday News,* Oct. 13, 1946; *San Francisco Examiner,* Oct. 13, 1946; *Chicago Daily Tribune,* Oct. 13, 1946; *Washington Post,* Oct. 13, 1946; *Evening Examiner* (Los Angeles), Oct. 13, 1946; *San Diego Union,* Oct. 13, 1946; *Houston Post,* Oct. 13, 1946; *Los Angeles Times,* Oct. 13, 1946; *Seattle Post-Intelligencer,* Oct. 13, 1946; *San Antonio Light,* Oct. 13, 1946; *Fort Worth Star-Telegram,* Oct. 13, 1946; *San Jose Mercury News,* Oct. 13, 1946; *New York Times,* Oct. 13, 1946; *Dallas Morning News,* Oct. 13, 1946; *New York Herald Tribune,* Oct. 13, 1946.

12. *Yonkers (N.Y.) Herald Statesman,* Oct. 14, 1946; *Miami Herald,* Oct. 13, 1946; *Chicago Daily News,* Oct. 14, 1946; *Newark Evening News,* Oct. 14, 1946; *Dallas Morning News,* Oct. 14, 1946; *Philadelphia Inquirer,* Oct. 14, 1946; *Houston Post,* Oct. 15, 1946; *Cleveland Plain Dealer,* Oct. 14, 1946; *Times-Picayune* (New Orleans), Oct. 14, 1946; *Philadelphia Record,* Oct. 14, 1946; *Baltimore Sun,* Oct. 14, 1946; *New York World Telegram,* Oct. 14, 1946; *San Francisco Chronicle,* Oct. 15, 1946; *New York Sun,* Oct. 14, 1946; *New York Herald Tribune,* Oct. 14, 1946; *Chicago Sun,* Oct. 14, 1946; *Boston Globe,* Oct. 14, 1946; *Washington Evening Star,* Oct. 14, 1946; *Columbus (Ga.) Enquirer,* Oct. 14, 1946; *Honolulu Advertiser,* Oct. 14, 1946; *Atlanta Constitution,* Oct. 15, 1946; *Washington Post,* Oct. 13, 1946.

13. *Western Star* (Sixth Army), Nov. 1, 1946; *Carmel (Calif.) Pine Cone–Cymbal,* Oct. 18, 1946.

14. *Ladies' Home Journal,* Apr., 1948, 42–45, 166–216; *Infantry Journal,* June, 1948, 12–22; *San Francisco Chronicle,* July 25–Aug. 11, 1948.

15. *New Yorker,* May 29, 1948, 70.

16. *Chicago Daily Tribune,* Apr. 2, 1948

17. *New York Times Book Review,* May 23, 1948; *New York Herald Tribune Weekly Book Review,* May 30, 1948; *Saturday Review of Literature,* May 29, 1948.

18. *Denver Post,* May 23, 1946; *Atlanta Journal,* May 28, 1946; *Richmond Times-Dispatch,* May 23, 1948; *Cincinnati Enquirer,* May 29, 1948; *Houston Press,* May 28, 1948; *St. Louis Post-Dispatch,* May 29, 1948; *Brooklyn Eagle,* May 30, 1948; *Boston Post,* June 6, 1948; *Arkansas Gazette,* June 27, 1948; *Tulsa World,* May 23, 1948; *Lexington Leader,* May 30, 1948.

19. *Time,* Apr. 5, 1948, 24–25; *New York Herald Tribune Weekly Book Review,* May 30, 1948.

20. *Seattle Times,* May 23, 1971; *Honolulu Star-Bulletin,* Mar. 29, 1971.

21. Gary Sheffield, *Forgotten Victory: The First World War, Myths and Realities,* 116, 118–19, 145–48, 218–19.

22. Williamson Murray and Allan R. Millett, *A War to Be Won: Fighting the Second World*

War, 514–15; William L. O'Neill, *A Democracy at War: America's Fight at Home and Abroad in World War II,* 413–14.

23. Frank and Shaw, *Victory and Occupation,* 390–91, 665.

24. Diary entry, July 2, 1945, vol. 52 (microfilm ed.), reel 9, Henry Stimson Papers, Yale University Library, Yale University, New Haven, Conn., 5; Marshall interview with Forrest C. Pogue quoted in Forrest C. Pogue, *George C. Marshall,* vol. 5, *Statesman, 1945*–1959, 19.

25. Minutes of meeting held at the White House, June 18, 1945, *Foreign Relations of the United States: The Conference of Berlin, 1945,* 1:909.

26. Coakley and Leighton, *Global Logistics and Strategy,* 601.

27. The removal of the Tenth Army from the planes can be followed in either *Reports of General MacArthur,* vol. 1, *The Campaigns of MacArthur in the Pacific,* 396, 423; or in Skates, *Invasion of Japan,* 203. Richard B. Frank uses earlier drafts of invasion plans, which has the Tenth Army taking part (*Downfall: The End of the Imperial Japanese Empire,* 25, 118). He also discusses Nimitz's and King's opposition to the operation (ibid., 147, 212, 276).

28. Barton J. Bernstein, "The Alarming Japanese Buildup on Southern Kyushu, Growing U.S. Fears, and Counterfactual Analysis: Would the Planned November 1945 Invasion of Southern Kyushu Have Occurred?" *Pacific Historical Review* 68 (Nov., 1999): 561–609.

Appendix A: Glossary of Terms

1. Army and Army Air Forces units used the same numbering system for identifying staff functions. The letter varies depending on the size of the unit and branch of the service. For example, A1 refers to the personnel officer/staff section in an AAF unit, A2 refers to the military intelligence officer/staff section, and so forth. Similarly, S1, S2, and so on, apply to regimental and battalion staff officers/sections. G1, G2, and so on, refer to the same officers/ sections at division, corps, and field army level.

Bibliography

Archival Sources

Dwight D. Eisenhower Presidential Library, Abilene, Kans. Simon Bolivar Buckner Jr. Papers.

Hays Family Privately Held Papers, Gilroy, Calif. George P. Hays Papers.

Hoover Institute, Stanford University, Palo Alto, Calif. Joseph W. Stilwell Papers.

Marine Corps University, Quantico, Va. Oliver P. Smith Papers.

U.S. Army Military History Institute, Carlisle Barracks, Pa. Simon Bolivar Buckner Jr. Papers. Ryukyu Papers.

U.S. Marine Corps Historical Center, Washington Navy Yard, Washington, D.C. Oral Histories by Brig. Gen. Fred Beans, Maj. Gen. Wiburt S. Brown, Maj. Gen. John P. Condon, Gen. Vernon Megee, and Lt. Gen. Merwin Silverthorn.

U.S. National Archives, College Park, Md. Record Group 407, World War II Unit Operations Reports, Tenth Army Files.

Yale University, New Haven, Conn. Papers of Henry Stimson.

Newspapers and Magazines

Anchorage Times
Arkansas Gazette
Atlanta Constitution
Atlanta Journal
Baltimore Evening Sun
Baltimore Sun
Berkeley Gazette
Boston Daily Globe
Boston Globe
Boston Post
Brooklyn Eagle
Carmel (Calif.) Pine Cone–Cymbal
CBI Roundup
Chicago Daily News
Chicago Daily Tribune
Chicago Herald American
Chicago Sun
Cincinnati Enquirer
Cleveland Plain Dealer
Columbus Enquirer
Courier-Journal (Louisville)
Dallas Morning News
Denver Post
Detroit News
Fort Ord Panorama

Fort Worth Star-Telegram
Honolulu Advertiser
Honolulu Star-Bulletin
Houston Post
Houston Press
Infantry Journal
Ladies' Home Journal
Lexington Leader
Los Angeles Evening Examiner
Los Angeles Times
Louisville Times
Miami Herald
Monterey Peninsula Herald
New York Herald Tribune
New York Herald Tribune Weekly Book Review
New York Journal-American
New York Mirror
New York Sun
New York Sunday News
New York Times
New York Times Book Review
New York World Telegram
New Yorker
Newark Evening News
Newark Sunday Call
Newsweek
Ohio State Journal
Oregonian (Portland)
Philadelphia Inquirer
Philadelphia Record
PM
Richmond Times-Dispatch
San Antonio Light
San Diego Union
San Francisco Call-Bulletin
San Francisco Chronicle
San Francisco Examiner
San Francisco News
San Jose Mercury News
Saturday Review of Literature
Seattle Post-Intelligencer
Seattle Times
St. Louis Post Dispatch
This Week
Time
Times (London)
Times-Picayune (New Orleans)
Tulsa World
Washington Evening Star
Washington Post
Washington Sunday Star
Washington Times-Herald
Western Star (Sixth Army)
Yonkers (N.Y.) Herald Statesman

Government Publications

Reports of General MacArthur. Vol. 1, *The Campaigns of MacArthur in the Pacific*. Washington, D.C.: GPO, 1966.

U.S. Army. *Official Army Register.*

U.S. Congress. *Congressional Record.*

U.S. Department of State. *Foreign Relations of the United States: The Conference of Berlin, 1945*. Vols. 1 and 2. Washington, D.C: GPO, 1960.

U.S. Navy. *Register of Commissioned and Warrant Officers of the United States Navy and Marine Corps.*

Articles

Bernstein, Barton J. "The Alarming Japanese Buildup on Southern Kyushu, Growing U.S. Fears, and Counterfactual Analysis: Would the Planned November 1945 Invasion of Southern Kyushu Have Occurred?" *Pacific Historical Review* 68 (November, 1999): 561–609.

Graybar, Lloyd J. "The Buckners of Kentucky." *Filson Club History Quarterly* 58, no. 2 (April, 1984): 202–14.

Haley, J. Fred. "The Death of Gen. Simon Bolivar Buckner." *Marine Corps Gazette,* November, 1982, 100–106.

Jenkins, A. P., ed. "Lt. Gen. Simon Bolivar Buckner: Private Letters Relating to the Battle of Okinawa." *Ryudai Review of Euro-American Studies* 42 (December, 1997): 73.

———, ed. "The Battle Diary of Lt. Gen. Simon Bolivar Buckner, 1945." *Scripsimus* 6 (October, 1997): 69–122.

Books

Alexander, Joseph H. *The Final Campaign: Marines in the Victory on Okinawa.* Washington, D.C.: Marine Corps Historical Center, 1996.

Ancell, R. Manning, with Christine M. Miller. *The Biographical Dictionary of World War II Generals and Flag Officers: The U.S. Armed Forces.* Westport, Conn.: Greenwood, 1996.

Appleman, Roy E., James M. Burns, Russell A. Gugeler, and John Stevens. *Okinawa: The Last Battle.* Washington, D.C.: GPO, 1948.

Astor, Gerald. *Operation Iceberg: The Invasion and Conquest of Okinawa in World War II.* New York: Donald I. Fine, 1995.

Belote, James H., and William M. Belote. *Typhoon of Steel: The Battle for Okinawa.* New York: HarperCollins, 1970.

Bradley, Omar N., and Clay Blair. *A General's Life.* New York: Simon and Schuster, 1983.

Buell, Thomas B. *The Quiet Warrior: A Biography of Admiral Raymond A. Spruance.* Boston: Little, Brown, 1974.

Chandler, Alfred D., ed. *The Papers of Dwight D. Eisenhower.* Vol. 4, *The War Years.* Baltimore: Johns Hopkins University Press, 1970.

Coakley, Robert W., and Richard M. Leighton. *Global Logistics and Strategy, 1943–1945.* Washington, D.C.: GPO, 1968.

Craven, Wesley Frank, and James Lea Cate, eds. *The Army Air Forces in World War II.* Vol. 5, *The Pacific: Matterhorn to Nagasaki, June 1944 to August 1945.* Chicago: University of Chicago Press, 1983.

Cray, Ed. *General of the Army George C. Marshall: Soldier and Statesman.* New York: Simon and Schuster, 1990.

Desmond, Robert W. *Tides of War: World News Reporting, 1940–1945*. Iowa City: University of Iowa Press, 1984.

D'Este, Carlo. *Patton: A Genius for War.* New York: HarperCollins, 1995.

Dod, Karl C. *The Corps of Engineers: The War Against Japan*. Washington, D.C.: GPO, 1966.

Feifer, George. *Tennozan: The Battle of Okinawa and the Atomic Bomb.* New York: Ticknor and Fields, 1992.

Frank, Benis M., and Henry I. Shaw. *Victory and Occupation*. Vol. 5. History of U.S. Marine Corps Operations in World War II. Washington, D.C.: Headquarters, U.S. Marine Corps, 1968.

Frank, Richard B. *Downfall: The End of the Imperial Japanese Empire.* New York: Random House, 1999.

Franzwa, Gregory M., and William J. Ely. *Leif Sverdrup: Engineering Soldier at His Best.* Gerald, Mo.: Patrice Press, 1980.

Freeman, Douglas Southall. *Lee's Lieutenants: A Study in Command.* Vol. 2, *Cedar Mountain to Chancellorsville.* New York: Scribners, 1943.

———. *Lee's Lieutenants: A Study in Command.* Vol. 3, *Gettysburg to Appomattox.* New York: Scribners, 1944.

Gailey, Harry A. *'Howlin Mad' vs. the Army: Conflict in Command, Saipan 1944*. Novato, Calif.: Presidio Press, 1986.

Hayes, Grace Peron. *The History of the Joint Chiefs of Staff in World War II: The War Against Japan*. Annapolis, Md.: Naval Institute Press, 1982.

Hersey, John. *A Bell for Adano.* New York: Knopf, 1944.

Hiroaki Sato. *Legends of the Samurai*. Woodstock, N.Y.: Overlook Press, 1995.

Hiromichi Yahara. *The Battle for Okinawa.* Trans. Roger Pineau and Masatoshi Uehara. New York: J. Wiley, 1995.

Hoopes, Townsend, and Douglas Brinkley. *Driven Patriot: The Life and Times of James Forrestal*. New York: Knopf, 1992.

Huber, Thomas M. *Japan's Battle for Okinawa, April–June, 1945*. Leavenworth Paper no. 18. Fort Leavenworth, Kans.: Combat Studies Institute, 1990.

Hynd, Noel. *The Giants of the Polo Grounds: The Glorious Times of Baseball's New York Giants.* Garden City, N.Y.: Doubleday, 1988.

Isely, Jeter A., and Philip A. Crowl. *The U.S. Marines and Amphibious War: Its Theory and Its Practices in the Pacific.* Princeton, N.J.: Princeton University Press, 1951.

James, D. Clayton. *The Years of MacArthur.* Vol. 1, *1880–1941*. Boston: Houghton Mifflin, 1970.

———. *The Years of MacArthur.* Vol. 2, *1941–1945*. Boston: Houghton Mifflin, 1975.

Japan and the Japanese. New York: *Fortune* magazine, 1944.

Kinnard, Douglas. *The Certain Trumpet: Maxwell Taylor and the American Experience in Vietnam*. New York: Brassey's, 1991.

Kluger, Richard. *The Paper: The Life and Death of the New York Herald Tribune.* New York: Random House, 1986.

La Bree, Clifton. *The Gentle Warrior: Oliver Price Smith, USMC.* Kent, Ohio: Kent State University Press, 2001.

Lewis, Adrian R. *Omaha Beach: A Flawed Victory.* Chapel Hill: University of North Carolina Press, 2001.

Luvaas, Jay, ed. *Dear Miss Em: General Eichelberger's War in the Pacific, 1942–1945.* Westport, Conn.: Greenwood, 1972.

Marder, Arthur J., Mark Jacobsen, and John Horsfield. *Old Friends, New Enemies: The Royal Navy and the Imperial Japanese Navy.* Vol. 2. *The Pacific War, 1942–1945.* New York: Oxford University Press, 1990.

Masters, Roger D., and Christopher Kelly, eds. *The Collected Writings of Rousseau.* Vol. 4. Trans. Judith R. Bush, Roger D. Masters, and Christopher Kelly. Hanover, N.H.: University Press of New England, 1994.

Mayo, Lida. *The Ordnance Department: On Beachhead and Battlefront.* U.S. Army in World War II. Washington, D.C.: GPO, 1968.

Millett, Allan R. *Semper Fidelis: The History of the United States Marine Corps.* New York: Free Press, 1980.

Morison, Samuel Eliot. *Victory in the Pacific, 1945.* Vol. 14. History of United States Naval Operations in World War II. Boston: Little, Brown, 1960.

Murray, Williamson, and Allan R. Millett. *A War to Be Won: Fighting the Second World War.* Cambridge, Mass.: Harvard University Press, 2000.

O'Neill, William L. *A Democracy at War: America's Fight at Home and Abroad in World War II.* New York: Free Press, 1993.

Osborn, Fairfield. *The Pacific World: Its Vast Distances, Its Lands and the Life upon Them, and its Peoples.* New York: W. W. Norton, 1944.

Potter, E. B. *Nimitz.* Annapolis, Md.: Naval Institute Press, 1976.

Pogue, Forrest C. *George C. Marshall.* Vol. 5, *Statesman, 1945–1959.* New York: Viking, 1987.

Rhoads, Weldon. *Flying MacArthur to Victory.* College Station: Texas A&M University Press, 1987.

Rhodes, Richard. *Dark Sun: The Making of the Hydrogen Bomb.* New York: Simon and Schuster, 1995.

Rogers, Paul P. *The Bitter Years: MacArthur and Sutherland.* New York: Praeger, 1990.

Sheffield, Gary. *Forgotten Victory: The First World War, Myths and Realities.* London: Headline, 2001.

Skates, John Ray. *The Invasion of Japan: Alternative to the Bomb.* Columbia: University of South Carolina Press, 1994.

Smyth, Henry D. *Atomic Energy for Military Purposes.* Princeton, N.J.: Princeton University Press, 1945.

Spector, Ronald H. *Eagle Against the Sun: The American War Against Japan.* New York: Free Press, 1985.

Totman, Conrad. *Early Modern Japan.* Los Angeles and Berkeley: University of California Press, 1993.

Tuchman, Barbara W. *Stilwell and the American Experience in China, 1911–1945.* New York: Macmillan, 1970.

Willock, Roger. *Unaccustomed to Fear: A Biography of the Late General Roy S. Geiger, U.S.M.C.* Quantico, Va.: Marine Corps Association, 1983.

Index

ISBN 1-58544-294-1
90000
9 781585 442942